M000222571

Sea Kayak

Desolation Sound
AND THE
Sunshine Coast

HEATHER HARBORD

To Anneke Gutter, a dependable
paddling companion of many years

Rocky
Mountain Books
Calgary–Victoria–Vancouver

Rocky Mountain Books
#108, 17665-66A Avenue
Surrey, BC V3S 2A7
RMB www.rmbooks.com

Library and Archives Canada Cataloguing in Publication

Harbord, Heather, 1939-
    Sea kayak Desolation Sound and the Sunshine Coast / Heather Harbord.

Includes index.
ISBN 1-894765-53-2

    1. Sea kayaking--British Columbia--Desolation Sound Region--Guidebooks. 2. Sea kayaking--British Columbia--Sunshine Coast--Guidebooks. 3. Desolation Sound Region (B.C.)--Guidebooks. 4. Sunshine Coast (B.C.)--Guidebooks. I. Title.

GV776.15.B7H368 2005   797.1'224'0971131   C2005-901250-1

Series design by Tony Daffern
Edited by Joe Wilderson
Cover design by John Luckhurst
Front cover by Bruce Kirkby
All photos by the author unless otherwise credited.

Printed in Canada

Rocky Mountain Books acknowledges the financial support for its publishing program from the Government of Canada through the Book Publishing Industry Development Program (BPIDP).

Contents

Introduction

Warm water, sandy beaches and the dry climate draw paddlers to Desolation Sound and the Sunshine Coast year after year. The ferry system and scheduled flights make it easy to access from big population centres.

~

On one of my early long weekend trips to the area, three friends and I caught the first ferry from Vancouver, drove the Sunshine Coast to Egmont, caught the second ferry to Saltery Bay and arrived in Lund about lunchtime. After putting in, we paddled to the Copeland Islands, where we camped on the edge of an arbutus forest. Mink caught shiners and played hide and seek among the rocks. Eagles and turkey vultures circled lazily overhead in a cloudless sky. Following a warm swim, we monitored the sunset while drinking hot chocolate laced with Triple Sec.

Next day, after Roberta, a newly qualified marine biologist, had introduced us to the finer points of a large orange sunflower sea star, we paddled around Sarah Point. Lunching at Flower Cove, we viewed the peaks of Desolation Sound before ducking into the shelter of Malaspina and Lancelot Inlets. On a tiny island in Isobel Bay, the men retired to their tents to nap while Roberta and I continued to the head of Theodosia Inlet. Though the tide was high, we couldn't get far up the river. Two hours we said we'd be gone, but four hours later dusk was deepening as we glided back over satin water. We fell asleep to the splashes of seals courting.

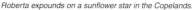

Roberta expounds on a sunflower star in the Copelands.

In the morning, we took out at the Okeover government wharf and John nobly volunteered to hitch a ride to bring the vehicle from Lund. We caught the last connecting ferry home. After many more such trips, I found an excuse to move to nearby Powell River to a house overlooking the islands, the ferries and the sunsets. Today paddlers doing this trip would probably start with a coffee and butter tart at Nancy's Bakery in Lund and end with a gourmet dinner at the Laughing Oyster at Okeover. Unfortunately, neither of those was around when I first ventured into this fabulous paddling area.

~

Okeover is one of the more sheltered places this book describes for beginners to both learn and practise their new skills. The information summaries at the beginning of each description identify others. Cottagers will enjoy finding additional places to paddle after they have explored their local waters or on days when the wind is in the wrong direction for their beach launches.

Experienced paddlers wanting long distance trips where they are free to paddle and camp governed only by wind and tide, will enjoy Desolation Sound, Texada Island, Powell Lake, Jervis Inlet and the upper areas of Howe Sound, but their territory is shrinking as the Vancouver conurbation creeps north. Already most of the mainland coast between Gibsons and Lund is a long line of waterfront residential development and aquaculture with few parks or campsites. Some areas like Toba Inlet and Jervis Inlet require advanced skills.

The 50 trips in this book are arranged in eight areas where details of launches and campsites are found. For planning purposes the trips are rated from Beginner to Advanced but last-minute weather changes can transform the former into the latter. The appendices include lists of sea kayak outfitters, visitors' bureaus, coastal campsites and B&Bs, instructions for hypothermia treatment, and equipment lists for day trips and longer expeditions, as well as metric conversions and further reading.

The Gulf Islands, with their sheltered waterways, many landing places and campsites, should still be the first choice for extended trips by unaccompanied beginning paddlers. Desolation Sound is a much more rugged territory, especially in the Redonda Islands. Cortes Island, being outside the park, is more populated. Like the Gulf Islands, the Sunshine Coast has lots of fancy B&Bs, good restaurants and interesting craft shops to visit—even by water. In most areas, you could either do a long trip or set up a base at a campsite or a B&B, drive to one of the many launches to paddle a different place every day.

Less sheltered than the Gulf Islands, Desolation Sound is a place where winds are more of a problem than currents. Paddlers need to pay attention to weather forecasts. Stores and medical help are relatively close by, but may not be available quite when you want them. Radios, satellite and cell phones work in most areas except up the inlets. Visitors should not disembark on private land without first obtaining the owners' permission, which is not always given. Plan to avoid having to ask for help except in extreme conditions.

There are many places to rent sea kayaks. Don't do this without first taking lessons. Certified Canadian Recreational Canoeing Association (CRCA) instructors offer an eight-hour beginner's package for sea kayakers which is a good start. Sea kayaking can be as easy as it looks, BUT if the weather changes, you will need more than the basic skills these lessons teach. First trips should be along shores you can land on in case of need. Don't attempt crossings till you've logged at least 25 nautical miles [designated throughout this book as "nmi"] close to the shoreline. Then study weather forecasting, navigation and seamanship. Know how to perform a surf landing, but plan not to have to use it. Surf landings on rocky shores are unpleasant to dangerous. Rescue practice both for groups and singles is mandatory.

There is a long tradition of paddling in the area. Before Europeans came, huge ocean-going Haida canoes swept down from the north at 7-knot speeds capturing slaves from the peaceable Salish people, who eventually learned to either fortify their dwellings or hide them. In the mid to late 19th century, Vancouver sawmills ran out of local lumber. Loggers rowed north in search of slopes steep enough that a single man aided by an axe and a knowledge of levers could slide tree trunks into the ocean to be towed south. Civil War veteran Joe Copeland, the Thulin Brothers, Mike Shuttler, James Palmer, the Gibson family and many others rowed up the coast to secluded bays where they lived a life of freedom no longer possible in today's bureaucratic jungle of tenures and government regulations. Some places are still beautiful but mind where you look.

Disclaimer

There are inherent risks in sea kayaking. While the author has done her best to provide accurate information and to point out potential hazards, conditions may change owing to weather and other factors. It is up to the users of this guide to learn the necessary skills for safe paddling and to exercise caution in potentially hazardous areas. Please read the introduction to this book and, in particular study the Trip Rating guidelines on pages 12 and 13.

Paddlers using this book do so entirely at their own risk and the author and publishers disclaim any liability for injury or other damage that may be sustained by anyone using the access and/or paddling routes described.

Acknowledgments

I greatly appreciate the help of many paddlers, friends, experts and advisors who assisted in a variety of ways. Thank you.

Anneke Gutter who:
- before her family arrived, came out Sunday after Sunday in all weather
- shared many gorgeous trips
- waited for me to catch up to her
- taught me to paddle more efficiently
- cured a frozen shoulder in half the time a sports medicine clinic took for a previous one
- steadied my boat when I got in or out in bad weather

Thank you for a job very well done.

Others who helped are:
Bowen Island Historians and Martin Clarke for solving the Bates mystery. Clyde Burton for his encyclopedic knowledge of birds and wildlife. Bryce Christie who advised on Jervis Inlet. Shirley Cole and Andy and Sue Ellingsen for advice on Cortes Island. Tony Clayton for information on Howe Sound. Vic Cole, Jessie Jones plus Rod Tysdale and Paul Kutz of Weyerhaeuser who advised on the circumnavigation of Powell Lake.

Ann Cooper who shared her knowledge of hypothermia treatment. Bette Cooper for information on Gambier Island. Doug Cooper for information on log sorting activities in the Port Mellon area. Jim Cosgrove, Manager, Natural History Section, Royal British Columbia Museum for advice on many of the natural history sidebars. John Dafoe, Coastwise Guide, who advised on the Sechelt-Pender Harbour area including Jervis Inlet. Desolation Sound pioneers and their descendants: Eleanor Anderson, Ingrid Cowie, Pat Hanson, Moyra Palm, and Maria Zaikow. John Dove who advised on some of the petrology. Blake Fougere who advised on forest tenures and Toba Inlet. Marjorie Harding who advised on Nelson Island. Don and Fay Johnson who advised on Texada. Ralph Keller for advice on the Redonda Islands and Toba Inlet. Maurice Liebich, the first Treasurer of the Vancouver Ocean Touring Kayak Association (VOTKA) for information on Howe Sound. Fred Morton who advised on Hardy Island. Marg and Dale McNeill for checking the distances and other sundry details.

Randy Netter who described his playground at the head of Toba Inlet. Phyllis Ogis who helped record the distances to the Powell River launches. Bert Penny who advised on Toba Inlet. Ray Pillman for information on Worlcombe Island and Richard Bates. Hugh Pritchard and Christine Hollman of Terracentric who advised on Cortes Island and provided pictures of it. Heinz and Liz Prosch who helped with the Gibsons area. Laurie Reid of Pedals and Paddles who advised on the Sechelt Inlets

The Sechelt Band Office for information on Jervis and Sechelt Inlets

Sliammon elders and others: the late Chief Joe Mitchell and his sister, Sue Pielle; Elsie Paul; and Murray Mitchell. Bob Spence for his Toba memories and his son, Bill, for details of the mill. Caroline Stoddart who helped record the distances to the Sechelt launches. John and Joan Treen for advice on Savary Island and on currents.

The Treen family and Rick Davies who advised on the hypothermia section. Adam Vallance of Powell River Sea Kayaks for advice on the Okeover dispute, Desolation Sound and Toba Inlet. Margaret Waddington who knows more about Northwest history than I ever will. Peter Waddington who took many of the pictures and has co-led many trips to this area.

If I have omitted anyone, please accept my apologies.

Exploring the Copeland Islands. Cortes Island in the background.

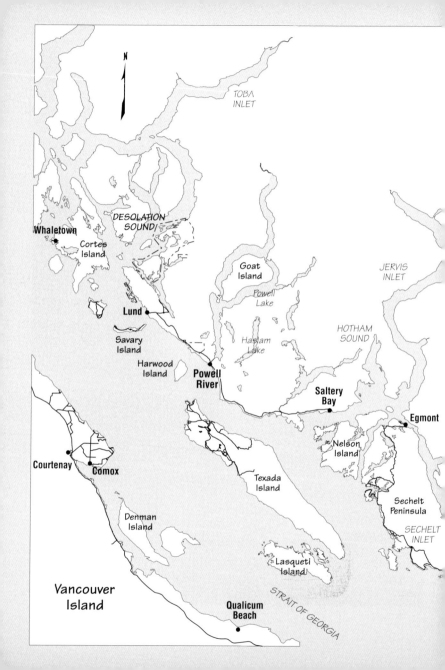

Desolation Sound
and the
Sunshine Coast
Area Map

0   nmi   10

Squamish

ALMON INLET

*HOWE
SOUND*

Gambier
Island

Sechelt

Langdale

Bowen
Island

Gibsons

Horseshoe
Bay

Trip Rating

Routes described in this guide have been rated according to the paddling skills required, normal sea and shoreline conditions and the level of risk normally associated with such conditions. The rating given to a trip is an indication of what to expect in good, summer conditions. It is an assessment of risk, taking into account paddling skill level and difficulties likely to be encountered.

Difficulty is a measure of sea conditions: wind, waves, currents, tide rips and length of open–water crossings, and shoreline conditions: surf and infrequent and/or difficult landings.

Risk is the possibility of inconvenience, discomfort, injury or even loss of life. For the paddler, the level of risk is not constant. Along the same route and with the same paddling conditions, different paddlers will encounter different levels of risk. For a beginner, risky conditions may include small wavelets that arise before white–capped waves appear. For a more skilled paddler the same waves may hardly be noticeable. Risk can be reduced by good paddling skills, knowledge and judgement. Risk is increased in worsening conditions, remote locations and with poor decision–making.

There is a complex relationship between paddling skills, difficulty and risk. The individual paddler's skill level, the nature of the route, changing weather, and the presence of a competent leader are essential factors in determining the difficulty and risk of a sea kayak journey.

Sound decision–making is critical to the enjoyment and safety of sea kayaking touring and an experienced leader will often reduce difficulty and risk to acceptable levels. In the company of a skilled leader, a beginner can paddle safely along a coast rated intermediate. With good leadership a large portion of the Gulf Islands coastline is accessible to beginner–level paddlers and a coastline rated as "advanced" is by no means the sole domain of the advanced paddler.

The rating descriptions below cover many, but not all of the factors required to assess difficulty and risk. There may be other factors to be considered such as river outflows, reflected waves, the profile of a surf beach and the limitations of gear and cold water.

The skill levels referred to below correspond to the conditions i.e. intermediate paddlers have the attributes necessary to safely travel in intermediate conditions.

Novice conditions – minimal risk
- Sheltered locations with stable conditions.
- Wind calm (less than 8 knots); sea state calm to rippled.
- Travel is along shore with abundant easy landing sites.
- Frequent opportunities for communication and road access; assistance is nearby.

Trip Rating courtesy Doug Alderson.

A group of novice paddlers can travel safely on day trips along the shore. Poor decisions or misinterpreting changing weather or sea conditions is unlikely to cause harm or significant inconvenience.

Beginner conditions – low risk
- Mostly sheltered locations with stable conditions.
- Light winds (0–11 knots); current (0–0.5 knots) Sea state calm to light chop.
- Abundant easy landing sites and short open crossings less than 1.5 nmi.
- Frequent opportunities for communication and access; assistance may be up to an hour away.

A group of beginners can travel safely on day trips. Intermediate paddlers familiar with the area could lead beginners on an overnight trip. Poor decisions or misinterpreting changing weather or sea conditions is likely to cause inconvenience but unlikely to cause harm.

Intermediate conditions – moderate risk
- A complex open water environment with the potential for moderate change in conditions.
- Moderate winds (12–19 knots); sea state moderate with wind waves near 0.5 meters; surf less than 1 meter; current less than 3 knots.
- Intermittent landing opportunities with some difficult landing sites; open water crossings less than 5 nmi (nautical miles).
- Communication may be interrupted; assistance may be more than one hour away.

A group of intermediate paddlers can travel safely on day trips. Advanced paddlers familiar with the area could lead intermediate paddlers on an extended overnight trip. Poor decisions or misinterpreting changing weather or sea conditions is likely to cause great inconvenience, the need for external rescue and possibly personal harm.

Advanced conditions – considerable risk
- Complex open water environment with frequently changing conditions.
- Continuous exposure to wind, swell or current.
- Strong winds (near 20 knots); sea state rough with wind waves near 1 metre; surf greater than 1 metre or tide rips greater than 3 knots are routine.
- Infrequent landing opportunities with some difficult landing sites; open water crossings greater than 5 nmi.
- Remote locations where communications can be difficult or unavailable; assistance may be a day or more away.

A mix of intermediate and advanced paddlers can travel safely on day trips. On extended overnight trips all paddlers should have advanced skills. Poor decisions or misinterpreting changing weather or sea conditions is likely to cause personal harm, without the availability of prompt external rescue.

Weather, Climate and Sea Conditions

Weather

The best months for sea kayakers are May through September and sometimes April and October. November is usually wet and stormy. A high pressure system often provides calm sunny weather for day trips in January. Except for Jervis Inlet and Toba Inlet, you can paddle most places all year.

Carry a weather radio and listen to the marine forecast religiously, before setting out every morning and several times during the day. Barring Jervis Inlet and Toba Inlet, Comox Coast Guard Radio weather reports are easily available. Weather forecast regions for this area are the Strait of Georgia north of Nanaimo; in Desolation Sound listen also to the forecast for Johnstone Strait, as it is on the border of both. Use a weather radio for the forecasts instead of depleting the batteries of your VHF radio, which needs a lot of battery power to transmit.

Wind is the most important weather phenomenon for kayakers. The frequent small-craft warnings in the Strait of Georgia are a force to be reckoned with, especially in the southern area where northwest winds can force paddlers to do surf landings anywhere on "the stretch" from the Trail Islands to Gower Point. At the same time, the warning seldom applies inside the northern island groups, but trust your eyes.

The inlets, including the Powell River lake chain, are subject to katabatic/anabatic winds. In warm weather, the land heats up, causing air to rise up the valleys and slide down their slopes and down the inlets at night. In long, straight stretches of inlets, big waves build up. If caught in this situation, land and wait till dawn or dusk. Sometimes the winds die down during a tide change. Even strong paddlers make no headway in 17 knots of wind or greater. Wind and waves are stronger than you; don't fight them. Enjoy your time ashore. Relax in the sunshine, letting the pebbles run through your fingers as you watch eagles and ospreys circle overhead.

If you see tugs with log booms sitting waiting tied up at either the Trail Islands or in front of Westview at Powell River, think carefully before setting out. They are waiting for weather to blow through before proceeding farther, as they don't relish having booms break up in heavy seas.

Sea fog is a problem at times. Although it may be sunny inland, fog creeps up the centre of the Strait of Georgia, blanketing the coastal communities and refusing to burn off. Keep warm clothes on hand in your boat in case you have to put them on in a hurry to ward off hypothermia.

During the winter before your trip, study Owen Lange's *Living with Weather along the British Columbia Coast* and his earlier book *The Wind Came All Ways*. Buy a weather radio and listen to your local forecasts till you become familiar with the meteorological terms used. Look out the window and watch the sky as a front passes through. Reading the first part of Lange's book explains some of the variables that make it almost impossible to produce up-to-the-minute

Into the storm, Hotham Sound.

forecasts. A combination of listening and looking at the sky will show you that the forecasts should be respected. The weather sometimes comes in faster or slower than predicted. Weather knowledge is often more important than anything else.

Average temperature and precipitation

Daytime high temperatures in July vary from 18–30 °C (65–90 °F) and in January about 2.5–4 °C (36–42 °F). When rain clouds approach Vancouver Island, they drop most of their load on the western slopes of the island's mountain chain. The eastern slopes, the Gulf of Georgia and the Coastal Range adjacent to it are in a rain shadow. Average annual total precipitation is around 40 mm in July and over 180 mm in November.

This relatively dry climate, with 1,400–1,900 hours of sunshine per year, produces desert conditions on Mitlenatch and Texada Islands.

The average sea temperature is 6–7 °C (43–44 °F) in January and 16–18 °C (61–65 °F) in July. Seawater temperatures in the Strait of Georgia are warmer east of Mitlenatch Island, as the cold water from Johnstone Strait flows through Discovery Passage and remains on the western sides of Century Shoal and Grants Reef. This affects both marine and avian wildlife.

Predicted survival time in water of 10 °C is 2–3 hours. You'll only be able to swim a tenth of the distance you can cover in a warm swimming pool. Wetsuits and drysuits increase survival time. For details on the treatment of hypothermia, please see page 245.

Sea conditions

Incoming tides swirl around the north and south ends of Vancouver Island to meet on the north side of Savary Island. Southern tides relate to Point Atkinson, whereas northern tides (beyond Cortes and Desolation Sound) are on Campbell River. It was this change in the direction of the tides which alerted Captain Vancouver to the fact that there was a way out of the northern end of the Strait of Georgia.

While Vancouver Island protects the Strait from open ocean swells, outflow winds from the inlets have room to build up quite large waves. Even a low surf can make landing difficult. If you capsize when trying to land with a loaded boat, quickly move to one end of the hull so that the boat doesn't beat you to a pulp as the waves drive it up the beach and suck it out again.

In summer months, the lowest tides are nearly 15 cm below chart data and the highest are close to 5 metres above. Of the four tides each day, there is a high high tide and a low high tide. Similarly with the lows, one is a high low tide and the other a low low tide. When choosing campsites, remember that wind and swell on top of a high tide can push the water farther up the beach, and wakes from passing cruise ships can slosh water up another metre or so. Learn to look for the lines of seaweed marking the last high high tide and allow another metre.

Fast tidal currents can be crossed using the same ferry gliding technique used on rivers. Point your bow at an angle to the current and let it squeeze your boat sideways and across. As it

Landing on a southeast-facing shore is sometimes difficult.

does this, watch the angle of stationary objects on shore like mountains and light beacons and adjust your course accordingly.

To avoid confusing backwash from cliffs, paddle farther out. When going through a group of rocky skerries, watch the sideways sucking action of the waves ahead of you. If you get too close to a skerry, you may be washed up on a ledge and unable to get off till your boat is pounded to pieces. Study the rock symbols given in Chart No. 1 (a book that explains the symbols used to describe features on Cana-dian charts). A star symbol indicates a rock which will be above water at high tide. This is easy but check the chart for plus signs. Those with four dots mark the locations of rocks that appear above water at low tide. An unadorned plus sign indicates a rock just below the surface at low tide. At various tide levels, a wave can easily slam your boat down on one of these, cracking or holing it. This is when you need duct tape and a fibreglass repair kit that will work under water. Look ahead and avoid these potential hazards whenever possible.

First Nations

The territory covered by this book belongs to three Salish Nations: the Sliammon, the Sechelt and the Squamish.

The Sliammon include the Homalco, who occupied Bute Inlet (not covered in this book); the Klahoose of Toba Inlet, Desolation Sound and Cortes Island; and the Sliammon, who ranged from Desolation Sound south to Texada Island. Before 1800, the Island Comox division of the Sliammon occupied Quadra Island and the Campbell River area of Vancouver Island. Gun-toting Kwakwaka'wakw drove them into a small area near Comox Harbour. Today, the people who live in the village of Sliammon near Powell River have relatives in the Homalco and Klahoose areas as well as among the Island Comox, the Sechelt, and the Salish in Washington State. They visit back and forth frequently among all these areas.

The Sechelt extended from Palm Beach, near Powell River, south to Jervis Inlet and the Sechelt Peninsula. In 1986, they became the first band in Canada to have self-government.

The Squamish occupied Howe Sound.

Natural History

Glaciers ravaged the land, leaving deposits of sand, gravel and erratic boulders as they retreated, and sometimes hanging valleys up in the mountains. Savary Island, which is almost entirely sand, has a typical barkhan formation. As the ice melted, sea levels rose, creating drowned valleys in the inlets and covering the terminal moraines at their entrances.

The foundation rocks are largely metamorphic, often granodiorites. There are also sedimentary deposits of limestone. Mineral exploration in the late 19th century centred on Texada Island. The Marble Bay Mine in Van Anda operated from 1898 to about 1919 and produced about 10,000 to 15,000 tons of ore per year. The mineralization was gold, silver and copper with a combined value of around $25 per ton at a time when the daily wage of a skilled miner was $3.50. The deepest level in the mine was 1,300 feet below the surface. Other mines were smaller. Texada Mines Ltd., an iron mine near Gillies Bay, produced about a million tons a year for about 25 years. Similar formations in the Lund area were less successful. Today, four limestone quarries on Texada sort and export various sizes of rock to make everything from roads to toothpaste.

Apart from Savary and sections of a few nearby islands there are few sandy or even shingle beaches. Most are covered with large and small rocky boulders. Landings are scarce.

Glaucous-winged gulls have hybridized with Western gulls to produce many variations, all of which are attracted to the rich garbage around many settlements. Bald eagles, who have suffered from the diminishing fish stocks, feast on the gulls and winter sea ducks. Turkey vultures are common in summer skies. Marbled murrelets nest on the broad, mossy branches of the remaining old-growth forest stands around Desolation Sound and especially in the Bunster Hills above Okeover Inlet. Murres and

Orca whale.

ancient murrelets are encountered around islands like Mitlenatch and Vivian. In the forest, several varieties of woodpecker thrive along with kinglets, Swainson's and hermit thrushes. Red-tailed hawks are seen and heard in the open areas.

Although black bear and cougar frequent the mainland and Vancouver Island, there are none on Texada, Savary or Hernando. River otters are often common and mink used to be. Orca, two kinds of sea lions, harbour seals, harbour and Dall's porpoise, Pacific white-sided dolphins and the occasional humpback whale inhabit the marine environment.

Summer low tides are good times to beachcomb. Turn over one rock at a time, gently replacing it before going on to the next. Often, you'll find chitons, many of which are nocturnal. Another rock may have batches of yellow eggs the size of corn kernels clinging to its underside and guarded by a male plainfin midshipman fish. This fish uses its swim bladder to groan and consequently is called the singing fish. Tide pools have orange, brown and purple colonies of sponges and bryozoans. Orange and purple ochre sea stars are common, as are sunflower and morning stars. Several introduced species have overrun the beaches in recent years. The most obvious are the Japanese oyster, the dark mahogany clam with a brilliant purple inside, and the ubiquitous mud snail.

In spring the islands are covered in pink sea blush, yellow monkey flower, blue-eyed Mary and many other plants.

Bioluminescence

Those electric green or blue streaks along the shoreline at night are caused by bioluminescence. This is light produced by a chemical reaction within an organism. The bodies of millions of organisms from plankton to squid contain luciferins, which produce light, and luciferases, which catalyze the oxidation of the luciferins, resulting in light.

Bioluminescence is a different process from phosphorescence or fluorescence. In fluorescence, energy from an external source of light is absorbed and almost immediately re-emitted. Phosphorescence is a slower process producing a glow after the light has been removed. Chemiluminescence is light produced from a chemical reaction. Bioluminescence is a kind of chemiluminescence.

Paddling or swimming in bioluminescent water is an unforgettable experience.

Chiton.

Trip Planning

For day trips

Always carry spare clothes in water-proof bags. Dress in layers and bring along something warm to put on during a lunch break.

- Bring charts and know where you are going and where you will take out.
- Carry a thermos of hot fluid of some kind and don't finish it at lunchtime, because you may need it later to revive a hypothermia victim.
- Bring lunch and some extra snacks in case you are longer than you planned.
- Listen to the weather forecast before you go and perhaps again at lunchtime.
- Tell someone on shore where you are going.
- Be back before dusk.
- If making a big crossing, take overnight gear and a VHF just in case.

See the asterisked list page 268.

For a weekend, a week or longer

Select the group to go. Due to the difficulty of finding campsites, limit the size to 4–6 people maximum. Smaller is better. Put latecomers on a wait list who might travel as a second group a week later. Choose experienced paddlers who:

- habitually listen to the marine forecast and know how to interpret it
- can paddle strongly against at least a 20-knot wind
- know and have practised rescues
- can read charts and use a compass
- know how to ferry glide across a current

- know the marine rules of right-of-way
- if paddling in the lead, will check back frequently to see where others are
- can do surf landings (otherwise, be prepared to be restricted in where you can go)

If paddling alone, you should be both experienced and skilled. Plan a wider margin of safety.

Although July and August are the best months, off-season paddling is a good possibility, especially for day trips. Avoid November, which is often continuously wet. In the cold and dark months of winter, if you're doing a crossing, take emergency overnight gear and extra food. A winter storm could pin you down for three days to a week. Summer storms seldom last more than a day or two.

On week-long or longer trips, plan to be at the take-out a day early. This is the time to do short local trips that you can easily get back from if the wind comes up.

Are you going to set up a base camp and make daily forays from it or are you going to move every night? If so, plan to not move every third day. Lugging all that stuff up and down the beach gets tiring, **and** this is a way of building in a safety day in case you are storm stayed. If this happens early in the trip, be prepared to adjust your plan. Perhaps you won't be able to get as far afield as you'd hoped this year. If you don't drown, you can come back. Consider moving at dawn and dusk or when the tide changes. Often, winds diminish at these times.

Before leaving home, assemble the charts on a large table and, using parallel rules or a wooden dowel, pencil-in lines of magnetic north all across the chart so that you won't have to unfold it to find a compass rose all the time. Also, note the magnetic compass courses in both directions of proposed routes. This saves fiddling in fog. Fold your charts so they will not only fit into your waterproof case but also show a full day's paddle at a time—or at least minimize the number of times you have to unfold and refold them. Make sure everyone has a chart and knows how to read it and how to use a compass. This is still important even if you are using a GPS.

GPS owners will want to enter the latitude and longitude coordinates of prospective destinations before leaving home. On the water, a GPS can tell how far you have to paddle to the next waypoint and how fast you are going. These instruments are very useful in thick fog, which can be a problem at any season. They can also be used to accurately retrace a course.

Establish who will bring waterproofed VHF radios, and ask them to get their proficiency certificates. Who will bring weather radios?

Know how long your group likes to paddle in a day. Most vacationing groups prefer to paddle 6–8 nmi, sometimes 10–12. They want time to relax and enjoy the area as well as travel. Leave the 25 nmi days to the hotshots.

Tell the group members that no one should have a pressing appointment the day after they take out. Accidents happen most frequently when someone has to be somewhere at a set time. Build in a day's safety factor.

Appoint someone not going on the trip to be a contact person for the Coast Guard. This person should have the names, addresses and descriptions of all members of the party and their boats plus some idea of their skills.

During crossings, plan to keep the group together so that they are visible to other traffic, of which there is sometimes a lot. The lead boat is responsible for keeping the group together—the slow ones wouldn't be straggling if they could keep up the pace set by the racers ahead. Lead boats should look back at the rest of the group frequently. If this tactic doesn't work, the leader should have the boats paddle side by side in designated spots, e.g., Bob, you'll paddle between Jane and Sue. Each boat stays within easy talking distance of the others. However, in heavy seas, don't get too close to each other. Perhaps you should have remained stormbound on that last island.

Make sure everyone going has had a tetanus shot within the last 10 years. Plan what first aid items each person will carry.

Ask for volunteers to bring a bird book, a flower book, a tide pool book, star charts etc.

Consider drying your own food to take with you. Start months before and dry meal leftovers. Don't forget vegetables. Home-dried food is much cheaper and reduces weight to be loaded and unloaded or hung in a tree.

In addition to mandatory safety gear, put together a kayak repair kit, including duct tape, fibreglass or Kevlar repair and rudder repair kits. A pair of vise-grips and some odd bits of neoprene with glue are useful.

For a sample list of what to pack, see page 248.

Fishing licences are required both for fishing with a rod and for collecting shellfish. Find out if there is a PSP ban. If fishing with a rod, carry a net or gaff and something to put the fish in once you've caught them.

Shakedown trip

In this area, it's probably not necessary to do a weekend shakedown trip unless planning a lengthy expedition, but a day trip together can be useful, if only to see who can keep up and who can't. It is a good location for a shakedown trip prior to paddling the West Coast or the Queen Charlotte Islands.

- Listen to the marine forecast, not the land TV forecast, and talk about it with the group.
- Review rescue procedures and have everyone practise them. Discuss how to recognize and treat hypothermia, the greatest killer of kayakers. (See page 245) Practise the HELP and the HUDDLE positions.
- Erect a tarp at lunchtime just to show how it's done. Have four people use straps to haul a kayak up the beach. Does anyone have any particularly useful equipment which the others would like to acquire before the big trip?
- Try a food-hanging session to show how easy or difficult it is with your equipment. How would this work under different conditions—an absence of trees, say, or pouring rain or high winds?

Being stormbound

Enjoy the opportunity to set up camp properly, bake bread, make cinnamon buns, build a beach sauna, tell stories, read books, go for walks, watch birds,

Paralytic shellfish poisoning (PSP)

Periodically, Fisheries & Oceans Canada closes areas to shellfish harvesting because a sometimes invisible red tide has contaminated the shellfish. Oysters, mussels and clams can ingest the microscopic toxin without being affected. Animals and humans cannot. The toxin attacks your nervous system and kills you. There is no antidote. In a desperate situation, try vomiting.

After eating clams, when painter/paddler Stewart Marshall experienced his lips and hands numbing and his heart labouring, he used yoga techniques to breathe harder and harder to increase his blood circulation. He forced himself to gather wood for a huge fire. He swam vigorously, then ran back to the fire and jogged next to it to warm himself up. Then he ran up and down the beach and repeated the process for about an hour and a half. As he says: "A different body, a different state, a different degree of poisoning—any of these could have been devastating."[1]

If your lips tingle when touched by a piece of shellfish, don't eat it. Most paddlers don't think it's worth taking the risk and few now eat shellfish. Crabs, shrimp and non-filter feeders are not affected, but you need a licence to take them. See also page 189.

examine intertidal life, wash clothes, practise tai chi, write poetry, etc. Above all, relax. You can't go anywhere and no one starves on this coast with all the sea vegetables to stew and the shellfish to roast—or eat raw.

Packing for overnight trips

Pack before leaving home. Being able to pack your boat in a hurry is really important if you plan to launch on a ramp used by impatient power boats, especially at places like Lund or Westview. They hate kayaks because they themselves can be launched and away in two or three minutes. Whenever possible, pack kayaks away from the ramp and carry or wheel them over to launch.

At home, repackage to remove excess paper, and waterproof each item. If you have to eat a hurried meal in pouring rain, you should only have to open the items you're going to eat. If necessary, snip cooking instructions off packages and repack in ziploc bags—or write cooking instructions in waterproof ink on each bag. It pays to have a good supply of small, freezer quality ziploc bags on hand when you start. They can often be reused and later double as garbage bags.

After all the individual bags— kitchen bag, cockpit bag, food bags, etc.—are packed, assemble everything that is going in one pile as if you were going to load your boat in camp. Take two large net bags (1 m long if possible) or lightweight nylon bags which when empty can be crushed up in a corner, and fill them with small items. These will reduce the number of trips you'll have to make up and down the beach once you're out.

Put the kayak in the back yard and assemble your gear beside it so that items going in the bow are piled beside the bow etc. Heavier stuff goes in the stern. Pack everything, stuffing the net bags in last. If possible, avoid carrying anything on deck. Tarps, empty water containers and spare paddles are good candidates for this, as it doesn't matter if a wave washes over them. Rope them on as you would at the launch. Put the first chart in the chart case along with tide tables, and set up the deck load with flares and pump within reach. Now sit in the boat. Have you left room for last minute fresh food purchases?

Unpack the boat straight into your vehicle. Add only an overnight bag with your paddling clothes and clean clothes for when you return. Load the kayak itself and secure.

Wet weather camping

Tarps Set the tarps up first. Slant them so that rain pours off the side least used. Pitch your tent, which should be almost completely covered by its own fly, under a tarp so that it is totally protected. Having extra line to tie to distant trees and logs pays off. Use driftwood or paddles to raise the ceiling. It also helps to have a structural engineer, aka tarpmeister, in the party who knows how to put up tarps that stay up and don't flap in a wind. Contribute the second tarp to a communal kitchen area. Take extra grommets for repair jobs.

Rain gear All rain gear should be seam sealed. Check the seals before leaving home. Breathable rain gear is apt to leak in the kind of heavy, wind-driven rain that can occur in Desolation Sound or the Strait of Georgia even though some places are in a rain shadow. Where there's rain forest, there's rain. Don't worry if you sweat inside your rain gear. That's what polypropylene underwear, which wicks the moisture away from your skin, is for. In warm weather, that and watertight rain gear is all you need.

Ziploc bags For food especially, pack anything you don't want to get wet in ziploc bags of various sizes. One item per bag or one bag for the item in use. Keep the rest—of the powdered drink or whatever—safely dry in a larger bag.

Drying out Not likely, though I've singed a few sets of underwear trying. Hanging towels etc. up under tarps isn't effective when the air is moist. They end up wetter. Take clothes that are warm when wet, such as fleece and wool. No cottons. At night, pack day clothes into a dry bag. If the tent leaks, they'll still be dry. Try to keep one set of clothes dry at all costs. Put rain gear on as soon as it starts to rain and before your clothes get sodden.

Then, when the warm sun comes out, quickly unpack everything and spread it over the hot shingle and logs. Tents flown as kites dry out quickly.

Hot weather

Use the tarps to provide shade. Wear long-sleeved cotton shirts, long lightweight cotton pants, sunhats and neckerchiefs. Pack waterproof sunscreen of SPF 30 or higher and put it on exposed skin before leaving the tent in the morning. Carry and drink lots of water when paddling. Carry at least two pairs of sunglasses and a sun visor. Paddling westward into a setting sun reflected in the water can be excruciating.

Potable water

Carry enough water for three litres per day per person. This is for drinking or cooking. Take salt water soap for washing yourself and cooking utensils in the sea. Filter water before use. Giardia, which are in almost every creek, cause diarrhea. Fill up before launching or as soon as possible thereafter. Many islands have no water sources.

A cruise ship dwarfs the camp on south Texada Island.

Campsites

Choice is often limited. In the Desolation Sound area, the terrain is rocky. In the Strait of Georgia and Howe Sound, it's usually either rocky or private waterfront property. Unless aiming for a park campsite, start looking around 3 pm and take the first place. In summer, the tide will be lower in the morning. Watch there isn't a dropoff preventing a low-tide launch, or be prepared to wait. Avoid camping within 90 m (300 ft.) of a freshwater source, not only to avoid pollution but also to keep wildlife well away. Use established sites whenever possible and avoid creating new ones. Be prepared to share the site with others, especially if they arrive late in the day or in bad weather. Wilderness experiences ended about 50 years ago. Sharing a site can be an opportunity to meet some very nice people with similar interests. Recently, guides of commercial trips have been required to be licensed by the provincial government to use certain areas, but they do not have exclusive use of them. If you are camped in their favourite place, they should not ask you to leave. If the site has been prepared, likely they are the ones who did the work. Please respect their efforts.

Unload or carry loaded? This depends on the sea conditions. With carrying straps, four people can carry a loaded boat up the beach but two people often risk injury doing this. Find three thin logs and use them as rollers to push the boats up one by one. Even solo paddlers can do this except on steep banks. Then a small "come along" or hoist can be helpful.

Human waste

If you want to make money, invent a gadget small enough to stow in a kayak to evaporate human waste without polluting either the atmosphere or the environment. Hurry up!

The alternatives are explored in Kathleen Meyer's book *How to Shit in the Woods.*[2] Most BC Parks sites on the Strait of Georgia have pit toilets. Never use the beach, even to pee. Owners of oyster leases go ballistic when they see people polluting their product. (Use a pee bottle and take it with you.) At the least, groups should dig a biffy 100 metres away from camp and water sources. Consider storing used toilet paper and tampons and then burning them in a fire below the high tide line—or substituting non-poisonous leaves or smooth rocks for the toilet paper.

Once the boats are unloaded, **always** tie them up. Are you sure where the high tide came to last night? Do the tide tables say it will come higher tonight? Is there any extra surge from an approaching storm or passing boat that could push it several feet higher?

Is there room to make a communal kitchen? Where can a hole be dug for grey water disposal?

Where is the biffy going to be?

Use stoves and fuel for cooking, especially in dry weather when sparks can easily set a whole beach of logs alight or even an entire island.

Should you carry an army hammock with mosquito netting and a tarp roof? Although hammocks are bad for people with back problems, they are useful up Jervis Inlet where the only alternative may be lumpy rocks. Sling an extra regular tarp over the top to keep all gear dry and form a sheltered area to move about in.

Before leaving a campsite, always return poles used to erect tarps to their original places on the beach so that it looks untouched. Pack out all garbage and fill in the biffy.

Fires

The land and the islands are often tinder dry. Do without fires whenever possible and cover the ground under lighted stoves with a 1-metre-square sheet of aluminum foil. Too many campers, including kayakers, have left smouldering ashes which irate residents have had to put out later. Do not leave till the whole campfire area is cold to the touch. (Savary Island residents would like to ban all campfires.)

Gather driftwood only for small garbage fires. Locate them downwind and below tide. Never against a log. Pour water on the ashes each night before going to bed. In the morning, collect up and crush any burnt cans and pack them out. Wash plastic containers and pack them out instead of burning them.

Land Ownership

In addition to private ownership, there are ecological reserves, parks, forest and commercial recreational tenures, and Indian Reserves. The B.C. government claims that "The Province owns the foreshore (intertidal) areas of its coastline."[3] In addition, the province owns coastal "inland waters," or waters "within the jaws of the land" and the lands covered by these waters. The Supreme Court of Canada, in a 1984 decision, also confirmed the province's ownership of the waters and the lands, minerals and other natural resources of the seabed and subsoil in the Georgia, Juan de Fuca, Johnstone and Queen Charlotte Straits. Offshore areas along British Columbia's western coastline from the low water mark, or from the boundaries of inland waters, seaward to the territorial limit are owned by the federal government.

Indian Reserves

Six millennia and more ago when First Nations canoes swept down from the north after the ice ages, they camped where they pleased, which is why Indian Reserves often have two beaches for different kinds of weather. Before landing, ask permission at the band office of the First Nation concerned. They will give permission for some areas but not others. Harwood Island is definitely off limits for camping, though day visitors may picnic on it.

Ecological Reserves

These were created to preserve certain ecological treasures such as:
- representative samples of the province's ecosystems
- rare and endangered plant and animal species
- important genetic resources etc.

They are mainly used for scientific research and educational purposes. Our system of ecological reserves grew out of a 10-year international biological program (1964–74) in which 58 nations participated to identify representative terrestrial and aquatic ecosystems. In 1971 the B.C. legislature passed the Ecological Reserves Act giving permanently protected status to 29 reserves. Others have been added since. Camping is not allowed on ecological reserves except at designated sites.

Provincial Parks

B.C. Parks has a mandate to protect the natural environment, including recreational values and representative and special natural ecosystems, species, features and phenomena. It has been doing this since 1911. Desolation Sound has a series of provincial parks, mainly geared to sail and power boats. Other areas have a mix of provincial and municipal parks. The Sechelt Inlets, though not a park as a whole, contain seven campsites operated by the Sechelt Inlets Marine Provincial Park and three more operated by the Mount Richardson Provincial Park.

Crown Land

Many different organizations can apply for short- or long-term tenures of Crown land. These are now being managed by Land & Water British Columbia Inc. (LWBC), a corporation of the Government of British Columbia. Two tenures of interest to sea kayakers are commercial recreation tenures and forest tenures:

Commercial recreation tenures[4]

Sea kayak guides operating on a fee-for-service basis must obtain a permit for non-exclusive use of specified areas. Some permits allow them to build "improvements" such as campsites. In these cases, LWBC grants them exclusive use of these.

Guides who hold both kinds of tenures are obligated to keep logs of their use for government inspection, pay fees and take out expensive liability insurance. As of 2004, they have to use boom boxes to dispose of human waste.

Buried in their permit document is the statement that they must not interfere with other campers on the land.

My interpretation of this is that if non-fee groups are camped on an unimproved site of a commercial guide's tenure, they cannot be asked to leave. However, in the interests of peace, and space permitting, it would be a good idea if you would graciously share the site. The guide has gone through a great deal of red tape to get it! It would also be helpful if the government would not give out tenures for small sites.

Forest tenures

Under the Forestry Act, the B.C. government grants forest companies tree farm tenures to manage Crown timber sustainably. Definitions of the terms and conditions of these and similar arrangements have been fought over for the better part of the last century. Basically, areas currently being logged have to be reforested within a time limit to a predetermined acceptable standard. The Ministry of Forests permits camping and picnicking in designated recreation sites.

UREPs

These are Crown lands which a provincial government department has set aside for the "Use, Recreation and Enjoyment of the Public." Each has a key number. For example, No. 2406028 refers to the Coode Peninsula and Isbister Islands UREP, which the Ministry of Forests has also designated as an Old Growth Management Area (OGMA). There are several oyster leases on the Trevenen Bay side of the Coode Peninsula and the government has been asked to leave 1-metre corridors between them for public access.

Private land

Most of the waterfront in the Strait of Georgia is wall-to-wall cottage country from Gibsons to Lund. Ask permission before landing or camping. There is also a lot of private property on Cortes and Savary Islands. Hernando is totally private property.

Paddling Etiquette

Wildlife

On the water Carry waterproof binoculars so you can see without getting too close. Frightened seals and sea lions can crush their smaller animals when sliding into the water in a hurry to avoid you. The same is true of birds. If disturbed during nesting activities, gulls and other pelagic birds may give up altogether for the whole year. Back off before they start to move, especially if they are on nesting ledges.

Ashore If birds are pretending to be wounded, they are trying to draw you away from nests on the ground. Watch where you place your feet, and leave. The nests may be little more than shallow depressions in the shingle and very hard to see. On Mitlenatch, volunteer resident wardens make sure that visitors keep to the designated trails to avoid disturbing nesting gulls.

If you see someone else watching or photographing birds or wildlife, do not make a noise or try to attract their attention. Never feed wildlife or leave scraps of food out for them. The bear or wolf you feed may attack the next visitor. When examining low tide creatures, put them back exactly where you found them, replacing protective seaweed or rocks gently.

Dogs

Leave dogs at home. They chase shorebirds, often destroying a year's nesting activities, and they attract cougar and bear, which regard them as tasty morsels. You're next—especially children!

First Nations sites

Many of these, including middens, are protected by the B.C. Heritage Conservation Act, which heavily fines those who disturb or touch artifacts. For permission to visit, ask band offices, not individuals.

Local residents

Ask permission before landing on private property. Never take water from a pump without asking. It may be in short supply. Don't light fires near residences, especially in dry weather.

Coastal communities

If there's a store or restaurant, patronize it. Unemployment is high in coastal communities, and they need all the business they can get. It's both useful and pleasant to go over last-minute trip arrangements at a pretrip dinner, and relive experiences the same way after it's all over. Enjoy the same craft and gift shops patronized by other tourists in search of trip mementoes.

When camping, be prepared to share with local tour operators, who are probably the people who cleared rocks off the landing, smoothed the tent area, and built a fire ring and/or a biffy. In addition to these obvious costs, they pay fees to use both parks and Crown land, and in 2003 their sole underwriter tripled their already-expensive insurance premiums. Although small operations, sometimes they are the only employer in a remote community where cash is short. While living in rural B.C. is

Sliammon Village.

idyllic, finding sustainable work can be a nightmare. This is why oyster farmers are so protective of the pristine waters required for their product. Avoid walking on beaches marked as oyster leases.

Other paddlers

Seek another beach if someone is there ahead of you, or land a distance away. Do not play loud radios or recordings.

Be prepared to share even a small campsite if others arrive. There may not be another place to land nearby. In bad weather, assist others to land and launch. It may be too dangerous for the newcomers to continue. The old Canadian dream of wilderness camping is no longer possible in this area. Besides, you may make some lifelong friends.

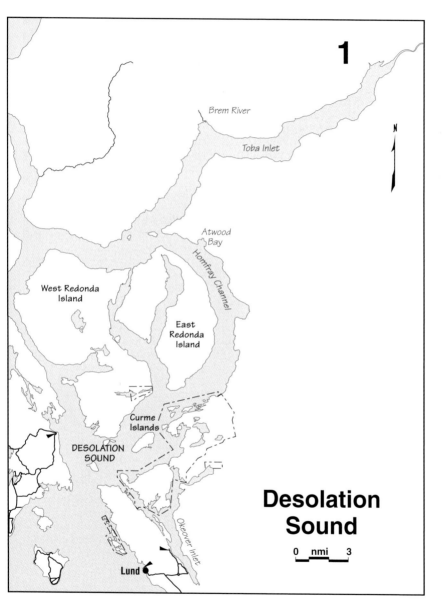

1

Brem River

Toba Inlet

Atwood Bay

Homfray Channel

West Redonda Island

East Redonda Island

N

Curme Islands

DESOLATION SOUND

Okeover Inlet

Desolation Sound

0   nmi   3

Lund

Desolation Sound's sheltered warm water coves dotted with tiny islands and surrounded by the lofty peaks of the Coastal Range have attracted sea kayakers and canoeists as well as the yachting public for many decades and the love affair goes on and on.

When Captain George Vancouver named the area in 1792, he didn't know what he was looking at. First Nations people knew it as a land of plenty with a snug winter village in Grace Harbour and many other summer houses safely hidden in the forest so that Haida slavers would pass them by. Thomas Copeland fleeing the U.S. Civil War, Mike Shuttler, James Palmer and other old timers who arrived by row boat in the 1890s thought it was paradise. So do the hundreds of sail and power boaters who jam its coves in July and August every year. Sea kayakers have been quietly frequenting the area since the 1940s. Cottagers arrived in the early '70s and some turned to oyster farming. In recent years the more radical growers have tried to ban kayakers from Okeover Inlet on the grounds of pollution. In Trevenen Bay especially, big aquaculture business with noisy machinery destroys views and peace.

"Noise is to sea kayakers what fecal coliform is to oyster farming," said Adam Vallance of Powell River Sea Kayaks at a February 2004 meeting where the Malaspina Okeover Coastal Plan was discussed. He can't take customers into Trevenen Bay because of the noise created by generators, sorters, washers and tumblers located on oyster farms there. Contiguous farms block access to some UREPs—areas supposedly set aside for the use, recreation and enjoyment of the public, e.g., the Isbister Islands at the mouth of Trevenen Bay. There is no noise bylaw and little point in passing one, as enforcement would be almost impossible.

Fortunately, parks protect several areas. Desolation Sound Marine Provincial Park encompasses the popular anchorages of Prideaux Haven, Tenedos Bay, the Curme Islands, Grace Harbour, etc. Parks at Teakerne Arm, Roscoe Bay and Walsh Cove protect small areas of West Redonda Island. The Copeland Islands Marine Provincial Park covers the Copelands but not the nearby Townley Islands or Powell Islets. Malaspina Peninsula Provincial Park protects the north end of the 180-km Sunshine Coast Trail. In addition the Okeover Arm Provincial Park (also called Tux'wnech), a joint effort of B.C. Parks and the Sliammon First Nation, ensures that kayakers have a place to launch in Okeover Inlet.

Authors who have written about the area include M. Wylie Blanchet (*The Curve of Time*) and Beth Hill, who edited Amy and Francis Barrow's 1933–1941 diaries, adding her own observations, in *Upcoast Summers* and *Seven-Knot Summers*.

Desolation Sound is accessible either from the Powell River area or from Cortes Island. Powell River is a mainland coastal community accessible only by ferries: two from Vancouver, one from Vancouver Island. Cortes Island is two ferry rides from Vancouver Island.

There are four approaches to Desolation Sound:

- From Lund by way of the Copeland Islands – See Trip Nos. 1, 2.
- From Okeover by way of Okeover Inlet and Malaspina Inlet – See Trip No. 3.
- From Squirrel Cove – See Trip Nos. 7, 8.
- By water taxi – The Lund Water Taxi service can take kayaks into Desolation Sound and beyond. If they are booked up, the Powell River Visitor Info Centre has a list of other operators, or look on the notice boards at Lund.

Launches

Lund area

Lund Harbour. From the Powell River Visitor Info Centre drive 27 km up Highway 101 and turn left at the T-junction after the Lund gas station (which is not always open). There are two launch ramps: a single concrete one at the bottom of the hill behind the hotel, and a double ramp into the boat harbour close by the vehicle-congested Savary Water Taxi.

The ramp behind the hotel, opposite where Rockfish Kayak and Terracentric Coastal Adventures are, is much less busy with power boats than the double ramp into the harbour. When using this ramp, keep gear to one side, as power boats sometimes use it too. There is a $3 in and out charge. Park up the hill at Dave's Parking Lot and tell the attendant how long you will be away. They will valet park your vehicle. On the way back,

Barge launch at the back of the hotel at Lund.

call them by cell phone and they'll drive your vehicle down to meet you on the dock.

If using the double launch ramp into the boat harbour, keep to the left-hand side, as the wharfinger prefers kayaks there. Take change to pay the $2 in or out charge. Before leaving Lund call in at Nancy's Bakery for a choice of seven varieties of coffee and lots of goodies, including three kinds of butter tarts. She also bakes bread.

Finn Bay

At the T-junction in Lund, turn right and drive for 1.2 km to where the pavement ends. Park on the right-hand side. A short narrow road on the left leads down to the rocky shore. Parking is limited and unattended vehicles have occasionally been vandalized.

Dinner Rock Forestry Campsite

From the Powell River Visitor Info Centre, drive 25.3 km north on Highway 101 and turn left at the sign.

Marbled murrelets

There is a community of marbled murrelets around Prideaux Haven. Simon Fraser University research on this colony has shown that the birds nest up to 50 km inland. As they are not proficient at landing, they require wide mossy branches of old growth trees on which to crash land and lay their eggs. They seem to like trees on edges, such as the steep slopes of East and West Redonda Islands.[5] In summer they are speckled brown birds usually in pairs. After breeding they moult, losing the ability to fly for a few weeks, so they dive instead. Their winter plumage is a smart suit of black and white. Marbled murrelets with dark beards are ancient murrelets and are more likely to be seen in winter in less-travelled areas such as between Savary and Harwood or around Mitlenatch.

Although this launch looks good on the map, it isn't. At the bottom, the road requires 4WD and the beach is too rocky to land on in any kind of a surf. This happens when the prevailing summer northwesterly blows.

Okeover area

Government wharf ramp. This charges $2 in and $2 out. Although the ramp has been improved somewhat, it is often in use by oyster farmers with big trucks. To reach it, drive up Highway 101 for 26.6 km and turn right at the Okeover sign. The wharf is another 4.1 km, at the end of the paved road. Before launching, walk up to the Laughing Oyster Restaurant and make a reservation for supper when you return. You won't get in at the last minute without one.

Tux'wnech Provincial Park

Also called Okeover Arm Provincial Park. Follow the same directions as above, but when the road curves down to the government wharf, drive straight ahead onto an unpaved road. The campsite is on your right and the park entrance about 50 m away. There is a small area where kayakers' vehicles can be parked overnight. You can't drive to the beach, just to the head of some broad steps down to it. A sign directs you to drop $4 a day in the box for "kayak parking."

Powell River Sea Kayaks

In Penrose Bay. They charge $4 a day for parking. To reach them, continue along the road past Tux'wnech Provincial Park for another 2.5 km. Their sign is on the right. You can drive to the edge of the shingle beach but not onto it, as it is an oyster lease. There is not a lot of space, especially if rental boats are launching at the same time. Phone ahead to book rental boats.

Y-Knot Campsite
Drive 3.1 km down the Okeover Road. Turn right at the sign for the campsite, which is on D'Angio Road. The road is unpaved and should be driven slowly. Register at the office. Back down a rough road to the beach. This launch is 1 nmi farther up Okeover Inlet than the government wharf. Their parking charge is similar to the others. Phone ahead to rent kayaks or canoes.

Campsites

Lund The private campsite Sunlund-by-the-Sea has tent sites, and tenters can leave vehicles there while off kayaking. Access from the water is up a steep trail and steps from a rocky landing. Alternatively, bring wheels, land at either boat launch ramp and wheel your boat 200–300 metres.

Tux'wnech Provincial Park
Fourteen sites, pit toilet, small area for overnight parking for kayakers at a $4 fee. Road access described above under Launches.

Y-Knot Campsite
A private campsite with a boat launch and dock. Access described above under Launches.

Cochrane Bay This campsite is shared with hikers on the Sunshine Coast Trail.

Grace Harbour Two tent pads and a pit toilet.

Curme Islands Rocky wilderness campsites with a pit toilet on one of the islands.

Teakerne Arm Marine Provincial Park
Although officially there are no campsites here, you may find space for a tent or two. Alternatives are very tough to find.

Tenedos Bay Two tent pads and a pit toilet on the east side of the bay where the creek comes down from Unwin Lake.

Otter Island An unorganized campsite on the mainland opposite Otter Island. Land in the bay behind the southern headland.

Roscoe Bay Provincial Park
Pit toilets and space for 4–5 tents at the head of the bay.

Walsh Cove Marine Provincial Park
Like Teakerne Arm Marine Provincial Park, kayakers have camped here and B.C. Parks has no plans to put in campsite or picnic site facilities.

Connis Point An unorganized campsite on the north side of East Redonda Island. Sometimes used by tour groups.

Forbes Bay An unorganized campsite on Homfray Channel.

Brem River An unorganized campsite at the mouth of the Brem River in Toba Inlet.

Some campsites out on the islands are very small. If you find something before you reach one of those mentioned above, take it.

The Copeland Islands from the air.

Thulin Passage pictograph.

1 Copeland Islands

Difficulty Beginner conditions – low risk
After Sarah Point, conditions change to Intermediate
Distance 8 nmi round trip
Duration 2–4 hours
Chart Sunshine Coast 3311 No. 5 Grief Point to Desolation Sound 1:40,000
Tides on Point Atkinson
Currents none

In addition to being one of the three approaches to Desolation Sound (see Trip Nos. 2, 3, 7, 8), the Copeland Islands (locally called "the Raggeds") are also a popular day trip, especially for paddlers renting kayaks at Lund. The islands are often full of campers on summer weekends. Some never get beyond them. Between Labour Day and Easter they're usually deserted.

Paddling considerations
• Wind direction and strength.
• Traffic in Thulin Passage.

The route
From Lund, paddle north along the coast and into nearby Finn Bay. At high tide you can negotiate a winding passage between Sevilla Island and the mainland past some funky little cottages. Once on the outside, cross over to the first island as traffic permits. Thulin Passage is quite busy with pleasure craft and commercial boats commuting to and from Desolation Sound. Rasmussen Bay, just before the islands, was once the scene of a terrible Indian massacre. There was a warrior camp above the cliffs at the south end of the bay, with lookouts posted on the islet below to guard it. One dark night, enemies crept up the rock and killed the lookouts as they slept, then wiped out the camp.

Landing is allowed anywhere in the Copeland Islands, as they are now a marine provincial park. Getting ashore is not always easy on the rocky beaches where, at low tide, razor-sharp oyster shells cut bare feet to ribbons. The narrow waist of the first island was where an old man and his dog lived in the 1940s. Once a week he would row to Lund for groceries. One day his boat was found floating without him. His dog was on shore in distress and no one saw him again. A picnic table marks the site of his cabin.

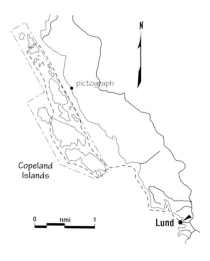

Mink used to run all over these islands but haven't been seen for over a decade. Since salmon stocks have been depleted, bald eagles have turned to alternative food sources. There is a strong possibility that mink are one of these.

An interesting way to approach the third island is to paddle the outer coast of the second to where a sheer cliff falls into the water between the second and next, unnumbered, island. The cliff always has lots of colourful purple and ochre sea stars cuddled together on the rock. In February one year we saw a hatch of shrimp fry there.

Behind the third island is a favourite anchorage for yachts, whose crews often come ashore to walk their dogs.

Manzanita tree in the Copelands.

The Epting family spent three weeks here in the 1970s. They packed their two double kayaks with colour-coded gear bags so that their two children could take an active share of the chores. The parents let them run wild and everyone had a wonderful time. One of their projects was to clear a way through the boulders on the beach to make it easier for their kayaks to launch. Others came later and widened the opening.

One Easter weekend, a group of kayak club members and I were storm stayed on this island while the northwest wind howled around us. We couldn't even get out of the bay. Even beginner's trips are not immune to the weather.

Across Thulin Passage from Third Island, high up on the cliff there's a pictograph which Sliammon guide Murray Mitchell thinks may have marked a fishing boundary.

The fourth island group is clustered around a lagoon which often provides overnight anchorage for power boats, so you may not have it to yourself. It's a good base for trips to the nearby Townley Islands, which are privately owned, and to the Powell Islets, which are too steep to land on. In spring these islands are particularly lovely for their wild flowers—pink sea blush, yellow monkey flower and blue-eyed Mary. Or go farther afield to explore Twin Islands and Cortes.

You can also paddle 13.2 nmi around Sarah Point to Okeover. Either shuttle a vehicle to the take-out or hike 7 km back to Lund.

Another pleasant short excursion from the islands is to visit Major Islet, a smooth, white rock that is home to pelagic and double-crested cormorants, pigeon guillemots and many harbour seals.

2 Copeland Islands to the Curme Islands

Difficulty Intermediate conditions – moderate risk
Distances Last Copeland to the Curme Islands via Mink Island 7 nmi
Last Copeland to the Curme Islands via Galley Bay 10.9 nmi
Duration Via Mink Island 3 hours
Via Galley Bay 4.5 hours
Charts No. 3538 Desolation Sound and Sutil Channel 1:40,000
No. 3312 Desolation Sound and Jervis Inlet pages 12–15 1:10,000
Tides on Point Atkinson
Currents none

The Curme Islands are magical rocky islands which tend to get overpopulated with kayakers but are beautiful all the same. They make a good base camp for day trips around Desolation Sound. They are one of three access points to Desolation Sound. Okeover and Squirrel Cove are the others.

Paddling considerations
- There's a lot of marine traffic in Thulin Passage.
- Crossing of Thulin Passage 0.3 nmi.
- It's best to do the crossing to Mink Island from Zephine Head (1.5 nmi) in the morning before the wind gets up.

The route
From the last Copeland Island, cross narrow Thulin Passage to the closed vacation community of Bliss Landing, where strata owners tie up their 20-metre yachts. Proceed north up Thulin Passage. Immediately before Sarah Point, a rocky cove is the start of the

Mount Denman and Desolation Sound.

180-km Sunshine Coast Trail. This is a good lunch stop and you can hike a bit of the trail for a change of pace. As this passes through a very dry arbutus forest, do not light fires or smoke.

Once past Sarah Point, if the wind is calm, head for Mink Island and the Curme Islands. Mink is privately owned and has few places to land. The Curme Islands are close to the east end of Mink.

If the crossing to Mink looks rough, paddle along the mainland coast via Galley Bay and Tenedos Bay and cross 0.4 nmi from Otter Island.

The approach to Galley Bay is festooned with No Trespassing signs. Please respect these. If you want to land, examine the sketch map and land on the areas which are not private property.

The Hansons

Axel and Amanda Hanson pre-empted land in the west corner of Galley Bay in 1911 and brought up a family of ten children there until the mid '50s. The Hansons smoked and dried their own fish and meat and lived to a ripe old age. Ingrid Cowie, who taught at Galley Bay at the time, recounted: "Pa Hanson made delicious wine which tasted like Cherry Heering. He served it a tumbler full at a time and it tasted like pop but when you tried to get up your legs wouldn't work."

Leaving Galley Bay, as you paddle along the rocky shore, watch for occasional flashes of scarlet hiding amongst the seaweed at low tide. They may be part of a blood or a vermilion star. Both are bright scarlet but the blood star has a smooth skin whereas the vermilion is covered in plates. They are quite different from the usual purple or orange ochre stars and much less common.

When you arrive at Portage Cove, don't land. It's private property and the owner has signs up forbidding trespassing. The cove provides a welcome respite when the wind is strong. Pause to think about Joe Copeland, who around 1890 rowed here from Vancouver, built a cabin and made a living trapping and hand logging. When the steamship arrived, he'd meet it wearing the full uniform of a Confederate bugler from the U.S. Civil War. His father was a colonel on the Union side. At the end of the war, Copeland lived with bands of stagecoach robbers while he worked his way north. The "Ragged Islands" near Lund are now named after him.

Since your destination is the Curme Islands and you'll have other days to explore, don't detour into Tenedos Bay. Follow the warm-pink cliffs to a narrow passage before a tall, rocky island. This is Otter Island. The Curme Islands are a short crossing back toward Mink Island. If this stretch of water is rough, retreat into the narrow passage, which opens into a small bay. On the mainland side of it is a camp spot overlooking the Curme Islands.

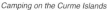
Camping on the Curme Islands.

3 Okeover Inlet

Difficulty Beginner conditions – low risk
Distances 23 nmi to explore all of it
         Freke Anchorage to the government wharf 2 nmi
         Government wharf to Grace Harbour 4 nmi
         Grace Harbour to Zephine Head 3.25 nmi
         Government wharf to head of Lancelot Inlet 5.5 nmi
         Theodosia Inlet 1 nmi at low water, 2 nmi at high water
Duration Okeover can be a day trip, a weekend or a week,
         or serve as the gateway to Desolation Sound.
Charts No. 3312 Desolation Sound and Jervis Inlet pages 12–15 1:10,000
         No. 3559 Malaspina Inlet, Okeover Inlet and Lancelot Inlet 1:12,000
         No. 3538 Desolation Sound and Sutil Channel 1:40,000
Tides on Point Atkinson
Currents The tidal current which swirls past the Isbister Islands is strong enough to
         produce boils which shift around the boats of unwary kayakers.
         If the current is against you at Zephine Head, cross to the other side of the
         inlet for relief.

Fringed with arbutus and shore pine, this lovely inlet has been enjoyed by beginning sea kayakers since the 1940s, but in the last 25 years, noisy oyster farmers have spoiled parts of it. On the plus side, most, though not all, of the industrialization is contained in Trevenen Bay, making it still possible to have safe, enjoyable paddles in other areas. This is just as well, as Okeover (pronounced OAK-over) is one of the few remaining sheltered places that is usually safe for beginners. It is also one of two access points to Desolation Sound from the mainland. Several days paddling can be enjoyed without going outside the inlet.

Paddling considerations

- Although a southeaster can make Okeover blow up, most of the time it is calm.
- Don't paddle through oyster farming equipment.

- Avoid landing on beaches signed as oyster leases.
- Don't try to portage at Portage Cove. Despite its traditional aboriginal use for that purpose, it is private property and trespassers are not welcome.

The route

Start at any of the three launches given above: Y-Knot, Tux'wnech or Powell River Sea Kayaks. If your destination is Desolation Sound, stay on the same side of the inlet as you launched on. At the end of the Coode Peninsula either cross the mouth of Trevenen Bay to Cochrane Bay or cross the inlet to Grace Harbour.

Cochrane Bay is part of the Desolation Sound Marine Provincial Park. There is a campsite, and a trail connecting to the Sunshine Coast Trail. On stormy days, use it to hike around Sarah Point to the start of the trail or hike in the opposite direction for a swim in Wednesday Lake.

Grace Harbour has a campsite in the inner bay and a short trail up to a marshy lake. The outer bay where a small cabin stands on the shore is the former site of the big winter village where the Sliammon people would gather after summering all through Bute Inlet and Toba Inlet, Squirrel Cove, Texada Island, etc. As each group returned, some by way of Portage Cove, they would walk at low tide out to the small island off the winter village, and the island

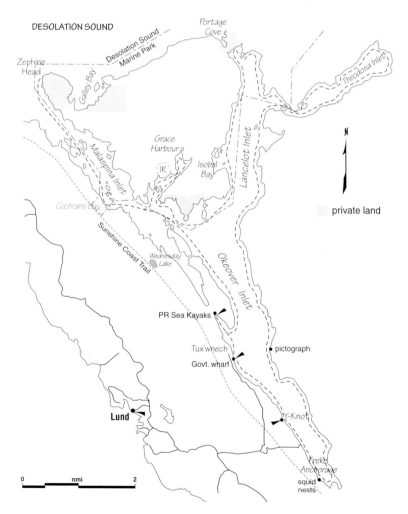

DESOLATION SOUND

Portage Cove

Zephine Head

Galley Bay

Desolation Sound Marine Park

Theodosa Inlet

Grace Harbour

IR

Isobel Bay

Lancelot Inlet

Malaspina Inlet

Cochrane Bay

Sunshine Coast Trail

Wednesday Lake

N

private land

Okeover Inlet

PR Sea Kayaks

Tux'wnech

Govt. wharf

pictograph

Lund

Y-Knot

Freke Anchorage

squid nests

0   nmi   2

would become a theatrical stage where the group would have until the next low tide to tell the stories of their summer exploits to the assembled people. Grace Harbour, and in fact the whole of the Okeover Inlet complex, should be a boaters no-discharge zone, but so far, although many people have recommended it, this hasn't happened. Don't swim where there are lots of yachts.

The Cochrane Bay or Grace Harbour stops can be lunch stops on the way to Desolation or they can be overnight camp spots prior to exploring Lancelot Inlet and Theodosia Inlet. For those heading out to Desolation Sound, if the tide is dropping, proceed along the east side of Malaspina Inlet to Zephine Head. If the tide is against you, avoid bucking the strong current by keeping to the western shore. At the mouth of the inlet, cross without going too close to Zephine Head, and follow Trip No. 2.

For those remaining within the Okeover Inlet system, Isobel Bay in Lancelot Inlet has some pretty islands to explore. From there follow the coast around the head of Lancelot Inlet till eventually the narrow hidden entrance to Theodosia Inlet is visible. Once inside, it's like being in a calm, landlocked lake with the tide still rising and falling. The head of Theodosia is a large mudflat. In the middle, there's a shallow waterway up the Theodosia River. If you paddle in at high tide, be sure to leave before you get stranded until the next high tide.

Leaving Theodosia, continue along the cliffs and back into Okeover. Watch for marbled murrelet chicks. These are the survivors of an incredible journey. Born on thick, mossy

Isobel Bay, Lancelot Inlet.

Okeover and Desolation Sound from the Bunster Hills.

branches of old growth forest in the Bunster Hills above the inlet, the tiny balls of fluff fledge by falling several metres to the ground and then make their way to the inlet. Not surprisingly, there's a high mortality rate.

Keep on the east side of Okeover and watch for some high cliffs opposite the government wharf. The smudged red ochre stains on them are pictographs whose message predates the Sliammon people and is lost in the mysteries of time.

Freke Anchorage at the head of Okeover dries to a mud flat encrusted with invading mud snails. Toquenatch Creek, which runs into it, used to be a favourite salmon fishing stream for the Sliammon people.

As the shore curves back into Okeover, the remains of a small log dump is where one August I found squid nests. These look as if someone had thrown a white sheepskin into the water. Look closer and it's a mass of tubular eggs, sometimes with a brown squid swimming above it in search of a mate. Within a week or two the nest turns brown and is almost impossible to see. The nests are likely to be found within 5 m of freshwater seeps, which occur throughout the inlet. These are the same squid that are harvested in California for calamari. Here, they are close to their northern limit, so their spawning grounds are too unpredictable for a commercial fishery.

James Palmer

In 1900, James Palmer pre-empted land at the head of Theodosia Inlet right next to the Sliammon village. Originally from Wisconsin, he and his family had lived in Oregon for 20 years until too many people arrived there. After a winter trapping in the Stillwater Valley south of Powell River, Palmer and his eldest son, Will, brought the rest of the family to Theodosia. But even this was not remote enough. In winter, Palmer left his wife and remaining children in Theodosia and rowed up Bute Inlet to run a trap line.

Pictograph in Oakover Inlet.

Y-Knot campsite and kayak rental is a possible launch or take-out at the road which comes down to the water just north of their dock. The massive floating oyster development beyond has been the centre of considerable controversy. Paddle around this, not through it.

Shortly after, there's a dock with a chainsaw carving on it. Above, in the trees, are several unusually designed cabins that look like tree houses. These belong to the popular Desolation Sound Resort. Although they have cooking facilities, most guests eat lunch and dinner at the Laughing Oyster restaurant, which is above the government wharf. The Tux'wnech steps come down to the beach about 100 m farther on.

The beach in front of the park is worth exploring at low tide. It is a favourite field trip for the Malaspina Naturalists, who have found all kinds of creatures, from mottled stars to baby octopi, squid nests to chitons, as well as the intriguing yellow eggs of the plainfin midshipman (*Porichthys notatus*) guarded by the male parent. Please return each creature to its exact habitat after you've looked at it. If possible, don't pick them up.

Plainfin midshipman with eggs.

4 Curme Islands to Tenedos Bay

Difficulty Intermediate conditions – moderate risk
Distance 4 nmi round trip
Duration 2–4 hours
Charts No. 3538 Desolation Sound and Sutil Channel 1:40,000
No. 3312 Desolation Sound and Jervis Inlet pages 6–7 1:40,000
Tides on Point Atkinson
Currents none

Tenedos Bay is a short day trip from the Curme Islands or Otter Island. It promises a freshwater bath in the warm creek, a walk up the trail and perhaps a swim in the colder lake. See sketchmap on page 48.

Paddling considerations
- Wind direction and strength
- Boat traffic

The route
From the Curme Islands, cross over to Otter Island. Instead of going through the narrow passage between it and the mainland, turn southeast and follow the warm-pink cliffs into Tenedos Bay, which is a popular yacht anchorage. Many people row ashore to follow the trail up to the lake and enjoy a freshwater bath in the warm creek pools slippery with moss. The lake itself is disappointingly jammed with logs, so it is difficult to reach the water to swim.

On the way back, circumnavigate the inside of Tenedos Bay, which has a beautiful shallow passage overhung with trees on the far side of an island. Off the mouth of Tenedos Bay a couple of rocky islets are home to a flock of glaucous-winged gulls.

Tenedos

In the 1920s, James Palmer's son, Will, had a logging camp in Tenedos Bay, then called Deep Bay. It was on floats but the Palmers' house, the commissary and the school were pulled up on the beach. By 1931 the men had finished logging the area around Unwin Lake and, after the last log had whooshed down the flume to the ocean, Palmer moved the camp to the head of Toba Inlet.

Twenty-year-old Eleanor Lusk, a Prairie neophyte, was the camp schoolteacher. The day of the move, she taught the whole way. The school's float was connected to those with the houses, so the children were able to go home for lunch. Her spelling test was much interrupted because the kids kept dashing to the windows to see interesting things. "I just let them because it was such a wonderful experience. I thought they should take advantage of it," she said.

5 Curme Islands to Prideaux Haven

Difficulty Intermediate conditions – moderate risk
Distance   Curme Islands to Roffey Island round trip 7.4 nmi
Duration   3–4 hours
Charts   No. 3538 Desolation Sound and Sutil Channel 1:40,000
            No. 3312 Desolation Sound and Jervis Inlet page 9 1:40,000,
            including a Roscoe Bay inset 1:10,000
Tides   on Point Atkinson
Currents   none

Prideaux Haven is the name given to a complex of coves including Laura Cove, Melanie Cove (pronounced muh-LAY-ni by the pioneers), Roffey Island, etc. First Nations people dug clams here; individualistic pioneers logged, fished and farmed here; and now boaters vie for places in the popular anchorages.

Paddling considerations
• Float plane traffic

The route
From the Curme Islands, head for the narrow opening between Otter Island and the mainland. On a high tide, you may be able to follow the coast and paddle between Eveleigh Island and the mainland. If not, paddle between Eveleigh and Mary Islands, turning in to Prideaux Haven between Lucy Point and Oriel Rocks before pass-

Melanie Cove as Mike would have seen it in winter. Photo: John Dafoe.

ing Scobell Island. Melanie Cove is straight ahead and east. For Laura Cove, paddle east if it's mid to high tide; otherwise, retreat and go in again by Copplestone Point.

In July and August the Prideaux Haven coves are full of expensive yachts, some of which are serviced by aircraft. It's quite a sight but don't swim there. In February, you can have it to yourself just as Mike Shuttler and Phil Lavigne did when they settled in Melanie and Laura Coves respectively in the early 20th century.

Mike Shuttler, also known as Andrew, lived for nearly 40 years in Melanie Cove, having arrived around 1890. He was born in Michigan and had worked there as a logger until a knife fight scarred half his face and left him near death.

"I decided then," he told M. Wylie Blanchet, author of *The Curve of Time*, who met him in the 1930s, "that if that was all there was to life, it wasn't worth living; and I was going off somewhere by myself to think it out." Armed with a small library of ancient philosophers, he built a snug cabin and set out to live in harmony with nature. Visitors were always welcome to come for a chat.

Blanchet tells of their first meeting when Mike rowed out to visit. Like many hand loggers, he stood up in the boat facing forward, pushing on the oars rather than pulling. He invited the Blanchets to come ashore to pick windfall apples. They found he had built terraces enclosed by an eight-foot cedar fence to keep the deer out. Inside, he grew apple trees and vegetables. For meat, he had chickens, goats and deer, plus fish and clams. The Palmer logging camp in Deep Bay

(Tenedos Bay) and the Refuge Cove store, where he and other Desolation Sound settlers went for mail, were glad to buy his excess.

When Stewart Edward White wrote his novel *Skookum Chuck*, he based the character of Tim in Chapter VII, "The Adventure of the Transcendental Hand Logger," on Mike.[6] There is a detailed description of how Mike felled a huge tree exactly where he wanted it and then used jacks and patience to slide it down into the ocean. When he had gathered enough logs for a boom, a tug towed it to Vancouver, where his wood was used to build some of the shipyards.

Mike was in his 70s when Cortes pioneer Ingrid Cowie, then a small child, met him. "His windows were darkened by grape vines with big white spider webs in between them," she said. "He used to drop flies in their webs, saying: 'These are my friends.' His floors were covered with scraped but otherwise untanned deer hides. Above them a layer of fleas bit anyone with bare feet like mine." She didn't like visiting him but her father, Jens Andersen, who had known Mike for 20 years, often took her there.

Today, Mike's cabin is gone but you can still see traces of his terraces and a few tangled fruit trees. There is a trail between the head of Melanie Cove and Laura Cove where his neighbour Phil Lavigne lived. Another trail goes to Unwin Lake.

Phil Lavigne, who was reputed to have killed a man in Quebec, settled in Laura Cove sometime in the early 20th century. He bought a fishing licence in 1924, and when Francis and Amy Barrows visited in 1933, he was already in his 70s and receiving $20 a month old-age pension.

Yachts in Prideaux Haven.

Entrance to Melanie Cove.

"Phil always took the Sunday paper," said Maria Christensen who as a child lived in Roscoe Bay in the 1930s and '40s. "He couldn't read but he enjoyed the funnies." After Mike died, Lavigne built shelves around his bunk and transferred Mike's book collection to them.

"All dem word and 'e 'ad to die like all de rest of us!" Lavigne told Blanchet.

Roffey Island hides the most famous place of all—Vancouver's flea village. Concealed from Haida slavers, the Sliammon people had a small, fortified village on the rocky peninsula behind the island. When Captain Vancouver and his men visited Roffey Island on June 30, 1792, they mistakenly thought the village had been abandoned.

"My grandfather said our people had the original mobile homes," said Murray Mitchell, who runs Ayjoo-mixw Tours in a traditional canoe. "Planks were lashed to posts and taken with them when they moved."

Vancouver's men saw the posts but didn't realize that the people had taken the planks with them for use elsewhere. The men also noticed that a cantilevered deck in front of the houses made scaling the cliff impossible. Mitchell said that when the villagers were in residence they would have piled rocks and heavy branches on the deck ready to hurl down on invaders. The small village at Lund had similar fortifications.

As Vancouver's men poked into piles of "filthy garments and apparel of the late inhabitants" they were attacked by a multitude of fleas. Although they jumped into water "up to their necks," they were unable to get rid of the creatures until they had boiled all their own clothes.

"The people hadn't fled," said Mitchell. "They had just been transformed into the fleas which Vancouver's men found there. The village was called Mah-choh-sah-yee, meaning flea village. It was not used for long."

6 Roscoe Bay and Black Lake

Difficulty Intermediate conditions – moderate risk
Distance 4.5 nmi
Duration 2–3 hours
Charts　No. 3538 Desolation Sound and Sutil Channel 1:40,000
　　　　　No. 3312 Desolation Sound and Jervis Inlet page 9 1:40,000,
　　　　　including a Roscoe Bay inset 1:10,000
Tides　on Point Atkinson
Currents none

Roscoe Bay on West Redonda Island is a Marine Provincial Park with camping facilities and a trail up to the warm sunny waters of Black Lake, which is excellent for swimming.

Paddling considerations
• Wind direction and strength
• Crossing Homfray Channel 1.5 nmi

The route
From the Curme Islands, head to the outside of Otter Island, pass Sky Pilot and Pringle Rock, where harbour seals bask, and stop at the end of Melville Island. Look up Homfray Channel and down Desolation Sound to assess the weather. How fast is this morning's forecast coming in? Cross the 1.5

The exit from Roscoe Bay.

nmi to Marylebone Point. Unless the tide is extremely low, kayaks should be able to make it into Roscoe Bay, though yachts have to wait till the water is deep enough. Halfway down the north side of the bay a pipe with fresh water enables you to replenish your supplies. Filter or boil it before using. Land at the end and pull your boats up to leave room for the dinghies from the anchored yachts. There is a pit toilet up a short trail on the north side and a camping area. Another trail follows the creek up to Black Lake.

Salt Lagoon

In 1927 when Carl and Bertha Christenson pre-empted land on Black Lake, Roscoe Bay was known as Salt Lagoon. Tragedy struck the following year. Bertha was alone with the two children, Maria and baby Joe, making fruit jelly. Maria aged three was stuffing paper into the stove.

"What's that crackling?" she asked her mother but Bertha was a bit deaf and didn't hear anything.

"Go outside and see if there's a bird on the roof," she told her daughter.

"There's flames out there," cried Maria running back inside.

Bertha picked up the bucket of water always kept handy, leaned a ladder against the house and climbed up. Maria had a little pail of water too. She climbed up behind her mother but unfortunately spilt it.

"It's too late," said Bertha climbing down. "Take your brother and go to the water and stay there." Maria grabbed Joe and took him to the well because she'd been told many times not to go near the lake.

Bertha ran back into the house and threw out two chairs and the sewing machine. Flames blocked the door. She was trapped. Throwing a felt mattress out of the bedroom window she jumped down on it. At the lake she couldn't find the children. Panicked, she called and found them at the well.

All three ran to Salt Lagoon where Jamieson Co. operated a logging camp. The men were out on the logs using a saw and didn't hear Bertha's cries so she took her bloomers off and waved them. That got their attention.

After the fire, Bertha went to Vancouver never to return. Her sister Peggy brought the children back on the Union steamship SS *Chelohsin*. The children and Carl had many happy years in the new house on Roscoe Bay.

Roscoe Bay.

Sunset on the Redondas and Desolation Sound.

7 West Redonda Island

Difficulty Intermediate conditions – moderate risk

Distances Round trip from Squirrel Cove 41.5 nmi
Squirrel Cove to Refuge Cove 2.8 nmi
Refuge Cove to Cassel Falls (Teakerne Arm) 7.5 nmi
Cassel Falls to Redonda Bay 9 nmi
Redonda Bay to Dean Point 8.5 nmi
Dean Point to the head of Roscoe Bay 9 nmi
Marylebone Point to Refuge Cove 6 nmi
Refuge Cove to Lund 9.7 nmi
Refuge Cove to Okeover 7.8 nmi

Duration 4–5 days

Charts No. 3538 Desolation Sound and Sutil Channel 1:40,000
No. 3312 Desolation Sound and Jervis Inlet page 9 1:40,000,
including a Roscoe Bay inset 1:10,000

Tides on Point Atkinson

Currents none

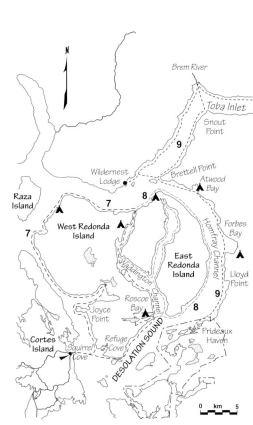

West Redonda is more visited than East Redonda. Most people want to call in at the Refuge Bay store, wash their hair in the waterfall in Teakerne Arm and visit Roscoe Bay to swim in Black Lake.

Paddling considerations
- Strong winds in Lewis Channel
- Few landings, usually rocky

The route

Although you can access West Redonda from Lund or Okeover, the closest launch is at Squirrel Cove on Cortes Island. Drive to Campbell River, take the Quadra ferry, drive across the island to Heriot Bay and take the Cortes ferry, then drive to Squirrel Cove.

Be wary of the wind as you cross Lewis Channel to visit Refuge Cove. As you approach, watch for other boat traffic and seaplanes landing. Over the years the store has gone through many transformations. Apart from general groceries, it also has a liquor store and a bakery. It is one of the oldest on the coast, dating back to the early years of last century.

Leaving Refuge Cove, paddle north to Teakerne Arm, where a large waterfall cascades down from Cassel Lake above. Land just before the waterfall and follow a 1-km trail up to the lake. Landing

Cassel Falls, Teakerne Arm.

On one trip some years ago we found a tiny beach behind a small point which made a lovely campsite from which we watched the seals courting. Redonda Bay, 9 nmi from Cassel Falls, was a lively settlement in the 1930s. Today, aquaculture, log booms and No Trespassing signs make this unattractive to campers. Proceed 1.5 nmi farther along Deer Passage just before Connis Point where a creek descends from a small lake. Black bear enjoy the creek too, so hang your food. Also watch for cougar. West Redonda is renowned for them, especially the one that followed a dog into someone's kitchen at Refuge Cove. That story and many others are in Beth Hill's *Seven-Knot Summers.*

From Connis Point, it's 5.5 nmi to Dean Point, which marks the narrow passage (0.15 nmi) between West and East Redonda. If you're planning to go up Toba Inlet (see Trip No. 9), continue for 2.3 nmi to Hepburn Point and cross the upper end of Homfray Channel (0.8 nmi) to Brettell Point and the start of Toba.

Otherwise, turn south down Waddington Channel.

There are pictographs and a potential camp spot in Walsh Cove and a fish farm in Doctor Bay. It's 3.5 nmi to Shirley Point and the same distance to Walter Point.

At the south end of Waddington Channel, spend a night in Roscoe Bay and have a swim in the warm waters of Black Lake. In the morning, head back along the rocky south coast of West Redonda. Off the southern tip, the Martin Islands, though quite rocky, are a potential camp spot.

at the waterfall itself is easy from a dinghy but tougher from a kayak. Camping is difficult. Joyce Point and Talbot Island are solid aquaculture, so you can no longer camp there. Some people have camped 0.4 km west of the trail up to the lake.

Coming out of Lewis Channel and into Deer Passage, the water turns noticeably colder. From Teakerne Arm, paddle north up Lewis Channel.

8 East Redonda Island

Difficulty Intermediate conditions – moderate risk
Distances 47 nmi round trip from Squirrel Cove,
plus 17 nmi up Pendrell Sound and back
Squirrel Cove to Marylebone Point via Refuge Cove 10 nmi
Marylebone Point to Horace Head 0.9 nmi
Horace Head to Booker Point 5.6 nmi
Booker Point to Forbes Bay 2 nmi
Booker Point to Hepburn Point 6.2 nmi
Hepburn Point to Dean Point 2.3 nmi
Dean Point to the head of Roscoe Bay 9 nmi
Marylebone Point to Durham Point 2.5 nmi
Durham Point to the head of Pendrell Sound 6 nmi
Duration 5–6 days
Charts No. 3538 Desolation Sound and Sutil Channel 1:40,000
No. 3312 Desolation Sound and Jervis Inlet page 9 1:40,000,
including a Roscoe Bay inset 1:10,000
Tides on Point Atkinson
Currents 1 knot in Waddington Channel

East Redonda is a steep wilderness island. Most of it is an ecological reserve. Pendrell Sound, which bisects it, has some of the warmest water on the coast. It is a prime area for spawning oysters. Unfortunately, there are few landing or camp spots. See sketchmap on page 55.

Paddling considerations
• Few landings, usually rocky
• Although Pendrell Sound on East Redonda has the warmest water in the Strait of Georgia, the water on the north side of the Redondas is apt to be cold.
• The winds in Waddington Channel are not usually as treacherous as those in Lewis Channel on the other side of West Redonda because the narrow entrance at Dean Point gives some protection.

• Crossing of Homfray Channel between Booker Point and Forbes Bay 1.5 nmi.

The route
Launch at Squirrel Cove, paddle along the south coast of West Redonda to Waddington Channel or come in from Desolation Sound, perhaps overnighting at Roscoe Bay. If you elect to go up Pendrell Sound, it's 5.5 nmi to the head of it, where, I've been told, there are some rocky beaches. As this is a prime place to breed oysters, there is a lot of aquaculture here. Explore the rest of the island and the upper end of Homfray Channel first.

The cliffs of Horace Head drop sheer into the water and you'd think it would be a good fishing place but the Sliammon people say otherwise.

Horace head, East Redonda Island.

Horace Head

"Our people never jig for cod off Horace Head," said the late Chief Joe Mitchell, who grew up at Squirrel Cove. "There is something bad there. The last person who fished there got something very heavy on his line. He rocked the boat and gradually pulled the line up. Suddenly it came up easily. It was a sunny day and when he looked down into the water he could see a mountain goat with pink hooves and nose and red eyes. Being very scared, he cut the line as big whirlpools tossed his boat.

"In Roscoe Bay, which we call Salt Lagoon, my grandfather caught a cod with huge horns on its head. It snapped at the line and got away. The female sea snake has been seen here and in Okeover. When the Transformer stabbed her mate and turned him into Savary Island, she lost her home in the cave at Hurtado Point near Lund. Now she surfaces anywhere."

Beyond Horace Head, the slopes of East Redonda fall sheer into the water. While uncertainty shrouds the pictographs and petroglyphs, many Sliammon legends are linked to clearly visible physical features. The battle between the mountain goat and the deer illustrates this.

"The mountain goat and the deer couldn't make up their minds which of them should live on the mainland and which on East Redonda Island," said Chief Joe Mitchell. "They went to war over it and, as the deer pulled the goat off the island, the goat's hooves left grooves on the rocks. That's why the mountain goat only lives on the mainland. If you look carefully, you will see black dots on the rocks all along the coast. These are the slugs, snails, mice and frogs that the mountain goat and the deer threw at each other during the war."

Archie Stewart homesteaded on the island opposite Lloyd Point. If you find old cherry trees, that's his place.

It was Stewart who told Jim Spilsbury about Joe Copeland and other old timers. Jim Spilsbury described Stewart as "an old hand logger with a beat-up cod boat with a four-horsepower Easthope engine in it." There are pictographs on the cliffs nearby.

For much of the first half of the 20th century, Lloyd Point was the site of a prosperous turkey farm run by Eric and Herman Lindberg, who supplied the Hotel Vancouver and many other well-known establishments via the Union steamships. The Lindbergs were Swedes who arrived via Minneapolis. In addition to turkeys, they also had goats, pigs, chickens and geese. They were reputed to be wealthy. Maria Christensen heard that Eric's brother-in-law had invented puffed wheat. Eric wouldn't buy cigarettes for Herman, as he disapproved of his smoking, so Herman used to row over to Laura Cove and get Phil Lavigne to buy tobacco for him.

Once when Carl Christensen was visiting the Lindbergs, he thought he saw another man but Eric firmly denied the man's existence. Later, Eric came over and asked Bertha Christensen how to treat diarrhea. He said he had his father with him illegally so he was afraid to take him to the Powell River hospital. Bertha told him to boil brown rice and make him drink the water from it. This remedy was commonly used.

Since East Redonda is a bit steep for camping, cross Homfray Channel and try your luck at Lloyd Point or in Forbes Bay or Atwood Bay.

In the 1930s, the Campbell Logging Company operated in Forbes Bay and was one of the first to depend on trucks. Their three Leyland trucks hauled logs over two miles of road which cost $10,000 a mile to build. Long ago the Sliammon people had a summer village here.

The upper reaches of Homfray Channel and the northeastern shores of East Redonda are much wilder than those closer to Prideaux Haven. Landings are rocky and scarce. At Pryce Channel the water turns cold as the glacial creeks cascading into Toba Inlet start intruding.

A mile west of Hepburn Point where a creek comes down there is a possible campsite if you don't think you can make it all the way around to Walsh Cove at the head of Waddington Channel. Now is the time to decide whether the long trip up Pendrell Sound is worth it or you'd prefer a side trip to Prideaux Haven before heading back to Squirrel Cove.

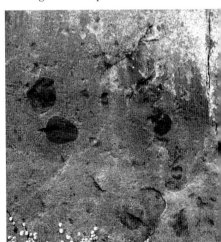

Remains of the slugs, snails, mice and frogs which the mountain goat and the deer threw at each other.

Toba waterfall. Photo: Adam Vallance.

9 Toba Inlet

Difficulty Advanced conditions – considerable risk
Distance 38 nmi round trip
         Brettell Point to Brem Bay 7 nmi
         Brem Bay to Toba River estuary 13.5 nmi
         Toba River estuary to Snout Point 12.5 nmi
         Snout Point to Brettell Point 6 nmi
Duration 4 days
Charts No. 3541 Approaches to Toba Inlet 1:40,000
       No. 3312 Desolation Sound and Jervis Inlet page 29 1:40,000
Tides on Point Atkinson
Currents none

Toba was named for the painted tablet which the Spaniards found when they explored the place in 1792. It's a steep-sided, cold inlet with wicked winds, beautiful waterfalls and no road access. At the head of it, the Toba River winds back and forth across a long flat valley. On a high tide, try paddling up it. See sketchmap on page 55.

Paddling considerations
- Sheer cliffs most of the way with very few landing places.
- Strong inflow/outflow winds.
- Clapotis waves of up to 2 m.
- Crossing — Snout Point to the Brem 1.5 nmi.
- This is grizzly country. Read up on how to cope with them before leaving.
- The glacier-fed water is very cold.
- VHF reception is problematical.

The route
Toba can be accessed either from Squirrel Cove and along the north coast of the Redonda Islands (see Trip No. 7) or via Desolation Sound (see Trip Nos. 2, 3). Another possibility is to hire the Lund water taxi to drop you off at the Brem River or at Wildernest Lodge behind Double Island.

From Prideaux Haven, follow the coast up Homfray Channel. Forbes Bay, 3 nmi farther on, has a couple of campsites. Atwood Bay is another possibility. Get as close to the entrance to Toba Inlet as you can because you'll need an early start to cross Toba and reach the Brem. I have never paddled or sailed up Toba, but the following is a distillation of what I've heard from people who have.

Brettell Point marks the entrance to Toba Inlet. Assess the weather conditions on the other side of it. If the winds are calm, cross the mouth of the inlet and paddle up the northern shore to the Brem River. If the winds have already picked up, head up the shore to Snout Point and then cross to the Brem, but expect a rough ride. If necessary, wait till the wind goes down before attempting it.

The estuary of the Brem River is moderately sheltered and has a sandy beach. There is a dock where the Lund water taxi could drop you. Camp to one

Toba Inlet from campsite. Photo: Andrew Vallance.

side of the Indian Reserve. Hang food out of the grizzlies' reach. You can hike up the valley a short distance.

After the Brem, you're on your own. No one lives up the inlet now and there is little traffic. Start early to paddle the 13.5 nmi to the head of the inlet, and make sure you can reach your lunch and snacks without having to land. The main attraction of the place is the scenery. Snow-capped mountains, waterfalls cascading down sheer cliffs into green glacial water. Take a camera and double the amount of film or digital media you think you'll need.

In the 1930s, Will Palmer had a floating logging camp at the head of the inlet, and when the Toba Valley was logged about 15 years ago there were two airstrips and a road. All are now choked by alders, though they may provide a camp spot. Since the logging, replacement plantings of black cottonwood, red alder, bigleaf maple, Douglas fir and Sitka spruce have grown up, though a weevil infestation has stunted much of the spruce.

Randy Netter, an experienced bush-man who worked and lived in a cabin by the river for several years, says, "It's a tough country. I broke both packboards and knives. You need to know what you are doing." He lived side by side with the grizzlies and watched a cub grow from making 5-cm pawprints to 20-cm ones. Since he left, a grizzly has trashed his cabin. Could it have been that cub?

Bear Attack

Bob Spence loves fishing and one of his favourite places when he worked at Weldwood's Toba logging camp in the 1970s was on the Klite River, which enters the Toba near its estuary. A short way in, there was a waterfall that was small enough for the fish to jump up, which we often watched them do. Behind it, there was a big pool with two big flat rocks and a ledge.

"One fall, I was fishing for coho," he recounted. "I caught two and put them on the ledge in the shade of a tree. Then I stepped down onto a lower ledge and caught a third. As I stepped back up to put it with the others, I surprised two grizzly bears eating the two I had caught before. I let out a yell. They roared. One spun me 'round, breaking a couple of my ribs, and pushed me at the other. The second bear caught me by the shoulder, dislocating it. I was wearing a big mackinaw jacket of heavy wool, which gave me some protection but not quite enough. The bear threw me into the river, where I lay for a while. After the bears left, I took the third fish and walked out.

"'Got any fish?' asked the foreman, who I met on the road.

"'Yes, but the bears got me,' I replied."

Netter thinks it would be fun to paddle around the estuary but says the river itself is fairly fast flowing. To be able to paddle up it, you need a high tide and then you can probably go upstream for about 5 nmi to "Big Bend." From there, you'll get good views of the rock faces of the mountains and some snow peaks.

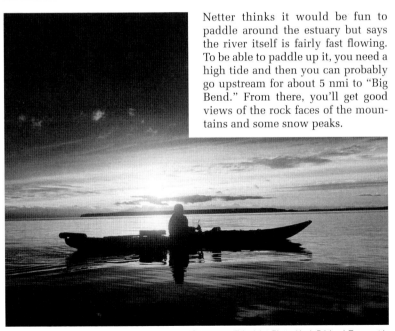

Sunset over Toba Inlet. Photo: Hugh Prichard, Terracentric.

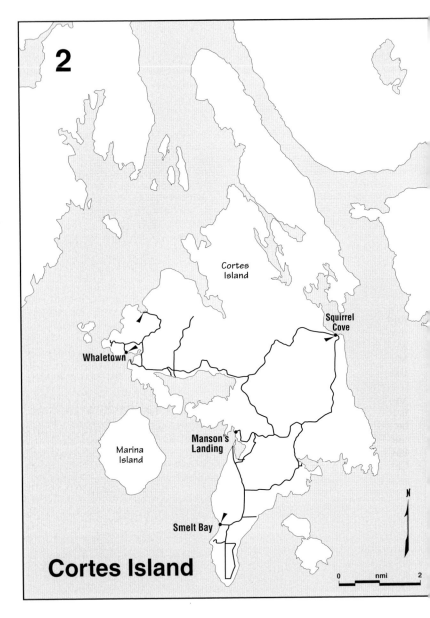

2

Cortes
Island

Squirrel
Cove

Whaletown

Marina
Island

Manson's
Landing

N

Smelt Bay

Cortes Island

0   nmi   2

The residents of Cortes Island (population 950) have long cherished the place for its warm sunny days and rich soils. It takes two ferries to reach it from Vancouver Island and no locals want any bridges. The Sliammon people loved it till small pox devastated them there in 1862. By 1919 the island was well settled by Europeans, who built trails all over it. Seaford pioneer Ingrid Cowie, née Andersen, says people living on the island and in Desolation Sound in the early decades of the 20th century were hand loggers, fishers, farmers or remittance men.

Although I have described the circumnavigation as a three-day trip, when friends and I did it we took five days. Much depends on the group and where you find campsites. The smaller the group, the easier it is to find sites. For local guided tours, mothership tours and kayak rentals, Misty Isles Adventures is based near Manson's Landing on Cortes. (See Useful Contacts on page 239.)

The multiple pages of Chart 3312 are awkward to use in a kayak, as it is necessary to weave back and forth between several pages. In addition, the southwest section between Smelt Bay and Sutil Point is missing. Use Chart Nos. 3538 and 3541 instead.

Launches

To reach Cortes Island, drive to Campbell River, take the ferry to Quathiaski Cove on Quadra Island (15 minutes). Drive 4.5 km across the island to Heriot Bay, from where the Cortes ferry leaves (45 minutes).

Squirrel Cove

After disembarking from the Quadra ferry at Whaletown, follow Harbour Road to the top of the hill where it meets Carrington Bay Road. Turn right and drive 13 km across the island to Squirrel Cove. The launch is just beyond the store, which may charge you to launch from either the ramp or the adjacent beach. Negotiate a group fee.

Coulter Bay

From the ferry, follow Harbour Road to the top of the hill and turn left on Carrington Bay Road. Drive past Sawmill Road on the left to another turnoff on the left, signposted Coulter Bay. By now the pavement is no more, but much dust is! At the bottom of the hill, the bay is on the right and parking space for maybe half a dozen cars is on the right side of the road, which continues on up a hill. You may be able to drive onto the right-hand side of the extensive mud flat to get as near as possible to the water. Check on foot first.

Whaletown

This is where the ferry from Quadra Island berths. Try launching in the northeast corner of the bay off Huck Road.

Smelt Bay. Photo: Hugh Prichard, Terracentric.

Manson's Landing Provincial Park
Launch on a sandy beach on the west side of the spit. The park is 14.5 km south of Whaletown.

Smelt Bay Provincial Park
Located 15 km south of Whaletown on the Sutil Point road. It has a boat launch, a sandy beach and a campsite (see Campsites).

Campsites

Ha'thayim (Von Donop) Marine Provincial Park Random wilderness campsites only.

Smelt Bay Provincial Park 22 vehicle-accessible campsites overlooking Smelt Bay. Reservations available. Some overflow camping in the day-use parking lot (adjacent to the beach).

10 Squirrel Cove to Von Donop Inlet

Difficulty Intermediate conditions – moderate risk
Distance 14.5 nmi (detour to Cassel Falls is an additional 7 nmi)
Duration 7–10 hours without the detour
Charts No. 3538 Desolation Sound and Sutil Channel 1:40,000
No. 3541 Approaches to Toba Inlet 1:40,000
No. 3312 Desolation Sound and Jervis Inlet, pp. 8, 17, 19, 1:40,000
Tides on Point Atkinson
Currents tidal flows in Lewis Channel

This is the wildest section of the circumnavigation of Cortes. Landings are limited and winds and tides in Lewis Channel can delay progress, so few paddlers attempt it. Von Donop Inlet became Ha'thayim Marine Provincial Park in 1994. Unorganized wilderness camping is permitted. Adventurous types with 4WD and high clearance may brave the road into the south end of the inlet.

Paddling considerations
• Winds in Lewis Channel.
• Scarce, rocky landings.
• To avoid the long paddle around Bullock Point, consider portaging the 0.5 km trail between Squirrel Cove and Von Donop Inlet.

The route
Launch at Squirrel Cove. If you cross Lewis Channel to Refuge Cove (3 nmi) and detour to Cassel Falls in Teakerne Arm, allow a full day for this (see Trip No. 7, West Redonda Island). Look for campsites early, as there are few places to get ashore. Corbie's Point, opposite the mouth of Teakerne Arm on Cortes, may be a possibility with a rocky landing. The slope above it has been recently logged, and since it is private land and now up for sale, it has unfortunately not been replanted.

If your plan is to circumnavigate Cortes, defer the exploration of yacht-filled Squirrel Cove till your return and paddle north. It's a long haul to Bullock Bluff. In bad weather, miss it altogether by portaging into Von Donop Inlet along a short trail that ascends a height of a little over 30 metres before returning to sea level.

Although no currents are marked on the chart for Lewis Channel, any time water or winds are forced through a narrow opening, they increase. Plan to paddle this section with the tide. As landing places are scarce, you may have to eat lunch in your boat, so keep food and snacks within reach.

At Bullock Bluff, there are good views of Raza Island, the Rendezvous Islands and Read Island. If you divert to them, you've added an extra day or more to your trip.

Continue around and into Von Donop Inlet. It is a lovely, sheltered place with many hidden nooks to explore. The area was logged in 1925, so there is no old growth. There once were at least two Indian villages in the inlet, so look for flat spots for camping.

The end of the inlet is a favourite yacht anchorage. Don't swim there.

Bullock
Bluff

N

Von Donop Inlet

Corbie's
Point

log jam

Quartz Bay

Carrington Bay

Coulter Bay

Cortes
Island

Squirrel
Cove

Squirrel
Cove

Subtle
Islands

Whaletown

Shark Spit

Gorge
Harbour

Seaford

Marina
Island

**Manson's
Landing**

Frabjous
Bay

Tiber Bay

Cortes
Bay

Three
Islets

Mary
Point

Smelt Bay

Hollyhock
Farm

Twin
Islands

Sutil Point

0   nmi   2

68 – Sea Kayak Desolation Sound and the Sunshine Coast

Paddling the lagoon, Squirrel Cove. Photo: Hugh Prichard, Terracentric.

Although Carrington Bay, Manson's Landing/Gorge Harbour and Cortes Bay are all boat "no-discharge zones," Von Donop isn't, but it should be. A short trail leads through to Squirrel Cove where, in July and August of some years, a restaurant serves traditional native food.

On the east side of Von Donop, a tidal lagoon is only accessible at high tide. In the late 1940s, a pod of 6–8 killer whales swam in at high tide. People came from miles around to see this unusual phenomenon. One by one the whales died. None escaped.

You can escape the yachts if you go into the lagoon, but watch the state of the tide if you plan a short visit. There are boulders in the waterfall which appears as the water drains out. The cleared area on the point at the mouth of it may have been the site of one of the villages.

11 Von Donop Inlet to Smelt Bay

Difficulty Intermediate conditions – moderate risk
Distance   13.5 nmi from the mouth of Von Donop
Duration   6–8 hours
Charts   No. 3538 Desolation Sound and Sutil Channel 1:40,000
        No. 3541 Approaches to Toba Inlet 1:40,000
        No. 3312 Desolation Sound and Jervis Inlet pages 5, 19 1:40,000
Tides   on Point Atkinson
Currents   none

This part of the coast is not as rugged as the part up Lewis Channel and there are several intriguing bays to explore as well as a warm, freshwater lake to swim in at Manson's Landing. See sketchmap on page 68.

Paddling considerations

• Prevailing northwest winds in summer can be strong especially when combined with inflow/outflow winds from nearby Bute Inlet.
• Landings are scarce and rocky.
• Ask permission if landing on private land.

The route

To the west, Quartz Bay, Carrington Bay and Coulter Bay were all well-kept homesteads at one time. We found Quartz Bay more interesting to explore than Carrington Bay, probably because a large log-jam prevented us from slipping through into Carrington Lagoon. If you're persistent, you can portage it, apparently. Swedish loggers once blasted the rock to widen the channel so they could get their logs through, but obviously that's not possible now. In 1898 there were 17 mineral claims in Carrington Bay, but the small amount of molybdenite that was found was not commercially viable. The public land at the entrance to the lagoon is a potential camp spot.

The Sutil Islands look intriguing from a distance, but No Trespassing signs repel visitors, so don't plan on stopping there. The land on the Cortes side of Plunger Pass is also privately owned.

Whaletown is where the Quadra ferry docks. The Dawson Whaling Company operated a whaling station there 1869–70. Those were the days when whaling was done from small boats lowered from schooners. Nothing remains of this enterprise. Launching in the northeast corner of the bay off Huck Road is a possibility.

Shark Spit on Marina Island is a good lunch spot and may be a potential camp spot also. In 1792, Galiano and Valdes named Cortes Island after Hernando Cortes, the conqueror of Mexico. At the same time, they named Marina Island after a beautiful captive whom Cortes made his mistress. A native legend relates that an adulterer was stuck on Marina Island. He built a reef toward the mainland and when he had almost reached it, he was turned into a rock which is still there.

Gorge Harbour has a narrow and easily defended passage into it. Look for red ochre pictographs on the cliff walls. Tradition has it that the natives hurled rocks down on invaders, probably very effectively. The east side of the quiet lagoon is noisy with aquaculture. On the west side, the Gorge Harbour Marina rents kayaks and tent sites in an old apple orchard. Their store sells fresh produce and groceries. Ask them to direct you to Trude's Café on the Whaletown road for decadent desserts and espresso. The Old Floathouse Restaurant serves meals, but you may need reservations. In November, chum salmon spawn in Gorge Channel.

Manson's Landing is one of the oldest settlements on Cortes. Mike Manson was a Shetland Islander who arrived in 1886. While working in Nanaimo, he eloped in an Indian dugout canoe with his partner's daughter, Jane. The happy couple lost four of their five children to diphtheria and then had five more. On Cortes, they opened the first store. They traded with the Indians for dogfish oil which they sold as lubricant to the coal mines in Nanaimo. Mike's younger brother, John, rowed everywhere delivering meat from wild cattle on the island to logging camps. He also rowed over to Mitlenatch Island to pasture his sheep.

The museum at Manson's Landing is on the site of the original store. The community has a new store and post office, a farmer's market, a community hall with a restaurant in it and a dock where, during fishing season, fresh fish may be available from fishboats.

The white sand beaches of Manson's Landing Provincial Park are a picnic site and a potential kayak launch. A 10–15 minute walk up the road brings you to warm freshwater swimming in Hague Lake.

Smelt Bay is a full-blown provincial park complete with reservations for campsites etc. It too has a white sandy beach with shingle at low tide, making it an easy place to land. This is a good launch for Mitlenatch Island, 5 nmi out into the open Strait of Georgia (see Trip No. 18). Smelt Bay is named for the sardine-sized green and silver fish which spawn here in huge numbers, attracting salmon and other fish in search of a tasty meal.

From Cortes Island looking west.
Photo: Hugh Prichard, Terracentric.

12 Smelt Bay to Squirrel Cove

Difficulty Intermediate conditions – moderate risk
Distance 12 nmi
Duration 6–8 hours
Charts No.3538 Desolation Sound and Sutil Channel 1:40,000
No. 3541 Approaches to Toba Inlet 1:40,000
No. 3312 Desolation Sound and Jervis Inlet partly on pages 8 1:40,000
Tides on Point Atkinson
Currents none

This part of the coast is subject to southeast winds. It passes Hollyhock, a well-known educational centre; Cortes Bay; and the communities of Tiber Bay and Seaford. See sketchmap on page 68.

Paddling considerations
• Southeast winds can be unpleasant in this area because they have room to build up big waves.

The route
Paddle south. The point south of the campsite has a sandy beach which in August is the site of the annual sand castle competition. If it is low tide, keep your eyes peeled for erratic boulders just beneath the surface of the water between Smelt Bay and Sutil Point. Unwary kayaks running onto them can be damaged. This is particularly hazardous in rough seas.

The small rocky island in the distance is Mitlenatch. Don't detour that way without listening to the weather forecast, as the crossing is 4 nmi from Sutil Point and camping is not allowed on the island.

Past Sutil Point there is a line of cliffs surmounted by houses. Once the cliffs end, look for Hollyhock on the left. This 20-year establishment is "an international centre for the cultivation of human consciousness, well-being and social impact." It runs programs from March to October. If you're not participating in their programs, you may use their facilities at a daily cost of $15 plus GST. This allows you to use the swimsuit-optional hot tub and participate in naturalist-guided walks, morning meditation/movement/yoga etc. Camping for a two-person tent costs about five times provincial park rates.

Twin Islands, 0.5 nmi offshore, used to be owned by a German prince who periodically invited Queen Elizabeth II to stay when she visited British Columbia. The islands have since been sold and partly logged. Before the Second World War, multimillionaire R.M. (Dick) Andrews, who could see war coming, bought Twin Islands to live on till hostilities were over. Charlie Rasmussen from Lund built him a 14-room log cabin and Jim Spilsbury installed a radio in every bedroom. At high tide it is fun to paddle the shallow lagoon between the islands.

Cortes Bay is more geared for yachts than kayakers. Both the Seattle and Royal Vancouver Yacht Clubs have outstations there, in

The view to the south from Cortes Island. Photo: Hugh Prichard, Terracentric.

addition to the public wharf. Watch for approaching seaplanes as you near the latter. If you see a 13-metre, dark-hulled motor sailer with a schooner rig called *Misty Isles*, that is the mothership which Misty Isles Adventures uses for their trips to Desolation Sound and Toba Inlet. On the two occasions I have paddled into the bay, the weather has been cold and blustery to the point where a cup of hot coffee would have been welcome. Unfortunately, the establishment which once sold hot drinks no longer exists, so fill your Thermos before leaving in the morning in case you encounter the same experience. There are no camping facilities.

"Frabjous Bay," unofficially named after Lewis Carroll's *Jabberwocky*, is a small, unnamed bay about half a nautical mile east of Cortes Bay. It is a pleasant cove to duck into, but Three Islets off the coast here are a great place to see harlequin ducks, black oystercatchers and seals. Don't go too close to seal pups.

Captain Vancouver named Mary Point after one of his sisters, and Sarah Point, on the end of Malaspina Peninsula, after the other. Tiber Bay just beyond is a strata-titled cottage development. Bud Jarvis, who put it together, now lives farther north at Seaford. Jarvis is a kayaker and avid organic gardener. He's also a great spinner of yarns and is featured in several books, including some of mine.

Back at Squirrel Cove, explore the cove if you have time. Sometimes boats anchor there all summer selling homemade pies and cinnamon buns. In November, chum salmon spawn there.

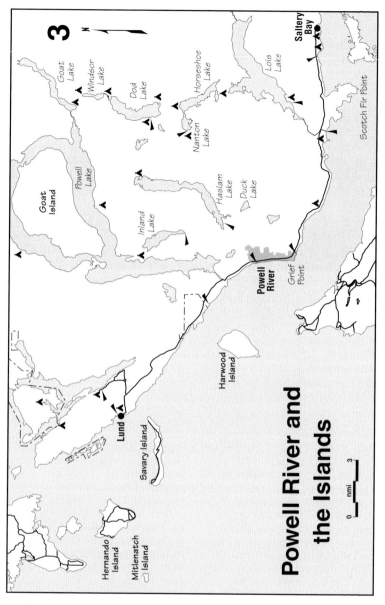

Powell River and the Islands

N

3

Goat Lake

Windsor Lake

Dod Lake

Horseshoe Lake

Lois Lake

Saltery Bay

Scotch Fir Point

Goat Island

Powell Lake

Nanton Lake

Haslam Lake

Duck Lake

Inland Lake

Powell River

Grief Point

Harwood Island

Lund

Savary Island

Hernando Island

Mitlenatch Island

0   nmi   3

Crossing by the second ferry from Vancouver gives safer access to Hardy Island and Hotham Sound as well as opening up new paddling areas. The coast itself has some interesting nooks and crannies to explore, and the north end includes launches for Desolation Sound as well as access to Savary, Texada and several other islands. Behind the coast, there are several lake trips, including the Powell River Canoe Route. Parts of these can be useful alternatives when storms lash the Gulf of Georgia.

As with the Sechelt Peninsula, there are many B&Bs on the water along the coast. Campsites, all of them organized, are easier to find here than farther south. Although the winds can still create problems for paddlers, there is a much shorter fetch along this coast than in the Gibsons/Sechelt area.

The town of Powell River (population 12,983) is halfway between Saltery Bay and Lund. It consists of four smaller communities: Westview, containing the main shopping centre and the harbour; Cranberry; Wildwood; and the Townsite, the historic company town where the pulp mill is located. With modern technology, the mill no longer smells like it used to.

Services in Westview include a visitors info centre, three large grocery stores, a liquor store, numerous wine and beer stores and a ferry to Comox. The Patricia Theatre, Canada's longest running movie theatre dates back to 1913. In addition, you may encounter a large choral festival called Kathaumixw, an orchestral school, the blackberry festival, loggers sports, and many other events.

Launches from south to north

Saltery Bay

Drive off the ferry and turn sharp right onto an unpaved road around the bay. At the fork where there's a sign for the Sunshine Coast Trail, bear right along a very rough road down to a rocky beach. Turn before unloading and park back up the hill in the lot above the small dock beside the ferry dock. It's about 0.6 km and the locals do it with 2WD vehicles, but gingerly.

Saltery Bay

Provincial Park boat launch is 1.5 km from the ferry. The sign for this comes after the one for the campsite of the same name.

Frolander Bay

Drive north on Highway 101 for 10.4 km from the ferry. Turn left on Loubert Road, which turns into Scotch Fir Point Road, and drive 1.7 km. Look for #12297. This used to be Ocean Shores B&B and may reopen under another name. Immediately to the right of its driveway, a narrow, bamboo-lined trail leads down to the beach. A rather hidden sign at the start proclaims Public Beach Access. Four uneven concrete steps at the end of the trail lead onto the rocky beach. Park on the road. There's very little space.

Palm Beach

From Highway 101 turn left on Lang Bay Road (13 km north of the Saltery Bay ferry terminal). After 0.6 km turn left on Palm Beach Road. Pass on by the regional park, as its parking lot is a long way from the water. You can get closer by driving a block past the park

Donkersly Beach launch.

and turning right onto McNair Road. Go to the end, turn and park.

Mahood Beach
Drive 15 km north of the Saltery Bay ferry terminal, and turn left on Brew Bay Road. After 0.5 km the road forks. Angle left onto Mahood Road. The beach is at the end.

Donkersley Beach
Turn left on Donkersley Road (about 1 km north of Brew Bay Road). The beach is about 0.5 km at the end.

Myrtle Rocks
This rocky cobble beach runs along Highway 101 about 24 km north of the Saltery Bay ferry. As the tide goes out a long way, it is best to launch when it is high. There is parking for several vehicles along the highway.

Grief Point Municipal Park
As you enter the Municipality of Powell River, pass the Beach Gardens Resort, continue through a flashing yellow light, and turn left on Windsor Road, which curves around to become Victoria Road. At the foot of the hill, turn left and park beside the park. Launching here is best done at high tide, as the beach is slippery cobbles.

Westview Harbour
Driving into Powell River from Saltery Bay, pass the Beach Gardens Resort and continue on Highway 101, which follows the coast. One block after the first

traffic light (Duncan Street), turn left down Courtenay. Watch for stop signs and ferry traffic. Past the ferry terminal, continue down a steep hill and turn right. The launch, which is often very busy with power boats, is on the left. For a quieter, if less convenient launch, drive into the parking lot beyond the launch. At the far end of this lot, a very short, rough road leads down to the beach. It's a pay parking lot.

Willingdon Beach Municipal Park

Drive along Marine Avenue and through the traffic lights on Alberni. The park is on your left. You have to park on the road and can't drive down to the water.

Gibsons Beach

From the Powell River Visitor Info Centre on Marine Avenue, drive north on Highway 101 for 11.5 km, turn left at the sign and follow the unpaved road another 1.2 km to the boat launch.

Dinner Rock
BC Forest Service campsite

From the Powell River Visitor Info Centre, drive north on Highway 101 for 25.3 km and turn left at the sign. Although this launch looks good on the map, it isn't. At the bottom, the road requires 4WD and the beach is too rocky to land on in any kind of a surf, which happens when the prevailing summer northwesterly blows.

Lund

From the Powell River Visitor Info Centre, drive up Highway 101 for 27 km and turn left at the T-junction after the Lund

gas station (which is not always open). There are two launch ramps: a single concrete one at the bottom of the hill behind the hotel, and a double one into the boat harbour close by the vehicle-congested Savary Water Taxi.

Lund – the ramp behind the hotel

Opposite where Rockfish Kayak and Terracentric Coastal Adventures are, is much less busy with power boats than the double ramp into the harbour. When using this ramp, keep gear to one side, as sometimes power boats use it too. There is a $3 in and out charge. Park up the hill at Dave's Parking Lot and tell the attendant how long you will be away. They will valet park your vehicle. On the way back, call them by cell phone and they'll drive your vehicle down to meet you on the dock.

Lund Harbour

If using the double launch ramp into the boat harbour, keep to the left-hand side, as the wharfinger prefers kayaks there. Take change to pay the $2 in or out charge. Before leaving Lund call in at Nancy's Bakery for a choice of seven kinds of coffee and lots of goodies, including three kinds of butter tarts. Nancy also bakes bread.

Finn Bay

At the T-junction in Lund, turn right and drive 1.2 km to where the pavement ends. Park on the right-hand side. A short, narrow road on the left leads down to the rocky shore. Parking is limited and unattended vehicles have occasionally been vandalized.

13 Saltery Bay to Westview, Powell River

Difficulty Intermediate conditions – moderate risk
Distance 21.2 nmi each way
Duration 2–3 days
Charts No. 3311 Sunshine Coast No. 4 Pender Harbour to Grief Point 1:40,000
No. 3512 Strait of Georgia 1:80,000
Tides on Point Atkinson
Currents 1 knot in Malaspina Strait near Grief Point

This somewhat urban paddle passes several sandy beaches with several sea-level B&Bs, good swimming and lots of sea stars. It could be three separate day paddles or shorter trips, depending on where you put in.

Paddling considerations

• Although this section of coast can blow up, the waves do not have the big fetch that makes the Gibsons to Halfmoon Bay trips hazardous.

The route

Before departing, call ahead to the B&B or campsite you are aiming for (see pages 240-241) and ask for directions on how to recognize them from the water. Points of interest along the coast in order of encounter:

Frank Jenkinson's house, 0.5 nmi from the Saltery Bay ferry, is a tiny old cottage perched on a rock. Jenkinson was featured in a 1979 13-minute National Film Board short called *The Man Who Dug for Fish* for his work preserving salmon spawning habitat in Bishop and Park Creeks. Over a 25-year period he increased the number of fish from 600 to 25,000. He had lived for almost 107 years when he died in July 2004.

Next door is the Saltery Bay Provincial Campsite. The sites are a long carry up from the water. At high tide, this place has a lovely pocket cove

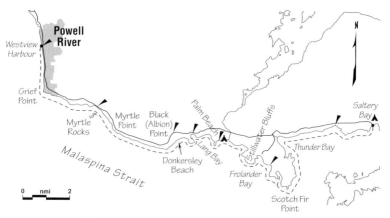

where a narrow concrete ramp enables even handicapped scuba divers to launch and visit the mermaid statue attached to a rock below the offshore buoy. Unfortunately the statue lies too deep to be visible from the surface.

1.0 nmi farther on, Kent's Beach is a private campsite which welcomes kayakers arriving by water. Next door to it is Saltery Bay Provincial Park boat launch and day-use area.

At low tide, the next 2.5 nmi are a good place to see a variety of sea stars—ochre, sunflower, mud, giant pink—as well as sea cucumbers and the bright pink and orange fronds of calcareous tubeworms.

The large house at the north end of Thunder Bay was a B&B until it was sold in 2004. The two small coves at the west end of Thunder Bay used to contain old summer cottages belonging to Powell River people.

Eclipse Plumage

Sea ducks lose their handsome suits of breeding plumage for about six weeks in August. Their strong flight feathers fall out and while the new ones are growing in they are flightless. Keep well back from them as they are under stress.

Scotch Fir Point sadly has only a few trees left after a developer raped it. It was named by Captain George Vancouver after he had explored Jervis Inlet in June 1792 and was on his way back to his ships and an encounter with the Spanish explorers Galiano and Valdes. The shingle cove on the north side of Scotch Fir Point is a traditional kayakers' lunch spot.

Mink at Myrtle Rocks.

It is to be hoped that this use will be respected once the developer starts building. At one stage he proposed to give the offshore islands to the Regional District as a kayakers' park. Unfortunately, they are too rocky for most paddlers to be able to scramble ashore comfortably.

McRae Cove, which is shallow and muddy, is often inhabited by Canada geese and harbour seals. It is where Farquhar (Fred) McRae homesteaded after pre-empting Scotch Fir Point. When he died the family wrangled for many years over the estate while his widow remained in her home. The land was then sold to a developer, who built a home on the edge of the property, on Frolander Bay.

Canoe Bay, the empty cove west of the first big house on Frolander Bay, was once a thriving summer cottage community until the cottagers were evicted. Four concrete steps in memory of Jean Lorraine Palliser lie to the left of a tiny creek on the southeast side of Frolander Bay, marking a short, bamboo-lined beach access trail to Loubert Road.

The northwest side of Frolander Bay has a neat little cove that is fun to explore. In August, shy brown ducks hiding in the crannies are likely harlequin ducks in eclipse.

On your way out of Frolander, the pink cliffs edging the shore are the Stillwater Bluffs, a mecca for would-be climbers. Paddlers get a front-row view of their efforts.

Stillwater Bluffs.

Westview Beach, Powell River.

Watch for otters among the floating logs in the Stillwater log sort and admire the boom boat ballet as these powerful little boats shuttle the logs around. At the end of this bay there's a way in to the power station below the tall white tower. Keep back from the outlet, as the current can increase without notice if the dam on Lois Lake above it is opened.

Palm Beach is a Sechelt Indian Reserve which leases land to happy cottagers. One of these is Sandy Shores, a sea-level B&B. This beach is a popular place to swim and the Palm Beach Regional Park beyond the cottages is home to a well-attended folk festival held on Labour Day. Unfortunately this is a day-use area and the adjacent RV park does not take campers. Taking out at Palm Beach Park means a long hike

to vehicles. This can be avoided by driving down McNair Road. Turn your vehicle around before leaving it, and don't park overnight, as space is very limited.

Below the Lifestyles Motel is an old concrete ramp into the water which is all that remains of the dock where the Union Steamships berthed. They serviced the Stillwater logging settlement, which predates Powell River. It flourished from the 1890s to the 1920s. Read about it in Golden Stanley's now-out-of-print *Pitlamping through Conscription, 1916–1923*. Farther along, Seabreeze Cottages & Campground is on the water but they want kayakers to camp about 200 metres up the hill. Land and check in at the office before pitching your tent.

At the west end of Lang Bay, the estuary of Lang Creek is a good place to see water birds which congregate here especially in winter. Beyond it, Mahood Road comes down. You can take out or launch on either side of the short spit.

Brew Bay (also known as Donkersley Beach) has a lovely big sandy beach at low tide where the gulls dig up giant cockles. In spring, among the rocks of the adjacent cobble beach, you may find plainfin midshipman fish fathers (*Porycthys notatus*) guarding a clutch of corn-yellow eggs. Turn large rocks over to find them but be sure to put them back gently afterwards. Groaning sounds come from this fish, which is also known as the singing fish.

Past Black Point (marked Albion Point on some charts), the beaches are cobbled and difficult to land on. There are two very picturesque B&Bs perched on top of the cliff. Leave your boat at sea level and climb up their private steps. North of them, Karen Southern's B&B by the Sea is at sea level. For any of these, phone first for a reservation and to receive detailed instructions on how to identify them from the water.

Myrtle Rocks is a Regional District Park proclaimed in recognition of Allen Roberts's 18 years of service as a director of the Regional District. Roberts was a mill worker who lived close by and died in 1986. At low tide, guests of the tightly packed Oceanside Resort can walk out over an oyster-encrusted beach. Canada geese, pelagic and double-crested cormorants, seals, sea lions and the odd mink inhabit the rocks. In March small numbers of migrating Brant geese can be seen here feeding on the eelgrass. These are part of the larger flock which feeds in Gillies Bay on Texada Island.

A breakwater below the Beach Gardens Resort provides moorage for a number of pleasure craft. A sandy beach just before it is a welcome pull-out spot.

Grief Point has a cobble beach. At high water, it is easy to land or launch at the foot of Malaspina Avenue. The light beacon beyond the small park officially marks Grief Point. Winds funnel around it, sometimes changing direction on the other side. The cobble beach develops some sandy areas as it heads toward the harbour. Three eagles' nests monitor the new sea walk which the municipality has recently built over the beach making landing at high tide difficult to impossible in many areas.

The barge terminal is slated to be relocated during a general restructuring of the Westview waterfront. If either the Comox or the Texada ferry is approaching, duck into the south harbour and explore it till the coast is clear. Ferries have right-of-way over other marine traffic and their backwash can dash small boats against the pilings. Keep well back.

Beyond the ferry dock and the north harbour, where resident pleasure craft and the Coast Guard berth and where there is a concrete launch ramp, there is another beach. There is a fairly easy kayak take-out at the beginning of it.

A rocky breakwater and a grassy area above a sandy beach signals Willingdon Beach Park and municipal campground. Camping is first come first served and the place is often full in summer.

14 Westview, Powell River to Lund

Difficulty Intermediate conditions – moderate risk
Distance 13.1 nmi each way
  Westview to Gibsons Beach 4 nmi
  Gibsons Beach to Dinner Rock 6 nmi
  Dinner Rock to Lund 2.5 nmi
Duration 4–5 hours one way
Chart No. 3311 Sunshine Coast No. 5 Grief Point to Desolation Sound 1:40,000
Tides on Point Atkinson
Currents 1 knot near the ends of Harwood Island and Savary Island

Although houses march along the shore for at least half the distance, settlement thins out after that. En route you get good views of Harwood Island and Savary Island.

Paddling considerations
- Wind direction and strength
- Lack of places for pit stops
- If camping, consider paddling

2 nmi farther to the Copeland Islands: see Trip No. 1.
- Concealed water outflow at the north end of the mill

The route
Launch on the north side of the boat harbour. If you use the interior boat ramp you'll be competing with power boaters.

Hulks.

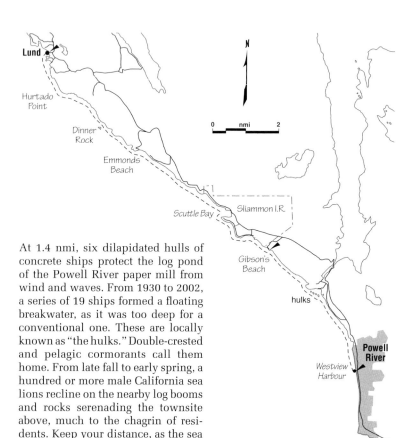

At 1.4 nmi, six dilapidated hulls of concrete ships protect the log pond of the Powell River paper mill from wind and waves. From 1930 to 2002, a series of 19 ships formed a floating breakwater, as it was too deep for a conventional one. These are locally known as "the hulks." Double-crested and pelagic cormorants call them home. From late fall to early spring, a hundred or more male California sea lions recline on the nearby log booms and rocks serenading the townsite above, much to the chagrin of residents. Keep your distance, as the sea lions could mistake your kayak for a nice comfortable log to rest on. Past the last hulk, there is a wharf and warehouse, then a steel breakwater followed by rocks. Between the steel breakwater and the rocks is a concealed water outflow. This is the tailrace from the hydro generating station. It produces fresh water, not sewage. The fresh water wants to rise above the salt water, creating an upwelling. The rate of flow depends on the number of generators in use at the time. Usually only a few operate in summer but up to five in early spring or late fall. At these times, either endure the chop or paddle about 100 m offshore. It is particularly noticeable at low tide.

Immediately past the mill are the remains of the Powell River. At 400 metres, this is Canada's shortest river. Before the mill was established in 1909, the river ended in a spectacular

The Iron Mines

The area around Hurtado Point is known locally as the "iron mines" because some of the rocks have a russet tinge caused by weathering of pyrite and chalcopyrite minerals.

The earliest reference to mineral claims in the Lund area occurred in 1896 when George Rawding recorded the Full Moon claim. By 1913 two shafts had been sunk, with negligible results.

In those days there were no welfare payments. Needy men took out Free Miner certificates and staked mineral claims. In exchange for work on a claim, the government provided grocery money.

The traces of gold, silver, copper and molybdenum they found were not economically viable. The best product of the claim is the following story.

Before roads and automobiles, Lund people thought nothing of rowing to Vancouver or Campbell River for supplies or social occasions. In January 1911, when the SS *Cottage City*, on its way to Skagway, ran aground at Willow Point, it was not surprising that passersby stopped and took off what they thought they could use, including the ship's bell.

Afterwards, the insurers, Lloyd's of London, tried to retrieve what was missing. When a Lloyd's representative found himself dining off *Cottage City* plates in Lund, he made sure the culprits were arrested.

waterfall which engineers converted into a power plant and dam. You can still paddle up the river a short distance to pools hedged by huge blocks of rock. It's a quiet sheltered place where you can contemplate the dry remains of the waterfall.

4 nmi – Gibsons Beach launch ramp with a popular swimming beach on the far side. It's one of the last easy places to stop before Emmonds Beach.

Before the church on the Sliammon Indian Reserve, a creek comes down which is a prime birding place. All kinds of gulls and sea ducks gather here. Use binoculars and don't get too close.

5.7 nmi – Scuttle Bay is a very shallow bay which dries at low tide. Usually 10–20 great blue herons stand guard on the rocks at the entrance. Once long ago the Sliammon people had a well-disguised sunken longhouse here with hidden exits into the forest. This was necessary to protect residents from the depredations of Haida slavers.

9 nmi – Emmonds Beach has a sandy beach where campers are welcome. Call at the house to pay the fee.

Cottages and houses line the shore almost all the way to Dinner Rock. Just before this island, a prominent long metal walkway to a private floating dock belongs to a large house concealed among the trees.

10.5 nmi – Dinner Rock is a rounded island with steep sides readily visible from a long way off. It is tough to land on but if you climb up to the top, you'll find a memorial to the two women and three children lost in the October 11, 1947, sinking of the *Gulf Stream*. The ship rests

Exploring the Cave of the Great Sea Snake at Hurtado Point.

in 50 metres of water. Beyond the island there's a rocky beach which is often hard to land on or leave. A 4WD road leads down to it from the B.C. Forest Service campsite above. The road down to the campsite is unsuitable for RVs and is gated during the winter months, which is a pity as the campsite has lovely trails and wonderful views over Savary Island, especially at sunset.

12 nmi – Hurtado Point opposite Savary Island heralds a large cave hidden from the north. On calm days at high tide when there's no traffic to make waves you can paddle into it and get soaked by the waterfall from above. Chief Joe Mitchell said this cave was home to the female sea snake before the Transformer turned her into Savary Island.

13.1 nmi – Lund, one of the oldest settlements on the coast established by the Thulin brothers in 1890. Recently, the original Lund Hotel has been refurbished from top to bottom. Both the dining room and the pub overlook the water. The launch ramp in the harbour charges in and out fees (see Launches). Ashore there's a general store, liquor store, post office, handicraft store and several other restaurants. The SunLund RV Park & Campground is accessed from steps near the water wheel. Next door, Nancy's Bakery serves seven different kinds of coffee and three kinds of butter tarts as well as several varieties of healthy breads.

Opposite: Quiet cove on Harwood Island.

15 Harwood Island

Difficulty Intermediate conditions – moderate risk
Distance 15 nmi round trip including Vivian Island and Rebecca Reef
(11 nmi without them)
Duration 7 hours
Chart Sunshine Coast 3311 No. 5 Grief Point to Desolation Sound 1:40,000
Tides on Point Atkinson
Currents a 1-knot flowing around the spit at the north end of Harwood

This is a beautiful day trip which can be done on calm January days. It has the added bonus of a possible side trip to Vivian Island when the sea lions are in residence. The Sliammon First Nation, which owns the island, has never permitted camping on it. Please respect this decision.

Paddling considerations
- Wind direction and strength.
- Watch for tugs with tows during crossings to and from the island.
- At mid to low tide, paddling on the inside of the exposed rocks on the south side may not be feasible even in a kayak. Portaging across the slippery cobbles is unpleasant to lethal.

- Crossings
  - Gibsons to the north spit of Harwood 2.2 nmi
  - Harwood to Vivian Island 1.1 nmi
  - Harwood to Rebecca Rock 1.5 nmi

The route
Launch at Gibsons Beach and head for whichever side of the island is sheltered from the wind. This usually means aiming for the spit on the north end, which is an hour's crossing. The Roman Catholic church at Sliammon is built on the site of another that burned on Easter morning 1918. In the early days when the priests came, men who wanted to gamble paddled over to Harwood to do so undisturbed. Today, the youth like to picnic on the south beaches.

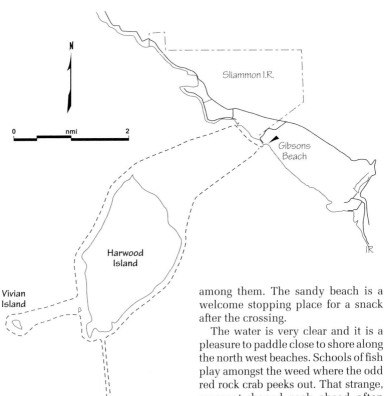

among them. The sandy beach is a welcome stopping place for a snack after the crossing.

The water is very clear and it is a pleasure to paddle close to shore along the north west beaches. Schools of fish play amongst the weed where the odd red rock crab peeks out. That strange, crescent-shaped rock ahead often turns out to be a basking seal. Listen for loon calls and watch for otter families busily hunting for fish. Halfway along, you'll hear the sea lions on Vivian Island if they are in residence.

For a number of years local people have requested that Vivian Island become an ecological reserve but the government has taken no action. Don't land on its rocky shores, as the nesting birds need their privacy. There used to be 14–15 pelagic cormorant nests but now there are none and no double-crested cormorants. Pigeon

On the crossing, don't get between tugs and their tows. They move faster than you think. Some of the boat traffic is on its way to Savary Island, which is spread out in front of you. As you approach the spit, watch the line of breaking waves stretching out from it. You have to paddle well out to round it. Check the gulls on the spit. Often there are California gulls

Steller's sea lions at Vivian Island.

Pacific white-sided dolphins

In the last few years, Pacific white-sided dolphins (*Lagenorhynchus obliquidens*), which previously kept to the open ocean, are now coming into the Strait of Georgia. No one quite knows why, but the theory gaining the broadest acceptance is that changes in the open ocean, both natural and human-caused, have reduced the availability of food.

The dolphins travel in herds of about 50 animals, sometimes playing in the wakes of power boats. When in the Powell River area they like to go over to Harwood and then down the inside of Texada. On calm days, listen for the gentle whoosh of their exhalations. They are pale grey with white markings on their sides.

Harbour porpoises are about the same size but black all over and travel in ones or twos. They are often seen between Harwood and Savary or on the north side of Savary.

guillemots still nest, so boats should stay well away. Hundreds of gulls used to nest here till people let dogs off on the island to run. Now there are three or four gulls, if any.

The sea lions, California and Steller's males, are only there from October to July, with the peak being in late winter. Kayaks seem to disturb them more than powerboats—perhaps because they approach quietly. On the way out to Vivian in winter, watch for ancient murrelets (*Synthliboramphus antiquus*)—small, fat, black and white birds the size of a robin which have a black beard. Don't confuse them with marbled murrelets (*Brachyramphus marmoratus*), which are brown in summer and black and white in winter but lack the beard. Murres and long-tailed ducks also congregate here in winter to feed on the convenient shoal between Harwood and Vivian.

At the south end of Harwood, there's a big sandy beach curved around a bay of warm water, which is great for swimming. Often a seal or two will put on a courting display here, slapping the water loudly with their flippers and generally splashing around. This or the bay on the other side of the point are good lunch spots.

From here, you may want to paddle out to Rebecca Reef, which is farther away than it looks—at least an hour's paddle. It has a very rocky landing, lots of harbour seals and a light beacon.

The extreme southerly tip of Harwood often has seals on it and sometimes dolphins.

Coming back along the east side of Harwood, you get good views of Powell River and Texada and far down Malaspina Strait to the distant Thormanby Islands. Harwood has some spectacular pink cliffs that drop sheer into the water. In the fall, hooded mergansers are sometimes seen here.

The next beach has a rough road going up into the interior of the island, which was logged a number of years ago. Somewhere in the interior a small, rough cabin has an old metal stove left there for emergencies. Reception is good for VHF or cell phones. If you carry either, you'll be able to call for help without needing the cabin.

Large boulders either sticking out of the water or just below the surface herald the shallows which, at low tide, cause even kayakers to take the outside route. This can be unpleasant if the weather has socked in and the sea has become lumpy. Grit your teeth and paddle steadily. You're about an hour away from take-out.

If you follow the island's coast before crossing, there are some nice sandy beaches on this side. On one of them a cross commemorates an unfortunate accident with a gun which terminated a young woman's life.

On the crossing back to Gibsons Beach, enjoy the view of the 2000-metre mountains of the Rainbow Range, including Beartooth Mountain beyond Powell Lake. One or two have snow even in summer.

16 Savary Island — circumnavigation

Difficulty Intermediate conditions – moderate risk
Distance 14.5 nmi round trip hugging the shore
Duration 7–9 hours
Chart No. 3311 Sunshine Coast No. 5 Grief Point to Desolation Sound 1:40,000
Tides on Point Atkinson
Currents 1–1.5 knots around Mace Point and in Manson Passage between Savary and Hernando. This becomes a factor when wind opposes tide.

A great day trip to and from Lund with lots of opportunities to enjoy extensive sandy beaches, swim in warm water, view seals, eagles and harbour porpoise. Savary belongs to the Garry Oak ecosystem—one of the most endangered habitats in the country.

Paddling considerations
- Winds tend to be calm in the morning, rising to prevailing northwesterlies in the afternoon and evening during summer.

- At least one paddler has drowned in rough weather on the way over to Savary from Lund. There are pay phones at both ends of the island, and in an emergency the water taxi can transport kayaks.
- Boat traffic heading to and from Thulin Passage and Desolation Sound
- Crossings
  – Hurtado Point to Mace Point 1 nmi
  – Indian Point directly back to Lund 4.3 nmi
- Bring water to drink.

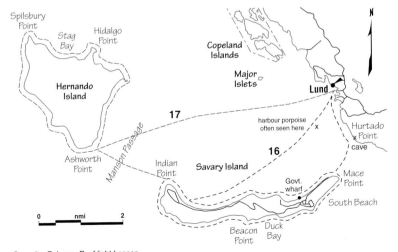

Opposite: Rebecca Reef light beacon.

The route

Launch at Lund and then, because of the boat traffic, hug the shore to Hurtado Point, visiting the giant sea snake's cave en route. Then carefully head over to Mace Point. Most paddlers take the south shore first. If the prevailing southeast wind comes up, the north shore will be sheltered on the way back.

Captain George Vancouver named the place Savary's Island in 1792, perhaps in honour of a French admiral, Daniel Savary, whom it is thought Vancouver met in the Caribbean.[7] Local residents and the Nature Trust of B.C. have combined to ensure that the middle third of the island is preserved in a natural state.

In the early 20th century, Savary Island lots were heavily marketed to the residents of Vancouver's upscale Shaughnessy district. The buyers hired the Maces and other locals to build their cottages before the 1914–18 war. Some remain. Whenever school was out, mothers and children would arrive by Union steamship and stay all summer. Fathers flew up for the weekend, landing on the sandy runway in the centre of the island. Today the "daddy planes" still bring fathers for weekends but they land in Powell River, as the Savary airstrip is closed, and the families come by car and ferry. In 1933, the Union Steamships ran day trips leaving Vancouver at 6 am, landing passengers for picnic lunches on Savary and returning late the same night.

Today the island has many cabins, even in the interior where they have no views. In July and August, parking at Lund is so tight that valet parking is the norm. Scheduled water taxi runs bring passengers and freight from Lund to the dock near Mace Point, where a land taxi takes over for those who don't keep vehicles on the island. There are several stores, restaurants and B&Bs but no hydro. Hikers and cyclists come over for the day. Pay phones at either end of the island are handy in an emergency. Paddlers can avoid most of the crowds, especially if they stick to weekdays in summer.

The south shore of the island has some beautiful sandy beaches with

Royal Savary Hotel

The prestigious Royal Savary Hotel welcomed visitors from 1928 to 1980. Guests came from Seattle, Vancouver and Victoria to enjoy what the brochure called "A South Sea Island Paradise… lovelier than Hawaii" with "absolutely no mosquitoes" (but there are today). Visitors swam in the warm water and played golf on the sand. Most were young people in search of an affordable vacation. Celebrities came too. An Alberta Premier's wife played the piano in the palm room in the early days. The manager of Vancouver's Orpheum Theatre brought crowds of friends with him in the 1940s. In 1979, I saw the conductor of the Vancouver Symphony Orchestra lounging on the sand in a deck chair. Everything ended in 1980, when the fire marshal and the health inspector enforced their regulations. Three years later, the building was dismantled and replaced with cottages.

Along the south coast of Savary Island.

lots of driftwood on them. At low tide, look for burrowing anemones in the sand. If they have a pink spot, this may be part of a shaggy mouse nudibranch (*Aeolidea papillosa*) eating the anemone. Both are the same colour.

The beaches close to Mace Point have had problems. In 2003, there were 20 fires on the beach during a tinder-dry hot spell and the locals feared for their cabins. The previous year a fire farther along raged from the beach to the top of the cliff, burning off one cabin's porch. Following this and some unpleasant all-night parties by yahoos, the locals have been trying to ban camping. If you camp, on no account light a fire, and pack out all garbage.

As you approach and round the third point, the high bank waterfront summer home area gives way to grass-covered dunes sloping back from the sea shore. This is Duck Bay. The wreck of a large, rusty logging grapple machine on the beach defines the western end of the bay. Duck Bay is a good stopping place, with easy access to the fragile dune ecology including some gnarled arbutus trees. The Nature Trust co-owns one third of the island in this area. There is a small sandy beach between the grapple and the next point, which is Beacon Point. The area on either side of Beacon Point is also suitable for stopping and exploring the dune area. Beyond it you paddle through a series of rocky reefs where seals bask on the rocks often supervised by bald eagles looking for fish. High cliffs, with cottages perched on top, edge the island. In places, owners have built extensive step systems down to the beach.

The next set of rocks may push you out a little but you can still thread your way through without going all the way out to Stradiotti Reef. Expect to see lots of seals on the rocks close by and bald eagles fishing. It's a great place to dally awhile. Ashore look for the wreck of a barge.

When the cliffs diminish to beach level, more cottages appear and you're getting close to the end of the island, though it may not look that way. The trees you're seeing are probably on nearby Hernando Island.

As you turn the corner, look off to the northwest. The small rocky island is Mitlenatch. It is 5 nmi away but looks closer. In the clear water beneath your kayak there are large beds of black sand dollars.

Indian Point is a good place to swim, though a little public. Anywhere on Savary, be prepared to change on the beach in front of an audience. Just inside the northeast side of the point is where the Royal Savary Hotel stood.

The mile of shallow water between Indian Point and the nearby island of Hernando tempts visitors to wade across. On the lowest tide it is less than a metre deep. However, when people did this the residents of that very private island soon asked the intruders to leave. A young man drowned trying to cross in 1970. His body was never found though his clothes were.

From Indian Point, there are two options. Either paddle direct for Lund at a distance of 4.3 nmi or follow the island's coast and then cross back to Hurtado Point. If you elect to paddle direct, it is rather a boring journey, with one exception. When you have

Savary Island lunch stop.

Sand Dollars

If you look closely at a sand dollar, there's a five-point star in the middle of it. This is because it is a member of the echinoid family of sea urchins. Like its larger siblings, it has spines that it uses to walk over the sand, which is its preferred habitat. It eats microscopic creatures in the water and positions itself in the sand so that the current brings them toward its body. The whole underside of its body (oral surface) catches bits of food and transports them via food grooves to the central mouth. When the tide goes out, the sand dollars burrow under the sand and disappear. White sand dollars on the beach are dead.

Major Islet at 90 degrees on your left and are midway across the passage between Mace Point and Hurtado Point, stop paddling and listen. I usually hear and see a couple of harbour porpoise at this point.

If you follow the coast, the water will get very shallow and the tide quickly recedes for almost a kilometre. Watch you don't get trapped. The inner crescent of Savary seems unpopulated because trees hide the cottages perched up on the cliffs. It's a popular place to walk or dig clams (if you have a fishing licence).

The area between the government dock and Mace Point was the first settlement. Nearby, Jack Green arrived in 1886 and opened a store. He was an elderly man crippled by arthritis so he hired a younger friend, Tom Taylor, to help him. As he distrusted banks, he kept his money in a strongbox. Once, thieves took $300, a tidy sum in those days. Green purchased several lots of Crown land and in October 1893 had just applied for another. On the last day of that fateful month, three men from Hernando Island found both Green and Taylor shot to death in the log cabin beside the store. The murderer was later caught and hanged.

Green's strongbox has never been found. A contemporary newspaper report speculated that it contained $10,000. For years, treasure seekers have dug all over the island but no one has ever admitted finding it. Jenny Botiko, the murderer's wife, reported that she had watched her husband count out $110 after the event but that was all. Green may have depleted his fortune by sending the money for the land to the government along with his application.

Early settlers like the Mace and the Spilsbury families located their homes here. Jim Spilsbury made a name for himself servicing radios in the early days and founding his "accidental airline," which was the first in the area.

Local people considered his mother eccentric. Before the days when pants were acceptable for women to wear, she wore jodhpurs. She and young Irene Mace hiked all over the island in the 1920s. They would take a pair of squabs (pigeons) with them to roast over an open fire for supper.

After the government dock, the beach narrows and becomes rocky near Mace Point. As you cross back to the mainland, check for oncoming boat traffic.

17 Hernando Island – circumnavigation

Difficulty Intermediate conditions – moderate risk
Distance 11 nmi round trip from Indian Point on Savary Island (or 20 nmi from Lund)
Duration 4–5 hours (or 7–10 hours from Lund)
Chart Sunshine Coast 3311 No. 5 Grief Point to Desolation Sound 1:40,000
Tides on Point Atkinson
Currents 1 knot in Manson Passage

Hernando is a museum piece where the wealthy are trying to relive their dreams of old-fashioned cottage country. They discourage uninvited visitors. As the island is 5 nmi from the nearest launch at Lund and another 8 nmi around it, most paddlers don't come. If you were staying on Savary, then Hernando becomes more attractive, as it is only a short distance away. See sketchmap on page 91.

Paddling considerations

- Although technically you can land if you remain below the high tide line, you may not be welcome. Try to do the trip without landing.
- Wind direction and strength.
- Crossing from Indian Point on Savary Island 2 nmi.

The route

Start out from Indian Point on Savary. If camping in high summer, there are so many people on Savary that it is probably a good idea not to leave your gear unattended, so take it with you.

To avoid the afternoon north-westerly winds, circumnavigate in a clockwise direction. The western shore is edged with cliffs and quite rocky. Stag Bay at the north end is where the dock is. The eastern side has some sandy beaches especially as you come south.

The Mansons from Cortes and others, whose children attended the first school to open in the area, in 1893, settled Hernando in the 1890s. Around 1970, a couple of Vancouver businessmen who had spent their childhoods on Savary bought the whole island and invited 50 friends to join them. They set up a company to own the island, with the cottagers as shareholders. Architect Geoffrey Massey was one of them. He surveyed the island and identified 75 potential building sites. The shareholders drew lots to decide who was to choose first, second etc. The last one had 26 sites to choose from.

An architectural and planning committee approved new building designs to maintain "the spirit of the island." Most cottages are unpretentious cedar buildings with large windows and decks hidden in the trees. Solar panels provide power and a caretaker delivers propane at the beginning of each season. A noise bylaw silences outdoor stereos and generators.

The residents want their children to have "the same summers we had." Kids play on the beach and collect low-tide critters with buckets and spades. With ice cubes clinking in glasses, the adults read books under beach umbrellas or play cards and chat on their decks. There are cell

En route to Hernando Island via Major Inlet.

phones but no TVs. Some families spend all summer on the island, with fathers commuting up by seaplane on the weekends. It's a utopia that many aspire to but fewer and fewer can afford. Paddle by without disturbing.

~

On an October day when the sea was platinum smooth, I paddled from Lund out to Major Islet and then on to Hernando. Pairs of marbled murrelets in smart black and white winter plumage accompanied me as far as the pink cliffs of Major Islet but the long hour's paddle between there and Hidalgo Point was barren of wildlife. As I approached Hernando, I heard a chain saw being used on the island but otherwise saw no sign of humans. Harlequin ducks sunned themselves on a rock in front of me while I ate lunch. Farther out, Pacific and common loons called.

Afterwards, paddling south along the shore, I saw a number of rustic cottages partly screened by trees. One had its own private pocket beach. Beyond a rocky islet a long stretch of shingle fringed a meadow with more cottages. Offshore a flock of about a hundred surf scoters chattered together. I skirted them as I headed back to Major Islet.

Within 50 metres of the pink cliffs, I heard a deep sigh behind me, and another to the south. As I watched, a pair of porpoise rolled up. Another pair surfaced within 10 metres of my boat, allowing me to see the distinctive white on their dorsal fins that identified them as Dall's porpoise (Phocoenoides dalli). They like to ride the bow waves of fast boats but quickly lost interest in me. An hour later, I was back in Lund—in time to catch Nancy's Bakery before it closed at 5 pm. It was a perfect day for this trip, as the stable air of a high-pressure system kept the sea unusually calm the whole way there and back.

18 Mitlenatch Island

Difficulty Advanced conditions – considerable risk
Distance 10 nmi round trip from Smelt Bay Park on Cortes and the same distance from Indian Point on Savary Island
Duration 4–5 hours
Chart No. 3538 Desolation Sound and Sutil Channel 1:40,000
Tides on Point Atkinson
Currents 2 knots in the middle of the Strait of Georgia

Mitlenatch, a dry, uninhabited island 3.5 nmi south of Cortes, is a favourite destination for cruising boaters and naturalists. Its 36 hectares of land fringed by 300 metres of ocean has been a provincial park since 1961.

Paddling considerations
- Wind direction and strength.
- Heed small craft warnings in the Strait of Georgia.
- You could be storm stayed. Take overnight gear, as there is no accommodation for visitors.

The route
Listen very carefully to the weather forecast before venturing toward Mitlenatch. It is in a very exposed position in the Strait of Georgia so you could easily be stormbound there for several days.

Possible launches are either Smelt Bay Provincial Park on Cortes Island or Lund and camp overnight on Savary.

On the way over, watch for murres, pigeon guillemots, marbled murrelets, ancient murrelets, Pacific loons and Western grebes. Also watch for marine mammals like orca, humpback whales, Pacific white-sided dolphins (usually 40–50 at a time) and harbour and Dall's porpoise (usually one to two at a time).

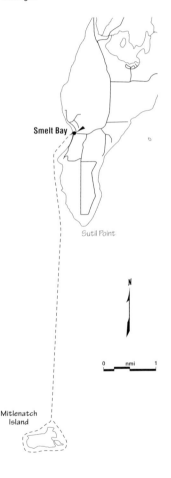

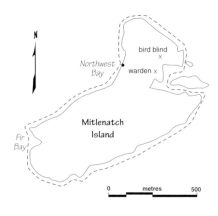

Traditionally, Sliammon people paddled over to the island to gather gull eggs. They called it Metlnech (Mitlenatch), which means "calm at one end." Later, Kwakwaka'wakw invaders named it "Mah-kwee-lay-ah," meaning "it looks close, but seems to move away as you approach it." As you paddle toward it, expect to see this phenomenon.

In 1894, John Manson and his wife, Margaret Ellen Smith, homesteaded on the island, thinking it resembled their Shetland Islands birthplace. John would leave his wife and toddler for long periods while he rowed up Homfray Channel to look after timber claims. When the isolation became too much, Maggie and the child returned to Cortes to live near John's brother, Mike. Until the 1940s,

Mitlenatch baby. Week-old Glaucous-winged Gull.

John continued to row sheep, two at a time, out to the island to graze.

Although Mitlenatch is not listed as an ecological reserve, the primary role of the provincial park is to protect "a unique island ecosystem... The 155-hectare park contains the second-largest seabird nesting colony in the Strait of Georgia as well as many rare plant and animal species." In summer, volunteers take turns supervising people who land, to make sure they keep to the trails and do not disturb either the nesting gulls or the unique flora.

Land in the Northwest Bay if possible. If not, land on the other side in Camp Bay. Check in with the volunteer wardens and pick up a brochure. On shore, you must stick to the marked trails.

Several notice boards illustrate the local wild flowers and birds. Although you can walk the trail through the meadow in minutes, dally to identify the colourful species in bloom. Tiny, delicate blue-eyed grass with their brilliant yellow centres are everywhere. Both white and blue camas flowers occur amongst the yellow umbels of the Indian consumption plant. Early in the season, look for chocolate lilies and orchids. Later on there will be orange tiger lilies. On sunny days watch for garter snakes basking on the trail and on the warm rocks. Some of the largest specimens in the province live here. They grow to over 90 cm. These snakes can act like boa constrictors—on mice.

As you turn left up the trail toward the bird blind, look for large pink patches of Hooker's Onion and the bright yellow flowers of Oregon Sunshine. Near the hide there's a patch of yellow and pink pricklypear cactus—an indication of how dry the island is.

On the trail to the hide, Mitlenatch Island.

A couple of years ago, the birdwatching blind was disappointing. Though still functional, it had fallen into disrepair. Sometimes the glaucous-winged gulls are so preoccupied with their courtship that you can get close enough to see the dark red orbital rings around the eyes of each breeding gull. Their white and grey plumage is perfection at this time of year. Once the female lays her two or three eggs, both sexes incubate them for 27–29 days. After the young hatch, it is a further 35–54 days before they fly, in early August.

Look back over the island from the hide for a panoramic view of Camp Bay where the warden's "cabin" is; Northwest Bay; the meadow between them; and behind it, the highest western cliffs, which are off-limits to everyone. The warden's residence is a log lean-to protecting a couple of tent pads from the wind. A pit toilet in the centre of the island serves everyone.

Wherever you land, also circumnavigate the island. There is more wildlife to be seen from the water than on land. Paddle slowly and stay far enough back that breeding birds don't start flying off the nesting ledges. If disturbed, they may abandon the nest and not breed again till the following year.

On the west side, halfway up the cliffs, pigeon guillemots and three species of cormorants vie for nesting space on ledges. Immature birds roost closer to the water. Their scarlet feet and mouths are an astonishing contrast to their smart black plumage and white wing patches. At the top of the cliff, glaucous-winged gulls and three kinds of cormorants nest. Most cormorants are the pelagic variety, which swim low in the water and sport white hip patches in flight. The bright orange throats of the double-crested show up well but the blue and yellow gullar pouches of the Brandt's are hard to see.

Predators are here too. There's a large bald eagle nest in a pocket bay, and immature birds from previous hatches send the pigeon guillemots, black oystercatchers, gulls and cormorants flying as they wheel over them. If eagles can't find enough fish, they will take other birds. Northwestern crows construct bulky platform nests in thickets and small trees. They eat anything so protect your lunch.

On the water, look for the distinctive pearl grey heads of Pacific loons. They are smaller than common loons. Small sooty birds flying past with rapid wing beats and bright yellow bills are likely rhinoceros auklets. They fly so fast they are hard to find in the binoculars.

Two kinds of sea lions haul out on the rocks from October to mid May, though the odd animal may linger all year. As you glide past, not too close, listen to the sounds they make. The larger, tawny, Steller's sea lions (*Eumetopias jubatus*) growl, whereas the smaller, darker, Californias (*Zalophus californianus*) bark. Both groups are non-breeding males. At the other end of the island, harbour seals of both sexes bask on the rocks. River otters frolic among the rocks and in the sea. These are smaller, slimmer animals than the sea otters found on the West Coast of Vancouver Island but just as fun to watch.

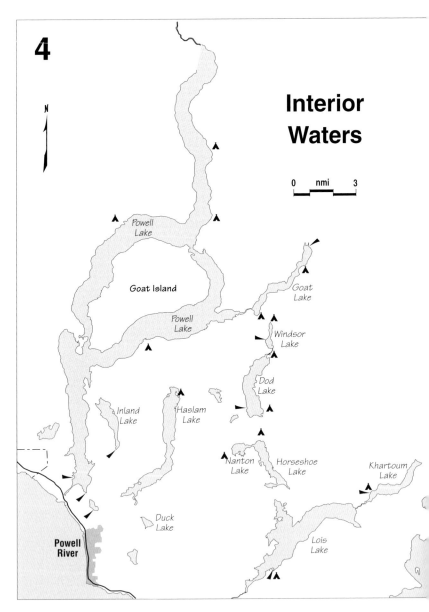

4

N

Interior Waters

0 nmi 3

Powell Lake

Goat Island

Powell Lake

Goat Lake

Windsor Lake

Dod Lake

Inland Lake

Haslam Lake

Nanton Lake

Horseshoe Lake

Khartoum Lake

Duck Lake

Lois Lake

Powell River

There's a variety of paddling areas on the freshwater lakes behind Powell River. Powell Lake is a landlocked version of inlets like Jervis, Toba, Bute and others with the same inflow/outflow wind pattern. The Powell River Canoe Route, although designed for portageable boats, can also be accessed by road. The roads to the beginning lakes are open at any time but the others are restricted to weekends. If you want to fish, you need a freshwater fishing licence.

Launches

Shingle Mill
From the Powell River Visitor Info Centre on Marine Avenue, drive north past Willingdon Beach Park and into the historic townsite. There's a stop sign outside the Patricia Theatre, but continue straight through for another block. Turn right on Arbutus Avenue and cross a bridge over the lake. Turn right toward the Shingle Mill Pub. The concrete launch ramp is on the other side of it. Paid parking is up the hill. If the ramp is busy, drive into the parking lot and unload beside a small grassy park on the lakeshore. Then repark the vehicle.

Mowat Bay
From the Powell River Visitor Info Centre on Marine Avenue, drive north to the first set of traffic lights. Turn right up Alberni to another set of lights. Turn left on Joyce Avenue. This curves around past the hospital to a T-junction. Turn left on Manson, then right on Cassiar. Within a block, turn left on Yukon Avenue, which you follow till it becomes Cranberry Street and

passes both ends of Cranberry Lake. Turn right on Mowat Avenue. Parking is unpaid and unsupervised. Vehicles left there for more than 36 hours are considered abandoned. If staying longer, call Municipal Hall and give the Parks Department a description and licence number of the vehicle.

Lois Lake
From the Saltery Bay ferry, drive north on Highway 101 for 10.4 km and turn right up a rough gravel road whose surface improves slightly after the first hill. After 2.4 km, the road splits into three. Take the middle road, which is signed for the Canoe Route. After 2.1 km farther, turn left at the T-junction and go down the hill 0.7 km to Lois Lake.

Nanton Lake, Dodd Lake, Windsor Lake, and Goat Lake
Are all accessed from Goat Lake Main, an unpaved logging road open only on weekends. From the Saltery Bay ferry, drive north on Highway 101 for 13 km and turn right up Dixon Road. The pavement soon ends but the road continues to Lois Lake and the rest of the lake chain. Make sure you have the Ministry of Forests Powell Forest Canoe Route Recreation map with you.

Campsites

The campsites for the Canoe Route are described in the B.C. Forest Service map.

The campsites for Powell Lake and Haslam Lake are largely unorganized and are included in the route descriptions in this book.

Sunrise at Dodd Lake.

19 Powell Forest Canoe Route

Difficulty Beginner conditions – low risk
Distance 79.7 km on the water, 10.7 km on 6 portages
Duration 5–7 days to enjoy it
Map B.C. Forest Service Powell Forest Canoe Route Recreation Map
Scale 1:100,000. This details all the portages and campsites.
Tides none, but lake levels govern the availability of beaches on which to land.
Currents none

Although you can portage between the six lakes like the canoeists, you don't have to. All the big lakes and some of the tiny ones are road accessible though hours are restricted to weekends along Goat Lake Main. Lois Lake is always open.

Paddling considerations
• Wind direction and strength
• Portages
• Logging roads only open between 6 pm and 5 am Mon–Fri and all day on weekends—i.e., day trippers access this area only on weekends.

The route
Most canoeists start at Lois Lake and end at the shingle mill on Powell Lake so that they can portage the 2.4 km down, not up, "Cardiac Hill" between Windsor Lake and Goat Lake. Kayakers can cherry-pick the areas they want to visit, lunching at the head of the well-marked portages, then leaving their boats to casually stroll down and back unencumbered by heavy paraphernalia. Listen for woodpeckers.

Before 1931, when MacMillan Bloedel built the dam at the end of Lois Lake, Lois Lake and Khartoum Lakes were three lakes known as the Gordon Pasha lakes. The dam flooded

the valley and combined two of them into Lois Lake. This is why when water levels are low, quite large tree stumps emerge. If they're lurking just below the surface, you may not notice them till you're hung up on one. Winds can be strong on both lakes but the narrow waterway between them is almost always calm. At the far end of Khartoum, you get great views of often snow-capped Mount Diadem (1785 m). As you paddle through the

Woodpeckers

Pileated woodpeckers, *Dryocopus pileatus*, make an arresting hollow drumroll sound that is hard to miss. Red-shafted flickers, *Colaptes auratus*, (the yellow-shafted live beyond the Rockies) make a laughing sound and a sharper drum when they are hunting for insects in tree trunks. Hairy *Picoides villosus* and its lookalike cousin the downy woodpecker, *Picoides pubescens*, make softer taps. (The downy's bill is only a quarter of its head width, whereas the hairy's is about half.) The red-breasted sapsucker, *Sphyrapicus ruber*, makes rows of twin holes when it pecks tree trunks. Although the red-naped sapsucker, *Sphyrapicus nuchalis*, has been seen here in September, it is uncommon.

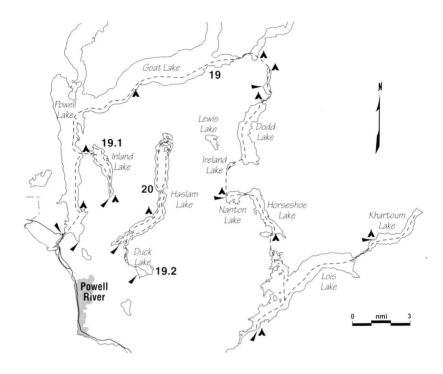

stump forest, watch for merganser nests in the sawed-off tree trunks, but leave quickly so that the female can return before the eggs get cold. Paddle a short way up the creek to find a nice lunch spot.

The portage between Lois Lake and Horseshoe Lake follows a rushing creek that has a beautiful quiet campsite by a big pool halfway along it. Look for merganser pairs here.

Horseshoe Lake, which is accessed from Nanton Lake, is also subject to strong winds but has a couple of quiet bays where you can shelter. Nanton is usually calm and the level 2.4-km

portage between it and Ireland is a pleasant stroll. Logs at the landing for the portage into Little Horseshoe Lake can be a problem for kayakers. The other end of it starts at Dodd Lake and goes a short distance to Beaver Lake, a secret gem where horned owls once greeted me as I examined the red carnivorous sundew plants clinging to a short dock.

If the winds are howling on the big lakes, head for Windsor Lake, which is too small for much fetch to build up. The launch is sometimes crowded with mushroom pickers but they should let you squeeze by.

The portage to Dodd Lake is an unattractive clear-cut but the one to Goat is not. Watch for the tree stump toilet on the right-hand side. "Cardiac Hill" doesn't start till after the portage has crossed Goat Lake Main, so you don't have to do it.

Goat Lake can be accessed from Goat Lake Main. If the water level is high, try paddling up the Eldred River, which is a glorious, shady cathedral of alder trees shimmering overhead. The lake itself has fierce winds. If they come up, stick to the shore or retreat to your vehicle. A beach within sight of the launch is often frequented by float planes from Seattle but there's lots of room, especially if you paddle south around the point.

Two more lakes, which are delightful for beginners and useful for others on stormy days, are Trip Nos. 19.1 and 19.2.

19.1 Inland Lake

(Also known as Loon Lake)
Although you can access this by a trail from one of the Powell Lake campsites, most people drive to it. Only 5 km long, it has a bicycle trail around it which is level enough for wheelchairs. Beginners can hike out if they get stuck.

Access

From the Visitor Info Centre on Marine Avenue, drive north one block to turn right at a traffic light and up Alberni Street. At a second traffic light, turn left on Joyce Avenue and follow it as it curves past the hospital to soon meet Manson Avenue at a T-junction. Turn left for one block and then right on Cassiar Street, which becomes

Bull frog.

Yukon Avenue. Glimpse tiny, water-lily-clogged Cranberry Lake on your left. Turn right on Haslam Street and go straight up the hill to the first curve. Here (4.7 km from the info centre), you veer left, leaving the pavement and entering the logging road to Inland Lake and Haywire Bay. Follow the unpaved road for 5 km till you come to a junction. Take the right branch for another 2 km, passing through a gate which is kept locked during the winter. Turn left at the next fork of the road and keep left as you descend steeply toward the parking lot near the boat launch.

Halfway down the east side of the lake there is a cove that often contains a loon. At the end of the lake, two small islands are interesting to explore. From time to time, you'll hear voices or see people on tiny beaches.

Contemplating Horseshoe Lake.

The trail around the lake sticks close to the shore and, at either end, connects to the 180-km Sunshine Coast hiking trail. Only small motors are allowed on the lake, so it is a peaceful place to paddle. Although it occasionally gets windy, it is not dangerous like the much larger Powell Lake, which is parallel to it.

19.2 Duck Lake

This is even smaller than Inland Lake (just over 1 km long) and never has a fetch higher than about 10 cm. To access it, proceed as for Inland Lake but at 4.7 km from the info centre remain on the paved road. When the pavement runs out, continue on the unpaved section. After a few kilometres, the lake appears on your left. Drive to the end of it and turn left over a bridge. The launch is on your immediate left.

The only danger on Duck Lake is the outlet, near the launch. Avoid it by paddling right or straight ahead. The outlet goes down a whitewater creek laden with sweeper logs, so it is not runnable even for those with whitewater skills.

Duck Lake has an island in the centre with a trail across it. Camping is not allowed there. Another point of interest is the creek, which comes into the eastern corner. Put your rudder up before entering it and be prepared to bushwhack a bit after the first 50 m. Watch for bufflehead or ring neck ducks and sometimes swans on this lake.

20 Haslam Lake

Difficulty Intermediate conditions – moderate risk
Distance 25 km (12.5 nmi) round trip
Duration 3–4 hours or 2 days
Maps Weyerhaeuser TFL 39 Block 1 Upper Sunshine Coast Recreation Map
1:75,000 includes logging roads
Topographical map sheets 92 F/16 Haslam Lake 1:50,000
Tides none
Currents none

This is Powell River's water supply, so motorboats are not allowed on it. For the same reason, access is difficult. This is unfortunate, as the slough where the lake drains into Duck Lake provides a welcome haven for paddlers, especially beginners, in bad weather. See sketchmap on page 106.

Paddling considerations

• Winds on the lake are strong in the daytime. Paddle in the early morning or evening.

The route

From the Visitor's Infocentre on Marine Ave, drive north one block and turn right at a traffic light onto Alberni Street. At a second traffic light, turn left on Joyce Ave and follow it as it curves past the hospital to a T-junction at Manson Ave. Turn left and drive one block, then turn right on Cassiar Street, which becomes Yukon Ave. Glimpse tiny water lily-clogged Cranberry Lake on your left. Turn right on Haslam Street and go straight up the hill staying on the paved road.

As you pass the water treatment building on your left, the lake appears ahead of it. Vehicle access is blocked off, but you can carry boats a few metres to the shore in several places.

Paddle northeast about 250 m along the lakeshore to the entrance to the slough. This is a calm sancturary for novices in rough weather. Pass the slough and cross to the other side of the lake. There is a beautiful camping spot on the point as the lake curves north. Stop and check it out before continuing up the same side to the islands at the head of the lake. Several of these have camping spots. Be sure to pack all garbage out.

From the head of the lake a mossy trail along a disused logging railway bed used to come down from Giovanni Lake. When Fiddlehead Farm was running, they kept canoes on it but no longer. Explore this if you're storm stayed.

Either get up early in the morning or wait till after 6 pm to come down the lake. Follow the east side and carry lights in case it is dark when you stumble ashore.

21 Powell Lake – 7-day trip

Difficulty Intermediate conditions – moderate risk
Distance 133 km (66.5 nmi) round trip
Duration 6 days but allow a 7th in case you're stormbound
Maps Weyerhaeuser TFL 39 Block 1 Upper Sunshine Coast Recreation Map
1:75,000 includes logging roads
Topographical map sheets: 92 F/15 Powell River, 92 F/16 Haslam Lake,
92 K/1 Powell Lake, 92 K/2 Desolation Sound.
These are all on a scale of 1:50,000 and do not include logging roads.
Tides none, but lake levels govern the availability of beaches on which to land.
See how much beach is showing above the water when you cross the road
bridge by the shingle mill.
Currents none

Although I've paddled the lower part of Powell Lake many times and thought about doing this trip, I've never actually done it. However, talking to the locals confirms my suspicions that this is a viable trip which could be quite interesting, especially if you take along a copy of Carla Mobley's out-of-print *Mysterious Powell Lake: A Collection Of Historical Tales*.[8] Renting one of the many floating cabins on the lake to use as a base for day trips is a popular and practical alternative. Check with the Powell River Visitor Info Centre for current lists.

Paddling considerations
- Winds on the lake are unpredictable and strong. Expect to be stormbound for a day or longer.
- At either end of Goat Island, the winds mix, requiring extra caution.
- Weekend cottager boat traffic when combined with wind can make for lumpy conditions.
- Hidden snags of flooded tree stumps are prevalent even at high water levels. Once stuck, try backpaddling hard.

- Infrequent opportunities to land, due to the many cliffs along the shoreline.
- Ask permission before landing at a cottage.
- Watch for fast-moving personal water craft in cottage and beach areas.
- No VHF reception, and cell reception is extremely patchy. Satellite phone is possible.
- Some cabin owners have been advised to boil their water for two minutes before drinking it. This is a problem in Smarge Bay (locally called Three Mile Bay), Henderson Bay and Hole in the Wall.

The route
When you cross the bridge to the shingle mill, if there is a lot of shingle along the lakeshore, this indicates that the water level everywhere is low and more landing places will be exposed than normal. If the water is high, there will be long stretches of shoreline where it is impossible to land.

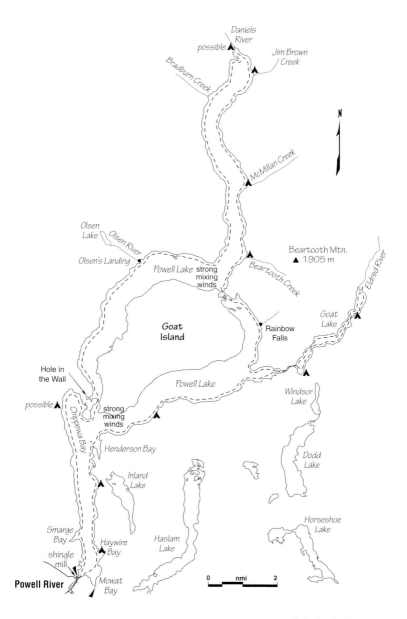

Interior Waters – 111

If the weather looks inclement, paddle under the road bridge and explore the boathouses. This is only a half-hour paddle at most, but it is interesting to see where the dam starts, though you can't get near it. The Powell Lake trip is best done with early starts when the wind is down.

Day 1 – 17 km (8.5 nmi)

Paddle up the east side of the lake. The small brown shore bird with the white rump flying just ahead of you from one cove to the next is a solitary sandpiper. You'll also hear many kingfishers chittering a warn-

Osprey nest.

ing when you enter their territories. Haywire Bay Municipal Park, with 12 waterfront campsites, is about 2.5 km along depending on where you launched. It has a sandy beach and a swimming area defined by logs. In summer, there's a fair bit of Sea-doo activity. If in a group, keep together for better visibility.

Five kilometres farther on, watch for steps coming down to the water in Thornton Bay. At high water it is rather dismal here but at low water one can see rails from the old logging days when they skidded logs down. This is the Lower Powell B.C. Forest Service recreation area. Sometimes scout groups camp here and if you got a late start or the wind came up, it would be wise to spend the night here, as the next camp spot is 10 km farther on. A 0.5-km trail leads up to Inland Lake.

Fiddlehead Farm

Japanese and Italians pioneered Fiddlehead Farm in the 1920s. Both logged selectively with horses. The Enrico brothers produced grapes, grain, vegetables and tobacco. After they left in the 1930s, the farm became overgrown till a back-to-the-land group established a commune there in the 1970s. One of them, Mark Vonnegut, wrote *The Eden Express* about his experience there. Other members of the collective established an alternative school called Total Education, which, under the direction of Peter Schreiber, ran a satellite program at the farm. After Peter's death, his wife Linda turned the farm into a very successful international youth hostel. When she grew older and wanted to retire she couldn't find anyone to take it over. She waited two years and then sold it to a buyer who promised to maintain the buildings but clear-cut the land the next week leaving one building standing.

Popular Haywire Bay campsite, Powell Lake.

Continue up the lake past many old cottages. On weekends the town of Powell River is deserted, as everyone gets in their boats and goes "up the lake." Some cottages are shared by three or four families. Others are enjoyed by extended families that come from far and near. In 2003, Weyerhaeuser identified 230 cabins on the lake.

After another 10 km you reach the Powell Lake B.C. Forest Service recreation site. This used to be the beginning of a trail into Fiddlehead Farm, an international youth hostel. The owner of the private float here is supposed to be building a separate float for recreational users, but until that is

completed, there is an agreement that they can use the private one.

You can hike into the clear-cut that was the farm and connect with the 180-km Sunshine Coast Trail that traverses it. The route is well signed. Tiny 1.5-km Giovanni Lake (unnamed on the Weyerhaeuser map) is also accessed from here. Follow the old wagon road and swing west for about 2 km to reach it. The far end of it has a 1-km trail down to the head of Haslam Lake (see Trip No. 20). When Fiddlehead Farm was in operation this was used frequently.

The Eldred River.

Day 2 – 24 km (12 nmi)

Paddle along the same shore and through the narrows into Goat Lake. This is the shorter of the two top arms of Powell Lake. There are usually buoys along the channel marking a clear passage through the sunken snags for powerboats that sometimes travel at high speed. Opposite the entrance to the narrows, the Powell River Canoe Route has a campsite below a very steep portage into Windsor Lake. Most canoeists prefer to come down this portage rather than up it. Leave the campsite to them and continue up the lake.

Within sight of the head of the lake, there is a long, sandy beach which curves around a point. This is a great campsite and is sometimes used by float plane pilots from Seattle or boaters putting in at the head of Goat Lake. Winds on Goat Lake blow up fiercely, so don't test them. Relax on the beach instead.

If the lake level is high, it's worth proceeding up to the head of Goat Lake and paddling up the Eldred River for a couple of kilometres. This is very pretty but at low water dangerous log sweepers repel entry. If they are visible, don't expose yourself to the possibility of being pinned against them by the current and drowned.

Day 3 – 25 km (12.5 nmi)

Cross over to the west side of the lake and watch for the Goat Lake mayor's funky little cabin sheltered behind a point. Go through the narrows and continue northward along the east side of the other arm of Powell Lake. About 3 km past the log sort, a cottage partly obscures the remains of beautiful Rainbow Falls which, when enough water comes down, produces a mist dancing with rainbows. In recent years, this has not happened often and consequently the falls are easily missed, though old timers will tell you to look for them.

Two kilometres beyond this is Rainbow Lodge. When MacMillan Bloedel owned the Powell River mill they used Rainbow Lodge as a place to entertain visitors. The lodge is now privately owned but is sometimes available for entertaining and renting. Contact the Visitor Info Centre for details. The lake narrows as the mainland almost joins the head of steep-sided Goat Island, and yes, wild goats are a feature of the cliffs. Also check the small islands for osprey nests. Beyond the narrows is one of the two areas where strong winds mix, so be prepared and if necessary wait till they drop. Continue to follow the eastern shoreline of the upper arm of Powell Lake for about 4 km to where Beartooth Creek comes down. Camp here. A hiking trail takes climbers up to Beartooth Mountain (1905 m). Some prefer to branch off up the logging road which crosses it.

Powell Lake cottages from the air.

Day 4 – 18 km (9 nmi)

Continue up the same coast for 5.5 km to McMillan Creek, which is a UREP and is a potential camping spot. A further 9.5 km brings you to Jim Brown Creek, another potential camp spot.

The colourful Billy Goat Smith had a homestead here, which is now under water. The Powell River Museum has a life-size exhibit of his cabin. Mobley's book *Mysterious Powell Lake* analyzes the rumours that Smith was a fugitive from U.S. justice and perhaps responsible for the 1906 murder of Stanford White in New York. A cantankerous crack shot, he was largely self-sufficient on this property from about 1910 till his death here in 1960.

An alternative to Jim Brown Creek is to paddle another 2.5 km to the remains of a permanent logging camp in the muddy estuary of the Daniels River. Crew boats bring workers here daily. Black bear and possibly the odd grizzly may visit, so hang food well out of reach.

Day 5 – 22 km (11 nmi)

Switch to the western shore. Five kilometres south of the Daniels River estuary, Bradburn Creek flows into Powell Lake. Originally this was called Siwash Creek and was homesteaded by Allen Farrell's father (See Allen Farrell sidebar on page 130). This is a good place to land and stretch before paddling south to around a steep point at the end of Upper Powell Lake. Watch for the shaggy white coats of wild goats high up on the mountains and be careful of strong winds where the two portions of the lake meet. At Olsen's Landing a rough road leads 5 km up to Olsen Lake and over to Theodosia, which is a further 10 km away. Olsen's Landing used to be a thriving settlement. Camping is a possibility near the beach/landing. A little farther south, there is the privately owned Powell River Lodge and some cottages.

Day 6 – 27 km (13.5 nmi)

Return down the west shore of the lake. Old-style logging with clear cuts are seen above this shore. Opposite on Goat Island are examples of the new-style, variable retention logging. As you approach First Narrows between Goat Island and the point containing Chippewa Bay there are more cabins. Hole in the Wall is full of them. Although there is nowhere to land, it is worth a paddle just to look. This is the other place where strong winds mix.

Chippewa Bay is almost always very windy in summer from 11 am to evening. The rollers pile right in. If necessary, stop and camp. There's a barge landing on the north side of the log dump in Chippewa Bay that is a possible camp spot. There is an access to an old steam donkey but it is getting less interesting now because the trail has been obliterated in parts from logging which is still active. Bears are very prevalent. The float cabins in the bay use the beach near the barge landing. When the wind calms, paddle back to where you put in.

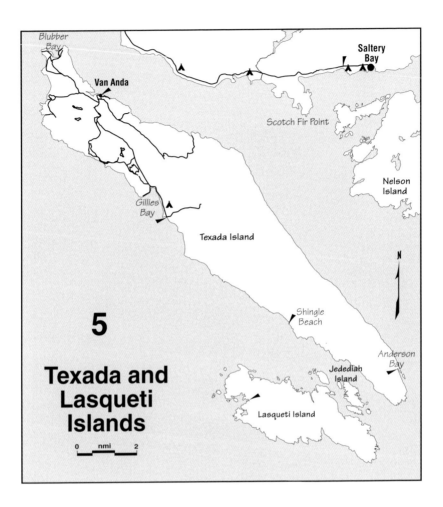

Blubber Bay

Saltery Bay

Van Anda

Scotch Fir Point

Nelson Island

Gillies Bay

Texada Island

N

5

Shingle Beach

Anderson Bay

Jedediah Island

Texada and Lasqueti Islands

Lasqueti Island

0   nmi   2

Although these two often forgotten islands lie beside each other in the Strait of Georgia, their ferry access comes from opposite sides. The Lasqueti ferry, which does not take vehicles, leaves from French Creek on Vancouver Island. while the Texada ferry, which does, leaves from Powell River on the mainland side. The voyage from Westview in Powell River to Blubber Bay on Texada takes 35 minutes. Texada repels visitors with an open pit quarry beside the ferry dock. Once past this, a long, beautiful, dry island opens up. Although there are two other quarries, they make up less than 1% of the shoreline. You'll need a vehicle, as you can't launch from the ferry dock and the launches are too far even for a wheeled kayak. At Lasqueti you can launch beside the ferry dock and then paddle in either direction around the island. The islands are often very dry, so don't light fires. Bring a stove to cook on and be careful to keep it away from vegetation.

Launches

Van Anda[9]

From Blubber Bay, drive approximately 7 km to the T-junction at Van Anda. Turn left down the hill. The hotel is immediately on your left. Call in to make arrangements to park vehicles there while you circumnavigate the island. In return for this courtesy, they ask that you eat a meal in the hotel, preferably before you go. Continue down the short hill and turn right to go along the road beside the ball field. Up the hill, pass the Texada Food Market and turn left again. Pass the Cheslakees monument and the old government wharf. As you start up the next hill watch for a sign for Erickson Park on your left. Drive in there and scout the road down to the beach before driving down it. This sheltered rocky beach is also the put-in for a high water exploration of the lagoon.

Shelter Point

From Blubber Bay, drive approximately 7 km to the T-junction at Van Anda and turn right. Drive another 20 km to Gillies Bay, through the village and out the other side to another T-junction. Turn right and the launch is a couple of blocks away, with the campsite on the right. You can leave vehicles overnight here but the concession manager can't always see what is happening and sometimes there are parties.

Shingle Beach

Follow the directions for Shelter Point. At the T-junction after Gillies Bay, turn left. Pass the overflow campground and turn right on an unpaved B.C. Hydro road. Continue on this for about 11 km. Past the hydro station the road climbs a hill and a smaller road goes off to the right. Take this. Shingle Beach is another couple of kilometres. The site has recently been enlarged considerably. In August 2004, about 700 people attended a music festival called Diversity here. Plans are to make this an annual event. Leave vehicles at your own risk. Vandalism sometimes occurs.

Northeast light, Texada Island.

Anderson Bay
4WD is mandatory. You might get down but you'd never get back up without it. Although the turns are signed, it's extra insurance to have the Texada map with you. Launch at high tide to avoid the mud. Parking is plentiful.

Pocahontas Bay
From Blubber Bay, drive approximately 7 km to the T-junction at Van Anda. Turn left down the hill and turn right at the bottom to go along the road beside the ball field. Go up the hill, but don't turn at the Texada Food Market. Go straight for another block, turn right on Columbia, which becomes Midas and then Central High Road. This is unpaved. Drive for about 9 km to where an unmarked but fairly well-travelled road goes off to the left. Take this and watch the potholes. Pocahontas Bay is about 5 km down it. There is usually lots of parking by the water.

Campsites

Shelter Point Regional Park See directions for the launch. Check in at the office. There are some sites on the water, a group campground sheltered from the wind, and an overflow campground back up the road. A small concession sells meals and snacks. The place is extremely popular on summer weekends.

Shingle Beach B.C. Forest Service campsite See directions for the launch. Most people camp up the hill above the launch, as there is no room to leave vehicles down by the beach.

Anderson Bay (in park) As you drive down to the bay, the camping area is to the left along an old roadbed.

Jedediah Marine Provincial Park
Random camping is allowed. Some beaches are muddy at low tide.

22 Texada Island – circumnavigation

Difficulty Intermediate conditions – moderate risk
Distance 59.4 nmi round trip
   Van Anda to Gillies Bay 15.4 nmi
   Gillies Bay to Shingle Beach 9 nmi
   Shingle Beach to Anderson Bay 11.5 nmi
   Anderson Bay to Northeast Point 15 nmi
   Northeast Point to Van Anda 8.5 nmi
Duration 5–6 days
Charts No. 3512 Strait of Georgia Central Portion 1:80,000
   No. 3513 Strait of Georgia Northern Portion 1:80,000
   Welcome to Texada Island brochure and map
Tides on Point Atkinson
Currents 1–2 knots in Sabine Channel: a hazardous area when wind opposes tide,
   as both funnel through the constricted channel

The joy of circumnavigating Texada is that you meet few other boats.

Paddling considerations
- Travel anticlockwise so that the summer prevailing northwest wind pushes you along.
- Plan to do Anderson Bay to Northeast Point in one day.
- Watch for the tail end of Qualicum winds in the Partington Point area.

The route
Launch at Erickson Park in Van Anda after first asking permission to leave vehicles at the Texada Island Inn. There are almost no landing places before Blubber Bay, so pack food and pee bottle where you can reach them. Also pack water for at least half the trip.

Leave the exploration of Sturt Bay to the return journey. You may have to paddle all the way to Gillies Bay before finding a camp spot, so get going.

The Texada coast is a continuous kaleidoscope of rugged rock formations surmounted by twisted shore pines and gleaming red russet-trunked arbutus trees. Almost every corner has a seal snoozing behind it, or a harlequin duck sunning itself on a rock, or a heron fishing. On a calm, warm summer day when the sea and the sky are the same blue, it's heaven. There are no bears or cougar on the island. As far away as Mexico, people prize Texada gold, which is grown here in illegal gardens. If you find one, back off immediately.

In Blubber Bay, stay well clear of the Powell River ferry. The Blubber Bay dock used to be accessible to other craft, but no more. There is nowhere to land till below the summer cottages west of the ferry. This is the last good landing place for a while though at high tide you may be able to scramble ashore at Kiddie Point, which has a nice flat spot suitable for camping. Kiddie Point, known by the locals as Cohoe Point, is a favourite fishing hole when there are fish.

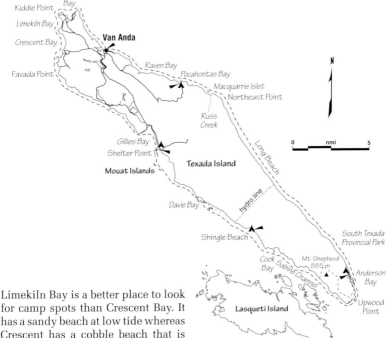

Limekiln Bay is a better place to look for camp spots than Crescent Bay. It has a sandy beach at low tide whereas Crescent has a cobble beach that is difficult to land on and launch from. On a very low tide, the rock pools at the south end of Limekiln Bay have orange and burgundy bryozoa as well as anemones and crabs. The Malaspina Naturalists from Powell River have hiked in on several occasions to see them.

From the water, the section from Crescent Bay to Favada Point and Davis Bay[10] appears uninhabited and very rocky, fun to paddle, with all kinds of little hidden nooks monitored by eagles and by seals basking on the rocks. Tiny Davis Bay is a possible landing and camp spot if no one builds a cottage there.

A couple of miles past Davis Bay, you'll start seeing the workings of a large quarry which seem to stretch a long way. This is the only quarry you'll see till just before Van Anda, which is several days away. Harlequin ducks often hang around the dock.

The next point of interest is an eroded cliff culminating in a sandy beach. The locals call this the "Sand Dunes" and some of them hike into it. It could yield a small camp spot and it is a pleasant place to rest and swim.

"Sand dunes," Texada Island.

Cross Gillies Bay to the Regional Park on the inside of tiny, privately owned Dick Island. There is a concession with a phone should you need one. It's also a last opportunity to buy chocolate bars or ice cream, and you could camp here. It's the only organized campsite on the island and very popular on weekends. The gap between Dick Island and the boat launch ramps is very shallow and has a fast tide that has drowned at least one person.

The rocky islands in Mouat Bay are home to a hostile colony of harbour seals, which have attacked a number of people in kayaks, canoes and zodiacs for the last 15 years. Give them a wide berth. Seal bites need to be treated with antibiotics. One person took two months to recover from one.

On the other hand, I've paddled and swum with the seals on these islands and not been attacked, but having since met some of their victims, I'm more wary.

Leaving Mouat Bay, the distant island is Flower Island in Davie Bay, another potential camp spot. Don't pitch your tent too close to the high tide line, because when the evening cruise ships pass, their wash can slosh up another metre or so. On going ashore in dry areas, watch where you step. This is cactus country. The flora is quite similar to that on Mitlenatch Island.

Farther down the coast, pass the hydro power line that crosses the Strait of Georgia. The seals on the rocks off it seem to be friendly.

Nine nautical miles south of Gillies Bay, there's a BC Forest Service campsite

Avian Recyclers

The Latin name for turkey vultures is *Cathartes aura*, meaning pacifier or cleanser. These much-maligned birds have several ways of avoiding being contaminated by the carrion they eat. Their heads, which come in contact with the carcasses, lack feathers, so they are easy for the birds to keep clean. In addition, sunlight on the bare skin kills bacteria and viruses. The birds spend several hours each day cleaning themselves. Internally, their stomach acids are strong enough to kill any viruses or bacteria in their food. During a hog cholera epidemic, the U.S. Department of Agriculture tested turkey vulture droppings and pellets and found them to be free of infection. Normally the pellets, which are regurgitated, do not smell, but if the bird is threatened, it may roll over and play dead or it may vomit foul smelling pellets. Although the majority of its diet consists of carrion, some sources claim that vegetation is also a significant part.

During the day they soar gracefully on the thermals, hardly moving their wings, which are tilted in a "V" shape and flap when there are no thermals. Turkey vultures are migratory in B.C. and do not over-winter. They may roost in the same tree every night while they are here and may return to the same area year after year. The tree is not a nest, however, as they lay their eggs on the bare ground or a cliff ledge.

Bird rehab workers have found turkey vultures to be gentle, inquisitive and very intelligent. They become attached to their caregivers and will bring them objects for a game of tug-of-war.

---

at Shingle Beach. If the few sites on the water are in use, walk up the road to the upper ones. You may want to avoid this place on a Saturday night, though.

Between Shingle Beach and Cook Bay, don't be surprised if you hear roosters. A number of isolated homesteads raise chickens. Although some of the cottagers at Cook Bay may welcome visitors, some don't, and as it is not a particularly scenic place, continue on past Partington Point. This is where paddlers going to Jedediah start wanting to cross.

Narrow Sabine Channel between Texada and Lasqueti (Jedediah) acts as a funnel for both wind and tide. The famous Qualicum gap winds scream up the Alberni Canal, cross the rest of Vancouver Island and head straight over to False Bay on Lasqueti. Sabine Channel gets some of this. In addition, all kinds of boat traffic from barges to cruise ships use it, so keep checking to see what is bearing down on you at speed. The best time to cross is at dusk or dawn. For more information on Jedediah Island, see Trip No. 24.

Beyond Partington Point, some private landowners allow camping, but as the ground is often very dry, don't light a fire. This southern part of the island is a provincial park, but the steep cliffs make access from the water difficult. Hike in from Anderson Bay if you want to see it.

The waterfall at Napier Creek is a popular water supply for campers who commute from Jedediah to get it. Unfortunately, there is no space to camp at the waterfall, and at low tide in a dry year, it is easy to miss.

The cove before Upwood Point contains a permanent residence but no landing. This south end of the island is a popular fishing hole for sport fishers from Pender Harbour. Follow the coast to Anderson Bay. The bunkhouse, which used to sit in the middle of the meadow has been moved. There is a rustic campsite beside the grassy old logging road on the east side of the bay. It's a snug place to be in a storm. The road, which comes down to Anderson Bay, is 4WD only. Hike back up to the fork and bear left. Soon you'll see a small quarry with lots of chips of flower rock. You can also climb up Mount Shepherd (885 m) for a view down to Vancouver and Mount Baker.

When I circumnavigated Texada in August 2002, I started out under a gunmetal sky. As I passed Kiddie Point, the wind rose and the sea became lumpy. A friend helped me ashore in Crescent Bay and arranged for similar help next morning. It was still rough but had calmed down by the time I reached Favada Point. It was smooth and beautiful all the way to Davie Bay, where I next camped within less than a metre of the wash from a cruise ship. In the morning, a fox sparrow pecked my toes as I ate breakfast.

That night I camped on a tiny peninsula south of Partington Point. As the weather had been so beautiful, I failed to put a tarp over my tent. A thunderstorm kept me awake most of the night and in the morning when

Anderson Bay.

Columbia Coast Mission

In 1904, John Antle, a maverick sea-going Anglican priest from Newfoundland who had grown up in the tradition of the Grenfell Mission, founded a medical mission serving the inner waters of Vancouver Island. In total, the mission operated about 20 ships with names like *Columbia I–IV* and *John Antle I–V.* Staffed by doctors and clergy, they visited every settlement and remote homestead up every inlet. Patients too sick to be treated on board were transported to hospitals at Rock Bay in Discovery Passage (1905), Van Anda (1907), Alert Bay (1909), Carriden Bay (1920), and Pender Harbour (1930). The service meant that people of all faiths, who otherwise would have died, survived frequent logging and other accidents.

In addition to this practical Christianity, marriages, christenings, funerals and regular Sunday services were performed on board or ashore by chaplain skippers. When Antle retired in 1939, Alan Greene took over from him. Gradually government services took over, making it difficult to raise funds to keep the mission going. In 1982 the remaining funds were split between the Anglican dioceses serving Vancouver and Victoria.

the rain finally came a corner of my sleeping bag got wet. I got up early and just had time to breakfast and load the kayak before the rain began again. Upwood Point was lumpy so I paddled hard for Anderson Bay, where a friend with a cabin helped me dry out. The forecast for the next day was bad so I stayed put.

I got an early start under rather poor conditions, but then the sea calmed. Far in the distance I could see the white water tower at Lang Bay on the mainland and knew I had to be level with it by evening. It seemed a long way away. Halfway along Long Beach, I capsized trying to launch on the slippery cobbles as the wake from a distant boat pounded the shore. The water was warm and I soon had the cockpit pumped out. I ate lunch in my boat and paddled hard till I came to a sun-drenched beach where I spread everything out to dry and had a swim.

The evening paddle past Northeast Point was magical. A heron held his position till I was almost within touching distance. The tide was high when I unloaded at Russ Creek and fell into my sleeping bag for a well-deserved rest.

Waiting for the tide to come up, I slept late and so did the seals on MacQuarrie Islet. At Pocahontas Bay, a family of river otter kits entertained me while I thought about the famous whiskey still located in the nearby forest in 1928. The sky began to cloud over again just as I reached my take-out at Van Anda. This is a typical weather pattern for August. Having already explored Sturt Bay on another occasion, I didn't do so again.

~

Get an early start from Anderson Bay. It's 15 nmi to Northeast Point, with few places to get ashore. The "Long Beach" marked on the Texada Island brochure is a cobble beach which is very slippery at low tide. Halfway along it, where the power line crosses

First landing at the north end of Long Beach.

the island, it may be possible to land at high tide. Watch for turkey vultures feasting on carrion on the beach and deer browsing on the seaweed. You're also likely to see seals on the rocks and harlequin ducks in the little coves.

Past Northeast Point, at the estuary of Russ Creek, there is a good campsite in the thick moss of an old logging road which extends back into the bush for a long way. It's best to land and leave at high tide. The trees on tiny MacQuarrie Islet are lovely against the sunset.

You can sleep late in the morning as the take-out at Van Anda is only 8.5 nmi away. If the tide is low, explore the mossy logging road behind the camp and have lunch. Then go and wake up the seals on MacQuarrie Islet.

Pocahontas Bay, which is accessible by logging road, is the site of an exciting raid on an illegal whisky still in 1928. Local filmmaker Bob Blackmore has made several videos about Texada, including one about the Pocahontas Still. These are available from the Holtenwood Gallery by the Blubber Bay ferry terminal. At low tide, a shingle bar uncovers to provide a sheltered landing.

The far side of Raven Bay is the site of another quarry, followed by an inactive one, and then you're back at Van Anda.

If the tide is high, don't forget to explore Sturt Bay. There are two marinas at the mouth of it, with a couple of lagoons in behind. Somewhere in there a trail runs up through the forest to a freshwater lake.

23 Lasqueti Island – circumnavigation

Difficulty Intermediate conditions – moderate risk
Distance 28 nmi round trip
Duration 3–5 days depending on where you camp
Charts No. 3312 Jervis Inlet and Desolation Sound, page 1, 1:40,000
No. 3512 Strait of Georgia Central Portion 1:80,000
Tides on Point Atkinson
Currents 2 knots in Sabine Channel

Lasqueti has some pretty offshore islands with good snorkelling in warm water. It has quite a number of cottages on it, so camping can be tricky. Side trips to Sangster Island and Jedediah Island are attractive extras.

Paddling considerations
- Both sides of the island, being in the middle of the Strait of Georgia, can be subject to strong winds.

The route
Even before the advent of Jedediah Marine Provincial Park, Lasqueti was a most enjoyable island to circumnavigate. Launching beside the ferry dock in False Bay, we always headed for the Finnerty Islands and the Fegan Islands first, because their rocky, narrow passages edged with arbutus trees are a joy to explore. Snorkelling in the warm water is a delight, so take fins and a mask. I stayed in for an hour one July, without a wetsuit.

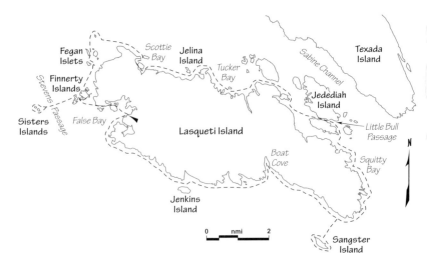

Narrow passage in the Finnerty Islands.

Unfortunately the islands don't have many camping spots and there seems to be a cottage in every cove. Start looking early and take what you can find. If you can find one near the Finnerty Islands, and if the weather forecast indicates calm seas with no wind for several hours, consider paddling the 1.2 nmi across to Sisters Island. The first lighthouse was established in 1898 but no one staffs it now. You probably won't be able to land on the windswept rock. On the way you may see ancient auklets, murres, pigeon guillemots, and the pearl grey heads of Pacific loons.

If the weather starts to look like a change, retreat. An experienced Lasqueti paddler who was flying a kite started out well but something happened and his body and boat were found later several miles apart. When flying a parabolic kite, always keep a knife on deck to cut the cord if things get hairy. Kite flying is best done by the bow paddler of a double while the stern person steers and braces.

~

After snorkelling and fishing in the Finnerty Islands a friend and I moved on to the Fegans, where we found a camp spot with a view of the sunset. We had caught a coho but had no frying pan so we improvised with an old grate which we propped over the fire. Then we wrapped the fish in aluminum foil and set it on top. If you lack foil, wrap the fish in seaweed. The outside will be a bit charred but the inside will be fine.

Arriving at the bay inside of Jelina Island we walked up to the veranda of an old house, where we met an elderly man of the same vintage. He kindly

Allen Farrell

In the summer of 1973, they circumnavigated Lasqueti in a 5-metre dory starting at Lennie's Lagoon. Reaching Tucker Bay, they slept in the moss and were eaten by mosquitoes. Next night they slept on the gravel on Sangster Island. "You just move around and it gives way to conform to your body." In the Finnerties it was raining so they turned the boat over and slept under it. This trip convinced

Allen Farrell (1912–2002) grew up on a homestead at Siwash Creek on the upper reaches of Powell Lake. A largely self-taught boat builder, he constructed the 12-metre schooner *Wind Song* at Bargain Harbour in 1951. He and his second wife, Sharie, sailed her to Fiji, where they sold her. When they returned, they homesteaded in Blind Bay on Nelson Island. They built a second schooner, the 10-metre gaff-rigged *Ocean Bird*, which they lived aboard. After selling the Nelson Island property, they built a 13-metre brigantine, *Ocean Girl*. In 1960 they set sail again for the South Pacific but only made it to Mexico and Hawaii. Back home, they built a 12.5-metre ketch, *Native Girl*, which they launched in 1965 and moved aboard. From 1965–69 they sailed up and down the coast, eventually settling inland on Lasqueti Island, where they moored *Native Girl* in Scottie Bay and sold her in 1972.

them to build a floathouse so that they could live by the sea. Unfortunately the people whose houses they anchored in front of objected.

Then Allen injured his back. All his life he had practised gymnastics and now he cured himself with exercises. Following this he built the dory *August Moon*, which had only a six-inch keel and cement ballast. After only two months living aboard her in 1975, they sold her and bought back *Native Girl*. Allen rerigged her in 1977 as a gaff ketch with a lug mizzen and sailed her to Mexico again. This was the last time they would sail offshore.

Now Allen began to study Chinese lug rigs and built the 14-metre junk *China Cloud*, which they launched in 1981. It had rocks under the floorboards for ballast and a 9-metre traditional Chinese sculling oar. They lived aboard her till 1995. Sharie died in 1996 and Allen went to live with his two sons on Lasqueti.

gave us permission to camp. Although we paddled by Jedediah, we didn't land on it but continued to Sangster Island. Next morning we had just finished packing when my friend said, "Look out there. What do you see?" The 1.2 nmi between us and Lasqueti was a mass of froth. We unpacked and repitched our tents in a sheltered hollow and hiked to the other side of the island, which was sheltered from the raging northwest wind. Next morning we crossed a calm sea in 15 minutes. It was definitely worth the wait.

~

Continuing past the Fegan Islands, duck into Scottie Bay and see if there are any junk-rigged sailboats there. Lasqueti was a favourite hangout for Allen Farrell, who built *China Cloud*. Someone in Scottie Bay built a smaller version. Farrell preferred windy False Bay because *China Cloud* had a flat bottom and he ran it up onto the shore of a sheltered shallow cove.

"She's a good old-man's boat," he told me when I went aboard. He demonstrated how easy it was for him to raise, lower and reef the small sails and manoeuvre the boat with the big sweep oar at the stern. Down below, his wife, Sharie, offered us fresh-baked bread and homemade jam. Next day I saw them sailing across the Strait at high speed. The Farrells lived aboard *China Cloud* for many years.

Somewhere on the way into Scottie Bay there's another good snorkelling place. Bubbles of old lava about a metre across have formed little gardens of emerald green seaweed through which brown and silver perch dart. They're just as spectacular as Australia's Great Barrier Reef, where much of the coral is dead and grey and the fish provide the colour. Here it's the weed that's vivid and there's more of it.

Whether you land on Jedediah or not, you should cross Bull Passage and paddle through Little Bull Passage. It's very quiet beneath the steep cliffs and sometimes you catch a glimpse of feral sheep or goats looking down from on high.

The southern coast of Lasqueti is rocky and hard to land on. Bigger boats can take refuge in Squitty Bay, but no camping is allowed in the park there, so it's only good for a lunch stop. It's also infested with mosquitoes.

Head for Sangster and hope the wind will let you cross. A strange rock formation at the southern tip of the island is reminiscent of an elephant's trunk. The nearby shingle beach is a good landing.

Paddling back to False Bay along the western shore, you'll pass a lot of cottages. This side, which can be battered by southwest winds, is less interesting than the northwest side.

24 Jedediah Island

Difficulty Intermediate conditions – moderate risk
Distance 4 nmi to circumnavigate the island
Duration 1-2 hours
Charts No. 3312 Jervis Inlet and Desolation Sound, page 1, 1:40,000
No. 3512 Strait of Georgia Central Portion 1:80,000
Bring photocopies of the map of the trails in Mary Palmer's book
Jedediah Days: One Woman's Island Paradise.[11]
Palmer lived there from 1949 to 1992.
Tides on Point Atkinson
Currents 2 knots in Sabine Channel

Jedediah is an uninhabited island which used to be a farm. The old homestead remains and the trails are kept open by boaters. Flocks of feral sheep and goats add to the ambiance. The old horse has died, perhaps from too many kind handouts!

Paddling considerations

- The approach is the tricky part. Lasqueti and Jedediah beside it lie in the middle of the Strait of Georgia, which often has a small craft warning posted.
- Water taxi from Pender Harbour. This is the safest way, as no crossings are involved.
- Drive to Frenchman's Creek on Vancouver Island and load boats and gear on the Lasqueti ferry, which does not take vehicles. On arriving in False Bay, paddle the 10 nmi around to Jedediah. This takes a bit longer but involves no crossings.
- Drive onto the Texada ferry at Powell River and then drive 27 km on pavement to Shelter Point at Gillies Bay or continue to Shingle Beach on another 13 km of unpaved road. Camp there and next day paddle 4 nmi down the coast to Partington

Point. When the weather allows, perhaps at dusk, cross Sabine Channel, 1.1 nmi (see Trip No. 22).
- Some writers have suggested paddling across Malaspina Strait to Texada and then across to Jedediah. This 4.2-nmi crossing is often subject to strong winds and is **not** recommended. It is much safer to take the Egmont/Saltery Bay and Texada ferries and then proceed as outlined above.

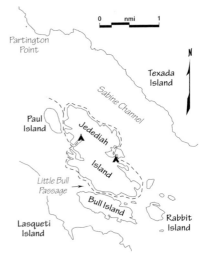

- The False Bay area of Lasqueti is subject to strong southwest Qualicum winds, which is why most yachts prefer to anchor on the other side of the island in Scottie Bay or Squitty Bay.

The route

Although Jedediah may live up to its marketing for power and sail boats, it is a bit overrated for sea kayakers. A lot of the bays where camping is good also dry to mud and become impassable at low tide. Take all the water you will need, as there is none easily found on the island.

Most people head for Home Bay, in the centre of the island. This too dries at low tide. Beside it there are two camping areas. One is for large groups which book it and the other is for drop-ins. If you want something more private, try Boom Bay, another that dries to mud at low tide. This can be a problem if low tide is in the morning when you want to leave to paddle back across Sabine Channel before the wind comes up. Camping at the head of Boom Bay means a stream of yachties strolling past on their way to Home Bay from their anchorage in Deep Bay. Codfish Bay is another popular anchorage.

~

Three of us arrived at high tide and camped at Boom Bay before we realized about the mud. We managed to skinny dip in between visitors, most of whom were on a trail up above us. At night we retreated to our tents to escape the mosquitoes, and watched the little brown bats fly around as dusk descended.

Mount Baker from Home Bay.

Texada and Lasqueti Islands – 133

Swimming in Long Bay.

At breakfast next day, raccoon families entertained us, even staying after the owner of the oyster lease appeared. A few yachts dropped anchor at the mouth of the bay, as inside was too shallow for them, and so we were spared having to listen to their noise.

We stayed several days, hiking all over the island enjoying the meadow flowers, the sheep and views of Mount Baker from Home Bay. In the evenings, after circumnavigating the island, we stuffed ourselves with Caroline's superb freshly made cinnamon buns.

The morning we left, we got up at 5 am and were away by 7. Even so, we had quite a bit of mud to contend with. Halfway across Sabine Channel the northwest wind came up and we had a hard pull back to our vehicles.

~

A good possibility for kayak camping is one of the coves on the outside of Long Bay. They're quite a hike from most of the other boaters, which cuts down on the visitors. Long Bay has the same mud problem as Boom Bay, so stay on the outside. There is lots of tent space on extensive grassy areas.

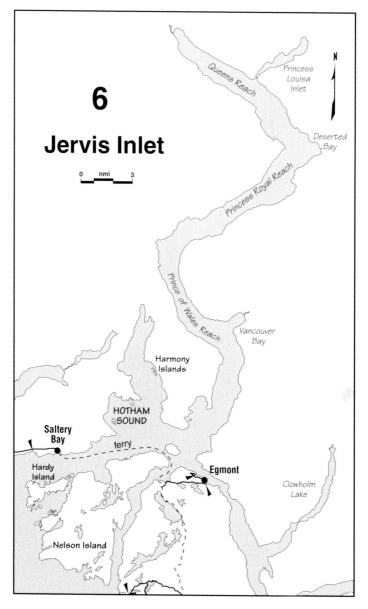

6
Jervis Inlet

Queens Reach

Princess
Louisa
Inlet

Deserted
Bay

Princess Royal Reach

Prince of Wales Reach

Vancouver
Bay

Harmony
Islands

HOTHAM
SOUND

Saltery
Bay

ferry

Hardy
Island

Egmont

Clowholm
Lake

Nelson Island

N

0   nmi   3

Nelson and Hardy Islands and the waters of Hotham Sound are good paddling but Jervis itself is much more hazardous. It is a narrow inlet whose inflow/outflow winds channel around the zigzags of its long, very steep coast. In summer, there's a small amount of recreational boat traffic to and from the famed Princess Louisa Inlet, which is guarded by a tidal rapid. In winter only work boats commute to logging camps and the First Nations camp.

Launches

Egmont
By the store or from the government floats. Check with the store about parking. Parking may be an issue because of hikers on the Skookumchuk Trail.

By the Back Eddy Pub. $3 in and out. Check with the pub about parking.

Saltery Bay
(near the ferry terminal) – Drive off the ferry and turn sharp right onto an unpaved road that leads around the bay. At the fork where there's a sign for the Sunshine Coast Trail, bear right along a very rough road down to a rocky beach. Turn before unloading and park back up the hill in the lot above the small dock beside the ferry dock. It's about 0.6 km and the locals do it with 2WD vehicles, but gingerly.

Saltery Bay Provincial Park
The boat launch is 1.5 km from the ferry. The sign for this comes after the one for the campsite of the same name.

Irvine's Landing
From Highway 101, turn off at the sign to Irvine's Landing and follow subsequent signs till you reach the pub. Pay the launch fee at the pub and ask them about parking.

Campsites

Saltery Bay Provincial Park Drive 1 km north of the Saltery Bay ferry terminal. The park is on the left. It has 42 vehicle sites, a 1-km trail through 90-year-old second-growth trees and a dive site with a 3-metre bronze mermaid statue underwater. At high tide, the diver's wheelchair ramp leads to a very pretty little cove that is worth a visit.

Harmony Islands Marine Provincial Park in Hotham Sound Only the southernmost island is park. The others are private and visitors are requested not to trespass on them.

Hardy Island Marine Provincial Park At the southwest end of Hardy Island is a possible campsite if you don't mind sleeping on a slope.

Nelson Island The meadow above the beach just east of Cape Cockburn has become a popular campsite.

Camping can be difficult. Photo: Cordula Thielke.

Princess Louisa Inlet
Macdonald Island Six bare-ground tent sites, each with a picnic table and one shared pit toilet.

Chatterbox Falls Four bare-ground tent sites, each with a picnic table. One communal fire pit for the tent sites. Water is available from the taps on the main dock and from a tap behind the Macdonald Memorial Shelter.

Jervis Inlet There are a number of places at creek mouths where camping may be possible. It's a matter of looking, especially in the McMurray Bay/Brittain River area.

Vancouver Bay, Deserted Bay and Skwakwa River At the head of the inlet, native watchmen are on duty all year. Check in with them before choosing a spot.

Elsewhere, scramble ashore where you can. Good luck! Consider taking a hammock tent.

25 Nelson Island

Difficulty Intermediate conditions – moderate risk
Distance Nelson Island circumnavigation from Irvine's Landing 35 nmi
Duration 2–3 days
Charts No. 3312 Desolation Sound and Jervis Inlet page 2 1:40,000
No. 3512 Strait of Georgia, Central Portion 1:80,000
No. 3311 Sunshine Coast No. 4 Pender Harbour to Grief Point 1:40,000
(only partial coverage)
Tides on Point Atkinson
Currents Hidden Basin, though not listed in the current tables, has a good
9-knot current. Enter and leave at slack.

Nelson Island is a destination easily reached from Pender Harbour. It has a lovely gravel beach on the south side, a tidal basin, and a sheltered waterway between it and neighbouring Hardy Island. There are many interesting stories about its early European settlers, whose old cabins are rapidly being replaced by large, modern retirement homes. Launch from Irvine's Landing, Egmont or Saltery Bay, depending on where you're coming from and how long you plan to be out.

Paddling considerations
• The south coast of Nelson Island is open to the prevailing southerly winds. If they're strong, reconsider the trip.

The route
Head out of Pender Harbour following the shore west around Henry Point, then past Lee Bay and Daniel Point, where there is a tiny Regional District park. Leaving Daniel Point, assess the wind situation in Agamemnon Channel. If the outflow from Jervis Inlet is blowing, you may want to reconsider and follow the coast around to the

portage into Sakinaw Lake instead. If conditions are favourable, cross to Fearney Point on Nelson Island. A neat alternative is to visit the Hodgson Islands en route. In spring, they are ornamented with yellow monkey flower, pink sea blush and blue-eyed Mary. They also have their own seal population.

Paddling west along the south side of Nelson, the pink rocks in the four coves before Mermaid Point are very attractive. When I first paddled into Quarry Bay it only had a couple of uninhabited old houses and an orchard. What a change! Now it's wall-to-wall pink monster palaces.

The quarry dates back to 1895. Stone from it was used to build the 240-metre Port Orchard dry dock in Seattle, the largest in the U.S. at that time. It also supplied stone for the B.C. legislature buildings in Victoria, the sea wall there, and many other commercial buildings in the city and in Vancouver.

In another 2 nmi there's a wide bay with a gravel beach. At the far end, a deserted cottage was once the beloved home of Sechelt pioneer Harry Roberts, which he built after his wife

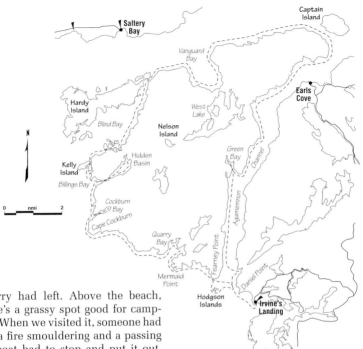

Cherry had left. Above the beach, there's a grassy spot good for camping. When we visited it, someone had left a fire smouldering and a passing fishboat had to stop and put it out. Don't light fires above the high tide line. This may be as far as you wish to go for a day trip.

Continuing on around Cape Cockburn, you'll get shelter from southerly winds but will be exposed to those from the northwest. In Cockburn Bay, a narrow inlet just beyond the cape, look for a funky log cabin called Sunray with windowpanes that match its cheerful name. This was the home Harry Roberts built for his second wife, Cherry. During construction, Roberts fell off the roof and had to be evacuated to the Pender Harbour hospital in thick fog.

A couple of islets give some protection to the coast between here and

Hidden Basin. In Billings Bay, hug the shore and land before the entrance to Hidden Basin. There are no tide tables for the torrent which rushes through the narrow passage, so either portage along the trail to it or reconnoite. At low tide the water is pretty shallow and rock-ridden. Slack water lasts for about 10 minutes and it is not much longer before the current becomes white water.

Inside the basin are many homes and cottages. The Wray family, who rowed up from Vancouver in the early 1890s but moved to Quarry Bay in 1895, initially settled it. Loggers followed, and during Prohibition both

Approaching the entrance to Hidden Basin.

Hidden Basin and Cockburn Bay were havens for rum-runners.

Between Hidden Basin and Blind Bay, Kelly Island, then called Granite Island, was another quarry that sent stone to the cities. Blind Bay, between Nelson and Hardy Islands, has been well populated for a long time. In the mid 20th century, loggers and fishers found cheap living here. Here, Alan Farrell hand-built several of his lug-rigged boats which he later sailed to the South Pacific. Today, most of the houses are summer homes.

The head of Blind Bay is a narrow waterway to Jervis Inlet. Check the weather, which is often sheltered on this side unless there's an outflow wind. Follow the coast of Nelson Island eastward back to Agamemnon Channel. Vanguard Bay is a deep bay separated from West Lake by only a narrow strip of land. West Lake is serious cottage country, with owners from Vancouver, the Island and as far away as California. It hasn't been wilderness for a long time.

Between Vanguard Bay and Captain Island at the head of Agamemnon Channel there are few landing places and those mostly rocky. You'll get great views up Hotham Sound to Freil Falls and the snow-capped mountains behind. The Earl's Cove/Saltery Bay ferry runs between Captain's Island and Nelson Island, so watch for its wake.

Toward the end of Agamemnon Channel you'll pass Green Bay, where author Howard White grew up.

26 Hardy Island

Difficulty Intermediate conditions – moderate risk
Distance Hardy Island circumnavigation from Saltery Bay 12 nmi
Duration 3–4 hours
Charts No. 3312 Desolation Sound and Jervis Inlet page 2 1:40,000
No. 3512 Strait of Georgia, Central Portion 1:80,000
No. 3311 Sunshine Coast No. 4 Pender Harbour to Grief Point
1:40,000 (only partial coverage).
Tides on Point Atkinson
Currents none

Hardy Island, named after the friend in whose arms Lord Nelson died, is a small island adjacent to Nelson Island. Hardy Island Marine Provincial Park (formerly Musket Island Marine Provincial Park), in the southwestern corner, is about the only place to land on these picturesque but rocky shores.

Paddling considerations
• Wind direction and strength

The route
From the Saltery Bay Provincial Park boat launch the shoreline of distant Hardy and Nelson Islands looks unbroken. Finding the gap between them requires a compass heading of 120°. En route there are views across the base of Hotham Sound and Jervis Inlet where the Saltery Bay ferry plies.

Crossing to Hardy Island.

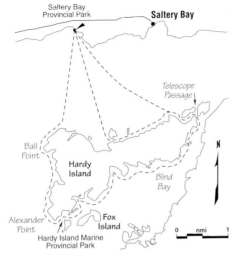

However, if you take this direct route, you may miss one of the treasures of the trip. Instead, head across on 200 °. You still get the views and this course brings you to some very pretty little islands off the coast of Hardy Island which are worth paddling in and out of. Then head east to Telescope Passage between Hardy Island and Nelson Island. At first the islands make the Passage seem like a another bay and then a very narrow inlet. Persevere, as it turns a corner and becomes the head of Blind Bay.

Entrance to Telescope Passage.

Dirty weather moving in.

If the wind is from the northwest, it may blow right in here. Most of the island has a single owner, but there are also a number of cottages on the Blind Bay side. At the Scotch Fir end, the Hardy Island Marine Provincial Park (formerly Musket Island Marine Provincial Park) sign is situated in front of a small sheltered bay that, at low tide, has the easiest landing for kayaks. Watch that the oysters don't cut your feet. Ashore, the grassy slope is a good lunch spot but a bit precipitous for comfortable camping.

Once you've rounded Alexander Point, hug the shore to avoid the flood tide current. Watch for eagles sitting on snags surveying the ocean waiting for their next meal. Also watch for some large blocks of concrete, which are all that remain of what once was a large saltwater swimming pool. When the drain out of the pool was plugged, the water inside would heat up very pleasantly. Unfortunately, little remains of it.

At Ball Point, the take-out comes into view and most groups seem to want to hightail it home. If you've already explored the islets on the north side, you won't miss much by doing this. In fog, use a compass course of 30 °. Often the wind comes up in the afternoon making this a choppy crossing with a slight surf landing onto either the concrete ramp or the cobble beach beside it.

The cliffs of Hotham Sound.

144 – Sea Kayak Desolation Sound and the Sunshine Coast

27 Hotham Sound

Difficulty Intermediate conditions – moderate risk
Distances From Egmont 27 nmi round trip
From Saltery Bay 28 nmi round trip
Duration 2 days
Charts No. 3312 Desolation Sound and Jervis Inlet page 3 1:40,000
No. 3512 Strait of Georgia, Central Portion 1:80,000
Tides on Point Atkinson
Currents none

With calmer winds than dangerous Jervis Inlet, Hotham Sound is often overlooked in the rush to get to popular spots like Desolation Sound. It is much less travelled and can be very beautiful.

Paddling considerations

- Inflow/outflow winds could be against you both ways and can be very strong. If they're raging, don't go.
- Steep cliffs edge much of the shoreline.
- Few landing places, so keep lunch and pee equipment within reach.
- No VHF reception.
- Crossings
  From Egmont
  Sechelt Inlet 0.5 nmi
  Egmont Point to Captain Island 1.0 nmi
  Captain Island to Foley Head 1.0 nmi
  Elephant Point to Mount Foley side 1.6 nmi
  Elephant Point to the Harmony Islands 1.7 nmi
  From Saltery Bay
  Granville Bay to Elephant Point 1.4 nmi
- Returning to Saltery Bay in the evening on a sunny day means paddling into the sun's strong glare

and reflection off the water. Bring sunglasses.

The route from Egmont

Hotham Sound can be accessed from the Egmont side, but as that involves braving the fierce inflow/outflow winds at the mouth of Jervis Inlet, it is much safer to take the ferry to Saltery Bay and put in there.

If you insist on starting at Egmont, cross Agamemnon Channel, watching for ferries as you go, and either paddle around the back of Captain Island and across to the inside of Foley Head or proceed along the north side of Nelson Island and cross to Culloden Point. Either way involves about 2 nmi of crossings.

The route from Saltery Bay

Saltery Bay is the closest launch. Watch for backwash from the ferry. Between Saltery Bay and Elephant Point there are three pictographs on the rocks. The first occurs within half a nautical mile of the put-in, and though small, it is readily visible. The second pictograph, a little farther along, is hard to find and often missed. The third is in Fairview Bay just beyond the beach where the Sunshine Coast Trail comes down. This beach

Pictographs

Pictographs are rock paintings done in red ochre long before the memories of today's First Nations people. They are usually the height of a man and are found above the high tide line. Some think they were made by a people who moved on to other places. Others think they mark fishing boundaries. No one knows for sure. The Heritage Act protects them.

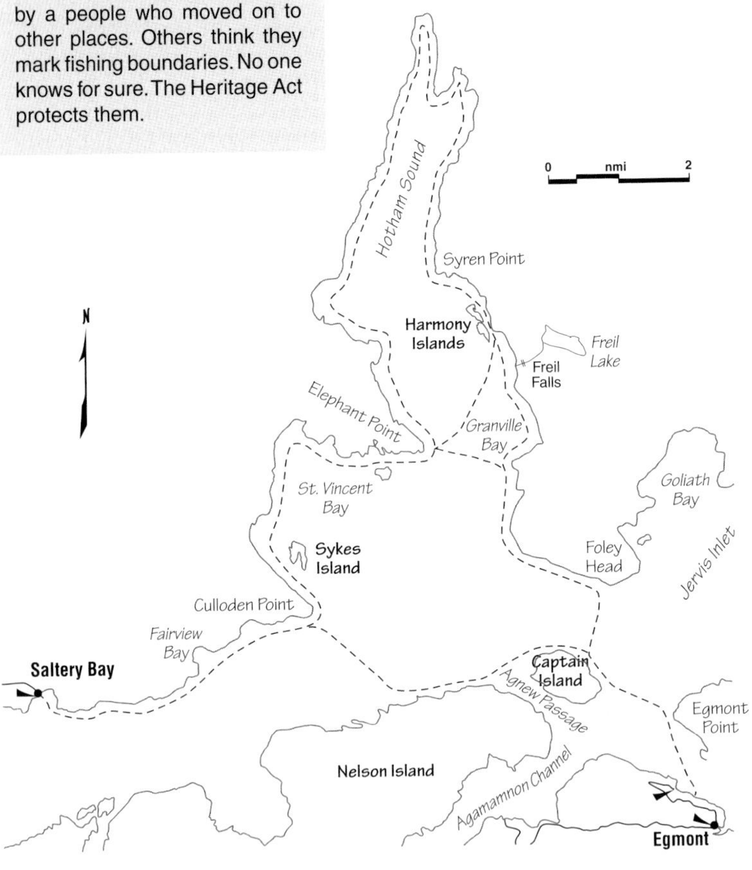

Hotham Sound

Syren Point

Harmony Islands

Freil Falls

Freil Lake

Elephant Point

Granville Bay

Goliath Bay

St. Vincent Bay

Sykes Island

Foley Head

Jervis Inlet

Culloden Point

Fairview Bay

Saltery Bay

Captain Island

Agnew Passage

Egmont Point

Nelson Island

Agamamnon Channel

Egmont

0   nmi   2

N

Friel Falls from a distance.

Fairview Bay pictograph.

St. Vincent's Bay

On February 14, 1797, Sir John Jervis (1735–1823) with a fleet of 15 ships met a Spanish fleet of 25 ships off Cape St. Vincent, Portugal. He overcame them, capturing four. Consequently, King George III created him Earl St. Vincent and granted him a pension of £3,000 a year. During this battle, Captain Thomas Troubridge aboard HMS *Culloden* held a collision course with a larger Spanish vessel, firing two double-shotted broadsides with such terrible precision that the Spaniard became too confused to fire back.

When Captain G.H. Richards surveyed Howe Sound in HMS *Plumper* in 1859–60 he commemorated the battle of Cape St. Vincent by naming many islands and points after the participants. *Agamemnon, Captain, Culloden, Diadem, Elephant, Goliath,* and *Vanguard* were all ships. Although all but Sykes eventually became admirals, at the time of the battle, Foley, Hardy and Troubridge were captains, Nelson was a commodore and Jervis an admiral. Sykes was and remained an able seaman and was with Nelson during much of the latter's career.

is a good lunch spot. Daytrippers may want to turn around here.

St. Vincent's Bay opens up beyond Culloden Point. If the place names remind you of English naval history, they should. When the Royal Navy survey vessel HMS *Plumper* charted the area in 1860, Captain George Henry Richards decided to commemorate the ships and commanders of the Battle of Cape St. Vincent.

Private cottages edge the shore in St. Vincent's Bay and there is a floating oyster farm in the middle of it. Dust rising above the trees behind the cottages means that a 4WD truck has ventured down the logging road from Saltery Bay.

Spectacular Freil Falls draws the eye to the other side of the Sound. The closer you paddle to it, the less you see of it, and its entry into the ocean is almost invisible. Take pictures from farther back. The water overflows from a lake above, but apart from the difficulty of finding a place to land, it would be a very tough slog to scramble up the steep slope to see it. On sunny days the water warms as it falls, which is nice for swimming where it flows out.

The Harmony Islands are a marine park but only the southernmost island is available for camping. The rest is private property. There is a small camping space on the mainland behind the islands. One couple who spent the night there got little sleep, as a bear prowled around their tent all night. Hang all food!

On the way to the head of Hotham Sound, try bouncing your voice off the high sheer, cliffs. There are few places to get ashore till you reach the end, where private cottages take up almost all of any flat land.

Returning to Saltery Bay on the west side, you pass more steep cliffs before reaching St. Vincent's Bay.

28 Jervis Inlet

Difficulty Advanced conditions – considerable risk
Distance 104 nmi round trip
Duration 8–10 days round trip
Chart No. 3312 Desolation Sound and Jervis Inlet pages 3, 6, and 7 1:40,000
includes Malibu Rapids inset 1:12,000 and Sechelt Rapids inset 1:20,000
No. 3514 Jervis Inlet 1:50,000 includes Malibu Rapids inset 1:12,000
and Sechelt Rapids inset 1:10,000
Tides on Point Atkinson
Currents Tidal rapids in and out of Princess Louisa Inlet

At 732 metres, Jervis is the deepest inlet on the coast. It is long and narrow with views of glaciers and a beautiful calm side inlet, Princess Louisa, 29.6 nmi in. Experienced paddlers who don't mind fierce winds and long distances between places to scramble ashore will enjoy paddling along the steep cliffs.

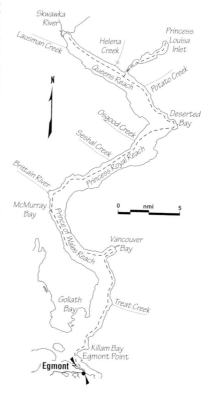

Paddling considerations

- Inflow/outflow winds could be against you both ways and can be very strong. If they're raging, don't go. The katabatic wind builds very quickly on summer afternoons. If you are anywhere north of Seshal Creek when the wind comes up, it will be very hard to land.
- Weather changes in minutes.
- Steep cliffs edge much of the shoreline.
- Few landing places, so keep lunch and pee equipment within reach.
- There is no VHF reception from beyond the inlet.
- Consider hitching a ride for the return trip. Some boats—but not the *Malibu Princess*—will take kayaks.
- Local people say there is a "very significant" outgoing current in the

Jervis Inlet from Egmont ferry dock.

inlet, perhaps 2 knots. It seems not to be related to the tide.

- Sechelt Band watchmen are on duty all year on band property at Vancouver Bay, Deserted Bay and Skwakwa River at the head of the inlet.

The route

Launch at Egmont very early in the morning to make as much progress as you can before the inflow wind whips up the water into waves of a metre and more. Only very experienced paddlers venture very far up this inlet, whose steep sides are almost impossible to either land or camp on. Consider taking a hammock tent. Fierce winds spring up at a moment's notice and there is little other boat traffic. Some creek mouths have relatively easy landings. Otherwise, when you scramble ashore, pull your boat up behind you and tie it securely to a tree. Launching may be difficult. Carry an orange distress flag with a black square and circle on it.

The Sechelt First Nation say that Miller Islet, just beyond Egmont Point, was once an orca whose pod left without it. Seals bask on its rocky shore. Farther on, Killam Bay has a gravel pit. Across the inlet, Goliath Bay and Dark Cove lose the sun early in the evening. Captain Vancouver made a brief stop here on his way out of the Inlet. He arrived at 9 pm and left at 4 am, so the lack of sunlight wouldn't have bothered him. Today there is an oyster farm on Sidney Is-

Clarence Joe

Sechelt leader Clarence Joe was born in Deserted Bay in 1908. The population was 82 at the time. Joe grew up to be a high rigger with his own logging company which he operated in the winter. In summer he fished. His wife and several of their sons contracted TB and were sent to live in the Coqualeetza Indian Hospital at Chilliwack.

Meanwhile Joe went into politics and dedicated himself to band work. He was one of the people instrumental in the band becoming the first one in Canada to have self-government. He also established a native environmental studies school in Deserted Bay attended by both native and European children. It opened in 1979 and ran for four years. He also helped found the National Indian Brotherhood and was active in the B.C. Native Brotherhood. Through the Raven Society of B.C. he raised money and obtained grants for native education. The United Nations once invited him to address them. Audrey Santiago, his granddaughter, says, "He was a great mentor to us and his legacy lives on in the videos he left in our language."

Waterfall at Helena Creek north of the entrance to Princess Louisa Inlet. Photo: Cordula Thielke.

land and some cottages in Dark Cove, but there's enough room in between them that you could probably find a camp spot there.

If you paddle on the eastern shore of the inlet and decide to camp at Treat Creek, make sure you pack your garbage out. The people who work at the gravel pit have had to clean up after kayakers on occasion. This en-courages bears, including grizzlies, to hang around hoping for a free meal.

Vancouver Bay was named in 1860 by Captain Richards on the survey ship HMS *Plumper* to commemorate Captain Vancouver's overnight camp on his way up the inlet in June 1792. The next day, Vancouver discovered that the head of the inlet did not lead to the Northwest Passage as he had hoped. All the Sechelt people who lived in Skwah'-kwee-ehm, the village in Vancouver Bay, died in the 1860 smallpox epidemic. Now the band operates Vancouver Bay Lodge, a drug treatment centre. Originally, the forest company Fletcher Challenge built the place as a retreat for their dignitaries. If you want to camp here, check with the native watch-

Brittain River, Jervis Inlet. Photo: Cordula Thielke.

The Solberg Sisters

Bergliot and Minnie Solberg were two sisters who lived much of their lives at Bear Bay, which is immediately north of Deserted Bay on Jervis Inlet. They lived off the land by fishing, hunting and trapping.

"They were known as the cougar ladies," said Audrey Santiago, who grew up in Deserted Bay. "Whenever they needed anything, they'd call for my grandfather, Clarence Joe. They always had lists for us. The Sechelt Legion uses the hide of one of the cougars they shot for its parades."

John Dafoe first met them when they offered him "an extremely warm bunkhouse to stay in on a bitterly cold December 1971 night." He left early next morning without seeing much of them. Over the years he ran into them on several occasions.

Bergie, who was living on Sechelt Inlet by this time, once asked Dafoe to take a few things up to Minnie. "Every time I saw her she added to the load with an array of sweets and fatty foods that would be considered most unhealthy fare. Finally I got away, and a good thing too or my little boat would not have managed the load. We went up to a camp just past Deserted Bay and were met by Minnie on a quad that she drove to the beach. This mountain of a woman was quite a sight driving down to the landing on that machine. We explained our mission and were well received by her, as she wanted us to unload an oil barrel from a stand by her cabin. It appeared that the cabin was somewhat supported by the stand and barrel and we thought better of removing it. Minnie accepted our explanation."

man. When leaving the bay, watch for mountain goats on the cliffs of Marlborough Heights.

McMurray Bay and Brittain River on the west side are possible landing spots. Brittain River was once the site of a native village of boat builders. Expect to find the remains of logging operations there.

On entering Princess Royal Reach, watch for strong changeable winds. Caution is advised. On the eastern shore, Soda Pop Falls, a slim thread of water falling down the cliff with such force that it creates a sea of frothy bubbles where it enters the inlet, is worth stopping to admire. Sechelt elders told children not to swim there because an octopus lives in the depths. There is some logging activity at Glacial Creek. Opposite and a little farther north, Osgoode Creek has camping possibilities but an application for a foreshore lease could change that. The neighbouring fish farm is about 20 years old.

Deserted Bay got its name when two men landed there in the 19th century to find all 10,000 people dead of smallpox except one baby girl. A few years later when Indian Reserves were created, this was a fairly large one. Pilings in Bear Bay on the north side of Deserted Bay are all that remain of several Japanese salteries.

The entrance to Princess Louisa Inlet is on the east side. If the tide is against you, paddle a mile farther north to view the beautiful Helena Creek waterfall while you wait.

Looking into Vancouver Bay. Photo: Cordula Thielke.

At the head of the inlet, there's the remains of another Indian village and some logging operations. On a rising tide, you can paddle up the swampy estuary of the Skwakwa River for some distance, depending on the water level and the number of sweeper logs in the river. This is a grizzly bear recovery area in which no hunting is allowed. In the fall when the salmon are running, the grizzlies definitely will be there and perhaps at other times as well, though in summer they are usually up in the high alpine stuffing themselves with berries. Ask the camp watchman if he has seen any. The views of mountains and glaciers in this area are spectacular. There is also some commercial activity at nearby Lausmann Creek.

Cordula Thielke took a week to paddle up to the mouth of Princess Louisa Inlet and back. She did not enter it, as the tide was against her, but she did refill her water bottles at the Helena Creek waterfall on the same side.

"I had four storms while I was there," she said. *"I almost capsized in Princess Royal Reach. The sunshine vanished, followed by rain and wind that whipped up the whitecaps just south of Stakawus Creek." Elsewhere on the coast, people were enjoying the calm July weather.*

"Be creative about finding camp-sites and be prepared to pull your kayak up behind you. I loved seeing the glaciers and would have stayed longer if I had the time." Thielke paddled up the west side and down the east side. "Sometimes I crossed back and forth."

29 Princess Louisa Inlet

Difficulty Intermediate conditions – moderate risk
Distance 4.2 nmi each way
Duration 1.5 hours
Charts No. 3312 Desolation Sound and Jervis Inlet page 7
1:40,000 includes Malibu Rapids inset 1:12,000
No. 3514 Jervis Inlet 1:50,000 includes Malibu Rapids inset 1:12,000
Tides on Point Atkinson
Currents On spring tides, rapids in the entrance run at 9 knots.
High water slack is 0–15 minutes after high tide at Point Atkinson and
low water slack is 20–50 minutes after low tide at Point Atkinson.

A mecca for boaters since Wylie Blanchet ventured in with her family during the 1930s, the inlet provides a welcome respite from the frequently fierce winds of Jervis Inlet. Chatterbox Falls at the far end is a must to visit.

Paddling considerations

- Sheer cliffs edge much of the shoreline.
- Few landing places, so keep lunch and pee equipment within reach.

- No VHF reception.
- It's relatively sheltered compared to Jervis Inlet.

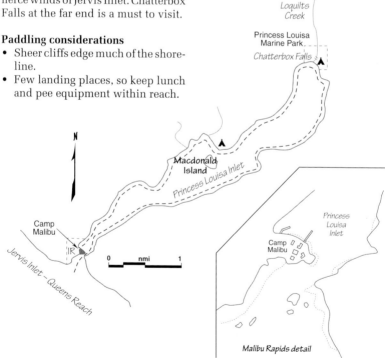

Malibu Rapids detail

Chatterbox Falls.

Camp Malibu.

The route

Either paddle up Jervis Inlet (see Trip No. 28) or take a water taxi from Egmont and have it come back to collect you. If taking it only one way, paddle up so that you know what you're getting into, rather than taking the taxi up and paddling back in the teeth of a headwind and unable, because of the topography, to call for help.

After carefully timing your entry, paddle to the left and land at Camp Malibu, which is operated by Young Life, a Christian camp that exposes adolescents from 50 countries to godly principles. If they are in operation, they sell ice cream but don't want unauthorized visitors wandering at will, so ask permission before landing. In the early days, Steve

Johnson, an unwashed hermit, lived in the inlet near Camp Malibu. He watched Thomas F. Hamilton struggle from 1947 to 1950 to make the luxury resort he had built to attract U.S. film stars become a profitable enterprise. Disappointed, Hamilton sold it to the present owners, who found Johnson a little too colourful for their liking.

Proceed down the inlet to behind Macdonald Island, which has the only sunny campsite. The other, at Chatterbox Falls, is shady. Adjacent to the public site is a private campsite belonging to the Young Life establishment.

Thin silver streams of water drop down the sheer cliffs deep into the inlet and stay there. They displace warm water, which floats to the

Princess Louisa Inlet.

top, producing 23 °C water that is lovely for swimming. "Nine degrees warmer than Porpoise Bay on the same day," says John Dafoe, who was involved in the research. At the head of the inlet, land and visit Chatterbox Falls. If you climb up the rock beside the falls, be aware that the moss is not only slippery but easily breaks away and can take you with it. Several people have slipped over the falls to their deaths. In wet weather, enjoy the visitor's shelter. At the back of the park, trails zigzag up the mountain. BC Parks recommends that you do **not** take these. Some were cut by Young Life and lead high up and back to their campsite by Macdonald Island. While this is useful knowledge in an emergency, it is best to follow Parks' advice unless you are an experienced alpine climber. This is grizzly bear territory.

Time your exit from Princess Louisa for an outgoing tide. Those with whitewater experience may elect to shoot the rapids. Before doing so, examine the chart carefully so you know where rocks close to the surface are located.

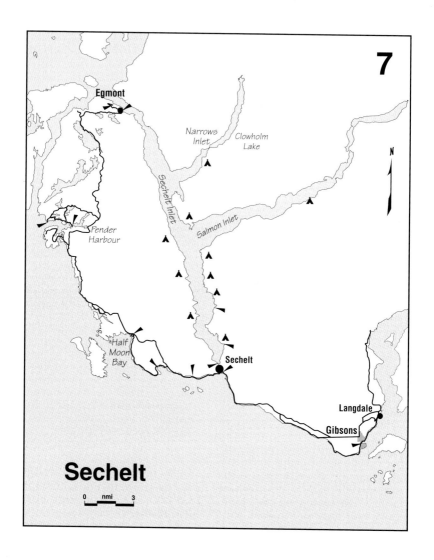

7

Egmont

Narrows
Inlet

Clowholm
Lake

N

Sechelt Inlet

Salmon Inlet

Pender
Harbour

Half
Moon
Bay

Sechelt

Langdale

Gibsons

Sechelt

0 ___ nmi ___ 3

The rocky coast between Gower Point and Pender Harbour is wall-to-wall waterfront homes just as Charlotte Roberts dreamed in 1900. When her family homesteaded Roberts Creek they commuted to Vancouver for groceries in an open rowboat. Today, they'd be run down by B.C. Ferries and a host of other craft from barges to high-speed pleasure craft. Paddling here is not unlike paddling along the waterfront in Vancouver, minus the high rises and industrial sites. A lot of the provincial and municipal parks are day-use only. They're designed by people who go home for the night, with no allowance for others who would rather camp out under the stars listening to the seals courting. Unless you have a friend with waterfront property, you likely won't be able to camp here, as summer cottages and even year-round residences have displaced campers. If you don't have access to a cottage, day trips from a campground or B&B are the way to go and there are lots to choose from though they are often not on the water.

There is no protection from strong winds between Gower Point and Sechelt, and more than 20 boats have been wrecked here. On the plus side, the three Sechelt Inlets immediately behind the town of Sechelt are more sheltered, especially from westerly winds.

In 1900, Charlotte Roberts was standing on the beach with her grandson Harry, enjoying the fragrance of wet earth and woods. Solid fir trees mixed with a few cedar surrounded them except for a patch of green grass and alders by the house. As watery

Early settlers

The first European settlers began arriving in the Sechelt area around 1859. About the same time, the colonial government began making a series of proclamations which gradually shaped its policy on pre-emption of Crown lands by individuals. In 1870 these numerous piecemeal enactments were consolidated into a single Ordinance allowing male British subjects over age 18, but not "Aborigines," to stake up to 160 acres for farming purposes. As it was easier to do this than qualify for a hand logger's licence, many loggers staked such parcels in the Gibsons area, only to abandon their claims once they had removed the timber.

The present town of Gibsons is located on the two lots pre-empted by George Gibson (1823–1913).

Many of the second wave of settlers were red Finns fleeing the disintegrating utopia they set up at Sointula in 1900. Their socialist ideas influenced a young Methodist minister, J.S. Woodsworth, who later went on to found the CCF party. His children, including Grace McInnes, MP, returned to live in the area.

sunshine turned a tiny bit of sea pearl-grey, she turned to him and said: "I want little cottages with gardens and little children to be playing in the sunshine all along right from here as far as Pratt's Point (now Gower Point). I want this part of the shore to be known as the Sunshine Belt. There are far more hours of sunshine than at any other part of this coast." He never forgot and painted "Sunshine Belt" on

Trail Island from Wakefield Creek.

a freight shed he built later on this site. Charlotte's wish has come true. Today cottages and houses line the shore and the whole coast from Gower Point to Lund is known as the Sunshine Coast. Rain clouds sweeping in from the Pacific Ocean drop their moisture on the west side of the Vancouver Island mountains, so they have little left by the time they cross the Strait.

Launches

Gibsons Harbour

From the Langdale ferry terminal, follow the signs for Gibsons, pass Molly's Reach and continue on the road by the water past the marina till you come to a T-junction. Turn left onto Headlands Road. You can drive down onto the beach to launch but park your car back on the road.

Davis Bay

Drive north on Highway 101, following the signs for Sechelt. After the Wilson Creek shopping centre, the road curves close to the seashore at Davis Bay. There's lots of day parking but no shelter if the winds have built up a surf.

Selma Park

Drive to Davis Bay (above) but continue past the small shopping centre on the right. Look for a boat launch sign on the left part way up the next hill. The road is narrow and there is little parking.

Snickett Park

Drive right into Sechelt, following the signs for Pender Harbour. Take the road on the left to the Driftwood Inn, park, and check out the weather and the best places for launching and parking vehicles. This launch is very exposed and only useful on calm days.

Wakefield Creek

From Sechelt, drive north on Highway 101 for 3 km till you see the sign for the Wakefield Inn. Immediately before it, a short road goes down to the water.

Sargeant Bay

Turn left off Highway 101 onto Redroofs Road and drive 1.7 km to the park. There is no boat launch but kayaks can put in from the beach. Sheltered from northwest winds but not from southeasters.

Cooper's Green

Turn off Highway 101 onto Redroofs Road. Cooper's Green Regional Park is 8.7 km along here on the left-hand side. Redroofs Road, which winds along the coast parallel to Highway 101, can also be accessed from just south of Halfmoon Bay. From this direction, the park is 1.6 km along it. There is a large shingle beach beside the concrete launch ramp, so there is no need to obstruct trailered boat traffic while loading and unloading.

Halfmoon Bay government wharf

From Highway 101, follow the signs to the Halfmoon Bay store. The wharf is beside it. On the south side, kayakers can scramble down onto the sandy beach to launch.

Brooks Road

From Highway 101, turn off at the sign to Smuggler Cove and drive to where the trail to it starts. Proceed another 50 metres to a small cove with a rocky beach. If there isn't a southwester blowing in here, it's a good place to launch for Merry Island, Smuggler Cove or the Thormanbys.

Secret Cove

Drive to the launch at the bottom of Secret Cove Road and park up the steep hill. This ramp belongs to Buccaneer Marina, so ask their permission to use it. There is also a government dock, which requires a long carry down a steep ramp to a float. There is no access to the rocky beach.

Madeira Park

From Highway 101, turn off at the sign to Madeira Park, drive past the shopping centre and then turn right. The launching ramp is 100 metres ahead.

Irvine's Landing

From Highway 101, turn off at the sign to Irvine's Landing and follow subsequent signs till you reach the pub. Pay the launch fee at the pub and ask them about parking.

Egmont

From Highway 101, turn off at the sign for Egmont (just before the ferry). There are two launches, one beside the general store and government dock, the other beside the Back Eddy pub. The latter has more parking space.

Sechelt Inlet launches

See Trip No. 39.

Campsites

Smuggler Cove Five walk-in tent sites at the head of the cove. Pit toilet but no water.

Roberts Creek Provincial Park Campsite On Highway 101, 14 km west of Gibsons and 12 km south of Sechelt. 21 gravel sites. It has a separate day-use area with a cobble beach 1.5 km south off Highway 101 at the end of Flume Road.

Thormanby Islands Rough camping is allowed in Simson Park and in the tiny Buccaneer Bay Provincial Park at the south end of North Thormanby. Watch the height of the tide here.

Porpoise Bay Provincial Park Campsite Drive north on Highway 101. At the second set of traffic lights in Sechelt, turn right on Porpoise Bay Road, which becomes Sechelt Inlet Road, and follow the signs to the park. This is the only road-accessible campsite on Sechelt Inlet. For those accessible by water, see Trip No. 39.

Garden Bay Marine Provincial Park in Pender Harbour Above a rocky landing there's a small, flat clearing on the left where Fred Claydon's house once stood. Try camping here. The park makes an L-shaped angle back and up 500-metre Mount Daniel. Fires are prohibited.

30 Gibsons to Selma Park, Sechelt

Difficulty Intermediate conditions – moderate risk
Distance 12 nmi each way
Duration 6 hours
Chart No. 3311 Sunshine Coast No. 3 Howe Sound to Pender Harbour 1:40,000
Tides on Point Atkinson
Currents 2–4 knot tidal current around Mission Point, which is between Wilson Creek and Davis Bay

Paddling here is similar to city paddles. You get an unusual view of the communities of Gibsons, Roberts Creek and Sechelt, which all meld into one long community. From the water you'll see and be able to land on all the tiny hidden beaches the residents think no one knows about. Consider combining it with a B&B stop en route.

Paddling considerations

- The locals call this portion of the coast "The stretch" because there is no shelter from the wind between Gower Point and the Trail Islands. Beginners should not set out unless the winds are calm and forecast to remain so.
- If the wind gets up, you may have to do a surf landing. Sheltered landings are few and far between and the shore is exposed to all that the Georgia Strait has to offer. Possible landings in these conditions are Beach Esplanade Park at Roberts Creek, Wilson Creek, Chapman Creek (on a high tide) and Selma Park.

The route

Launch at the Gibsons boat launch at the foot of Headlands Road and follow the coast around to Sechelt. Beginners may want to put a vehicle halfway at Roberts Road Park in case the weather turns sour or someone wants to take out early.

On the way out of Gibsons, enter Shoal Channel between Gibsons and Keats Island. On an ebb tide, when the wind is blowing into Howe Sound, there could be some standing waves here. The water is too shallow for most sailboats to go through at low tide. If you want to camp, make the short crossing to Plumper Cove and camp there. There are no other places to camp unless you know someone with waterfront property.

Although the shore is lined with private dwellings, there are a number of small parks where you can land and picnic. These are:

Georgia Beach Park, a tiny municipal park where the locals like to swim in the daytime. Much to their chagrin, it has become a party place at night.

Pebbles Beach Park with steps up to the foot of Burns Road comes next.

Attlee's Beach Park with steps up to Cochrane Road and limited parking.

Secret Beach Park with steps up to Mahon Road.

Gower Point is a gradual point more appreciated from a distance than close up. You're around it if you can't see Keats Island behind you.

Next, **Chaster Provincial Park** encompasses the beach where a monument to Captain Vancouver's 1791 visit has been erected. Behind it is the Regional District Park of Chaster House. In 1906, just after fire had ravaged the area, the James S. Chaster family bought Ralph Gibson's building for a store and post office. (Ralph Gibson was the son of George Gibson [1828–1913], who on May 2, 1887, made the original pre-emption of the land on which the town of Gibsons now sits.)

Oak Street A municipal park. Between Oak Street Park and Beach Esplanade Park, you'll pass Camp Byng, a well-known Scout camp that has been going since 1922. It was named after Lord Byng of Vimy, who

Gumboot Café, Roberts Creek.

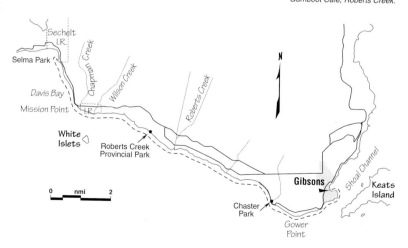

End of Roberts Creek esplanade.

opened it. He was Governor-General of Canada and Chief Scout at the time. Camp Byng's resident caretaker discourages visitors.

Beach Esplanade Park This is at the estuary of Roberts Creek. Somewhat confusingly, Roberts Creek Park is farther on. If you land at Beach Esplanade Park, which has picnic tables, outhouses and a beach trail, you can also access the community of Roberts Creek with its craft store, a general store, etc. Formal dining is available at the Creek House Restaurant or informal at the famous Gumboot Garden Café, which specializes in vegetarian dishes. The park is on the site of an orchard planted by Thomas and Charlotte Roberts.

Chaster Park.

Roberts Creek Provincial Park This is the picnic site on the water, complete with picnic benches, an outhouse and off-street parking.

Just past Roberts Creek picnic site at the mouth of Flume Creek is Douglas Camp on Beach Avenue. It is a Presbyterian church camp which is constantly in use. In summer, they discourage visitors when the camp is in session, starting the first weekend school is out in June and continuing through Labour Day. During the school year, a Waldorf school uses the buildings and the public is allowed to walk on the beach.

Wilson Creek used to be a gathering area for log booms. There is some protection from the wind. It was named after James Wilson, a blacksmith employed by Burns and Jackson Brothers logging camp in 1889.

In winter, Chapman Creek is often patrolled by sea lions in search of a meal courtesy of the fish hatchery. Just before Davis Bay, Mission Point has a 2–4 knot tidal current.

Davis Bay Waterfront This is one of the most used of the municipal parks. Low tide exposes a large sandy beach

Sea Lions

Larger sea lions that **roar** are the fast-disappearing Steller's, or northern, sea lion (*Eumetopias jubatus*). They are usually pale brown with a flat face. The males, which have a mane like a lion, grow 3 m in length and weigh up to 1,000 kg. The females are about a third that size. They breed on islands in northern B.C. and Alaska.

Smaller sea lions that bark are the commoner California sea lion (*Zalophus californianus*). While the males are dark brown to black, the females may be tan like the Steller's but with longer faces. They are about 2 m long and weigh just over 100 kg. The males have a prominent bump on their foreheads and grow to 2.4 m and nearly 400 kg. They breed on islands off the California and Mexico coasts. Male Californias migrate north in August and September, returning to their breeding grounds in March, April and May.

Steller's used to breed there too but haven't frequented the area much since the early 1980s. Their decline is even more dramatic in Alaska, where research has shown that decreasing fish stocks are a major factor. The Vancouver Aquarium is conducting a study of the diet, physiology and fishing behaviour of young animals. Although they will eat any kind of fish, and invertebrates including octopus and squid, the researchers have found that those living off the B.C. coast prefer mackerel and pollock. The deepest recorded dive for a Steller's is 424 m.

Selma Park take-out.

against a backdrop of the White Islets. If the wind is in the northwest, a surf landing will be necessary here. If you don't want to do this, continue on to Selma Park. Ashore, Davis Bay has plumbed washrooms, a selection of motels, restaurants and stores, including Pier 17, which features fresh produce, often organic and a well-patronized deli and magazine section.

If tempted to paddle out and circumnavigate the White Islets, be warned that they are a good 1.1 nmi from Wilson Creek even though they look closer. Don't land on them, as they are a bird sanctuary: glaucous-winged gulls and others breed there from April to August. In the spring and fall, immature male sea lions haul out there on their way to and from the breeding grounds off the California and Alaska coasts. When they are not there, harbour seals take over the ledges. Stay back at least 100 metres and use binoculars to observe.

Selma Park boat launch is protected by a rock wall. There is not much parking space here and it is popular with trailered boats, so park only the shuttle car here and leave the rest at Gibsons. Selma Park is named after the All Red Line's SS *Selma*, which ran a passenger service in the area before Union Steamships bought the property and cabins in 1917. Selma Park is on the southern edge of the community of Sechelt (population 7,775). It and Gibsons are the two main shopping centres of the area. Both offer a selection of stores and restaurants.

31 Selma Park, Sechelt to Half Moon Bay

Difficulty Intermediate conditions – moderate risk
Distance 9 nmi each way
Duration 3 hours
Chart No. 3311 Sunshine Coast No. 3 Howe Sound to Pender Harbour 1:40,000
Tides on Point Atkinson
Currents none

Urban and rural landscapes mix on this trip, starting with a water view of the Town of Sechelt, followed by the Trail Islands, Sargeant Bay Provincial Park and more waterfront homes.

Paddling considerations
• Wind direction and strength

The route
Launch at Selma Park, where you can drive to the water. Trail Bay, which is open to the prevailing southerly winds, has been the scene of many shipwrecks. Snickett Park along Sechelt's waterfront is a popular municipal park for walkers. The gravel beach is steep and not suitable for landing in southerly winds. In calm conditions, landing may be fine. Sechelt's main shopping mall is located a block away.

For a change of pace, consider a detour out to the Trail Islands. If you're short of time, you can put in at Wakefield Creek (see above) and then the crossing is only 0.6 nmi.

Weave in and out of the islands watching for seals, river otters, black turnstones and harlequin ducks. In August, keep away from the harlequin ducks to avoid stressing them during their eclipse period. They have shed their flight feathers and their

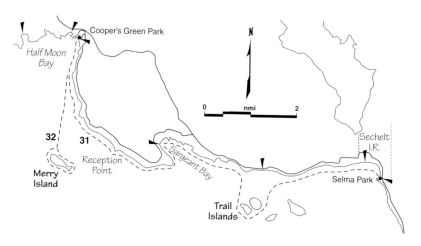

The Trail Islands

Long ago the Sechelt people lived, dug clams and fished off the Trail Islands. In 1884 the Canadian government refused to let them include the islands in their reserves. Chief Paull Policeman tried to pre-empt them but was told Indians couldn't do this. He tried to buy them but was denied for the same reason. In 1892 Arthur Prichard bought their 111 acres for $1 an acre. Policeman appealed the sale on the basis that he pastured his sheep there, but in 1916 the government turned him down again.

When tugboats towed booms of logs along the coast, skippers found the Trail Islands were a mixed blessing. No sooner would they tie up in a sheltered spot than the wind would change and they'd have to manoeuvre their booms to a different part of the islands.

Today the islands are privately owned by cottagers. At times, they are host to a large colony of sea lions. The west Trail Island has a cormorant nesting site.

Trail Islands from Sargeant Bay.

Cooper's Green Park take-out.

colourful breeding plumage so that the males look like the females. Their wing feathers take about six weeks to grow back.

Sargeant Bay is the next landmark. It's wide open to southerly winds, which may make landing on the cobble beach difficult, but it's a welcome refuge from northwesterlies. Look for the sandy areas. Although it is a provincial park, you can't camp here and there is no boat launch. A 300-metre trail leads along the beach past a wetland to a fish ladder. Another wind about a kilometre up fish-bearing Colvin Creek. The park extends back to Triangle Lake. The wetland is

an important stopover for waterfowl including trumpeter swans.

From Sargeant Bay it's about 1.5 nmi to Reception Point and about that distance again to Welcome Beach. This is also a cobble beach and hard to land on if a surf is running.

Cooper's Green Regional Park is just over a mile from Welcome Beach. Offshore islands shelter its pebble beach. It has a concrete boat launch and plumbed toilets. Although parking is limited, this is the easiest place to take out in this area.

Priestland Cove is the estuary for Halfmoon Creek, beside the government wharf.

32 Merry Island

Difficulty Intermediate conditions – moderate risk
Distance 2.5 nmi each way from Cooper's Green Park in Half Moon Bay
Duration 3 hours out and back
Chart No. 3311 Sunshine Coast No. 3 Howe Sound to Pender Harbour 1:40,000
Tides on Point Atkinson
Currents 3-knot currents swirl on either side of the island.

This offshore trip visits an intriguing island group with a historic lighthouse and a bird sanctuary.

Paddling considerations
- Wind warnings in the Strait of Georgia

The route
Launch at Cooper's Green Regional Park or beside the government dock at the Halfmoon Bay store, which is less accessible, or at Brooks Road. Assess the boat traffic. Often, tugs tow log booms across in front of Merry Island. See sketchmap on page 169.

It takes about an hour to paddle out to Merry, where the lighthouse is now automated. Franklin Islet, on the west side, is a bird sanctuary, so do not land there.

The first lighthouse keepers, Will and Mary Franklin, arrived in November 1902 and stayed 30 years. They pre-empted the land on the main island and raised sheep, ducks and chickens. In March 1915 they rescued a family whose boat was smashed on the island after its engine quit. During the daylight hours of May 1922 the Franklins recorded 90 passenger steamers, 127 tugs and three freighters as having passed

Merry Island light.

Will It Pass In Front or Behind?

To determine whether a ship will pass in front of you or behind you, look at the land behind it. If the ship is moving ahead of the land, it will pass in front of you. If it is losing ground and the land is moving ahead of it, it will pass behind you. If it appears to be stationary, you are on a collision course with it and should make an obvious and exaggerated change of course to avoid it. Freighters may take 11 nmi or more to stop, so don't expect them to turn on a dime. They won't. Commercial traffic has the right of way, including ferries.

The Merry Island lighthouse complex.

by the light. On March 22, 1927, radio operator Gerald Pike, who was smoking a pipe, leaned over a can of gasoline, which exploded. Snatching up the can, he ran outside but became a human torch. Franklin's mother-in-law threw water over him and pumped the hand foghorn to get Will's attention. While the women tended to Pike, Will put the fire out, saving the rest of the buildings. As the radio still worked, they were able to call a tug, but Pike died on reaching hospital in Vancouver. A later keeper,

George Potts, counted 680 boats passing the island one day as he was painting the roof. In his open, 3-metre skiff, he frequently braved heavy seas and rescued many people.

The main island has a couple of summer cottages on it. One of these was built in 1923 by Harry Roberts of Roberts Creek, who called it Bugaboo and lived there till he moved to Nelson Island in 1929. As the island has recently been sold, it could sprout more cottages soon.

33 Smuggler Cove and Secret Cove

Difficulty Beginner conditions – low risk
Distance 1.5 nmi each way from Brooks Road
Duration 2 hours
Chart No. 3311 Sunshine Coast No. 3 Howe Sound to Pender Harbour 1:40,000
Tides on Point Atkinson
Currents 3-knot tidal current between Grant Island and the mainland

Smuggler Cove (frequently called Smuggler's Cove) is a kayaker's heaven of little coves and islands with no crossings to frighten the timid.

Paddling considerations
- Plan to paddle with the tide in Welcome Passage.

The route
The closest launch is at the foot of Brooks Road, but the government wharf at Halfmoon Bay or Cooper's Green Regional Park are also possibilities. From the first two, follow the coast around till you come to Frenchman's Creek. This is a great place to explore when the wind is high though it's best when the tide is not too low. As you head out from it, there is a float beside an island on the left-hand side. Opposite this is a portage into Welcome Passage. This is easiest on a high tide if you want to check conditions before venturing out.

Once around Jeddah Point, mosey around the skerries admiring the seals and watching the cormorants, which often spread their wings to dry while perching on the rocks. When paddling north through the narrow passage into Welcome Passage, listen and watch for incoming speedboats, which have a tendency to tear through here without regard for others.

Hug the rocky shore for about 0.7 nmi. En route there are a few rocky coves where you could get ashore if you had to. People sitting on the rocks have likely hiked in from the trail to Smuggler Cove or come ashore from a sailboat in the cove.

At the end of Welcome Passage, between Grant Island and the mainland, the tide often runs at about 2–3 knots. If it is against you, you'll have a tough pull for a short distance. Once past the island, the current ceases and it's easy paddling into Smuggler Cove.

In summer, Smuggler is a popular anchorage stuffed with power and

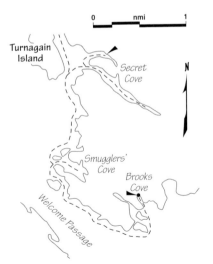

sail boats but it's still interesting to explore. Parts of it dry to mud at low tide, preventing access to one of the inner lagoons. Getting ashore is sometimes difficult but you are rewarded with great views if you scramble up on top of the ridge overlooking both the cove and Welcome Passage. At low tide, boulders ornamented with ochre starfish block some of the ways out.

The two cottages in the cove were built before the park was created in 1971. The owners retain a lifetime right to use them.

In several parts of the cove, the Sechelt people built weirs to catch fish as the tide receded. Short lines of rock across the entrances to shoreline indentations show where they were. When the weirs were in use, Sechelt canoes would paddle in from the outer entrance to the main cove, driving herring and salmon before them past the obstructions. Then, when the tide

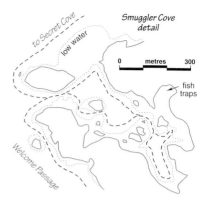

dropped, the people would gather a feast of fish and clams. The oysters so prevalent today had not yet been introduced to coastal waters.

Smuggler Cove got its name because it was reputed to have been used by Larry Kelly, a Royal Navy seaman

Inside Smuggler Cove.

Secret Cove marinas in front of the launch ramp.

who fought on the Confederate side in the U.S. Civil War and later smuggled Chinese labourers into the U.S. after they had been abandoned following completion of the CPR. The cove was also used by rum-runners during the 1920s, when liquor was prohibited in the U.S. Some of this liquor probably came from the large still at Pocahontas Bay on Texada Island.

If there's time, continue on to Secret Cove. Keep to the shore out of the way of speeding power boats. In the several small coves along here, watch for squid eggs and possible camp spots away from the yachts.

Once inside Secret Cove, you can either go straight ahead to the government dock and the store, which sells ice cream, or turn south to explore the floats of several marinas before returning to go up a long inlet. This used to contain the famous Secret Cove Yacht Club, which was formed to provide cheap moorage for a very expensive international racing yacht. It now has an outstation of the Royal Vancouver Yacht Club. Some very attractive cottages line the quiet inlet, which ends in a very shallow waterway into which a 6-metre waterfall empties from a creek.

It is possible to take out (or put in) at Secret Cove. Either land at the government dock float and carry the boats up a steep ramp, or thread your way in behind the marinas to the east of it. Well hidden, and north of the boat ways, there is a tiny, steep concrete boat launch belonging to Buccaneer Marina.

The inlet ends in mud.

34 Thormanby Islands

Difficulty Intermediate conditions – moderate risk
Distance 14 nmi round trip from Brooks Road
Duration 4–5 hours
Chart No. 3311 Sunshine Coast No. 3 Howe Sound to Pender Harbour 1:40,000
Tides on Point Atkinson
Currents A 3-knot tide runs through the north end of Welcome Passage,
diminishing by 1 knot as it reaches the south end.

Circumnavigating the Thormanbys or even just South Thormanby can be a satisfying day trip. It's also an ideal place for a shakedown trip in preparation for a more vigorous expedition or a weekend of lolling on the sand and finding where the sea stars and harlequin ducks hide in the rocky coves of Buccaneer Bay.

Paddling considerations

- Plan to paddle with the Welcome Passage tidal current.
- Watch the winds.
- Watch for other boating traffic, including log booms, in Welcome Passage.
- If the weather sours, portage into Buccaneer Bay and save North Thormanby for another day.

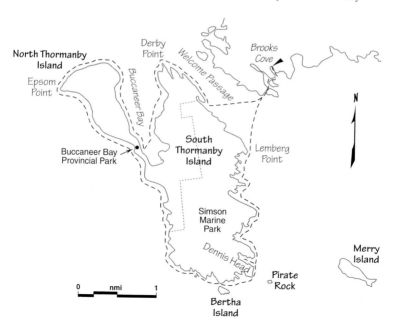

Tiny Buchaneer Marine Park at the bottom of the cliff on the right.

The route

Launch at Brooks Road or Halfmoon Bay and proceed as for Trip 33. From Jeddah Point and the skerries, cross over to Lemberg Point on South Thormanby and paddle along the rocky, indented south shore, which is open to the southeasterly winds. Watch for seals and cormorants.

The cove just before Dennis Point is a good spot to stop and explore if the wind is not blowing in there. The beach is quite rocky and not pleasant for a surf landing, to say nothing of trying to relaunch later. If you do get ashore, tie the boats up securely and hike up the trail to a lake where Canada geese nest and daffodils grow on an old homestead site. This area is all part of Simson Provincial Park.

There are usually lots of sport fishing boats around Pirate Rock, where a 2-knot current can run. Bertha Island often has seals on one end or the other. Beyond, there's a long paddle to the sandy beach where the two Thormanbys join. It's a very popular

Simson Provincial Park

In the late 19th century, ironmonger Calvert Simson emigrated from England to run a hardware store in the town of Granville, as Vancouver was then called. For vacations, he built a summer cottage on the sandy shores of Buccaneer Bay. He liked the islands so well that he homesteaded on South Thormanby, keeping his farm in manicured condition. His son, George Joe Simson, carried on the same way until 1975 when he donated the land to the province.

Derby Horse Race

When Captain G.H. Richards surveyed the Thormanby Islands in HMS *Plumper* in 1860 he must have had a bet on the popular English horse race called the Derby, because he named many of the physical features around the Thormanbys after the event and the racecourse itself. Welcome Passage was named for the "welcome" news that the racehorse named Thormanby won that year for his owner, J.C. Merry. Buccaneer was another racehorse of the time.

Established by the Earl of Derby in 1780, the race is run on a course near the market town of Epsom in the county of Surrey, 15 miles south of London. The Derby is held on the last Wednesday in May or sometimes on June 1. The following Friday, the Oaks, a race for three-year-old thoroughbred fillies, is run over the same course. Tattenham Corner is the name of the spot on the course where the horses turn onto the straightaway about half a mile from the finish line.

picnic place for day trippers brought over by water taxi from Secret Cove. The water at the outer beach is usually warmer for swimming than in Buccaneer Bay. If you want to avoid the crowds, either stop at one of the pocket beaches on South Thormanby or continue on to Epsom Point.

Choose whether to continue around the sandy cliffs of North Thormanby or portage into Buccaneer Bay. North Thormanby is much

Shake-down trip to South Thormanby. Landing to camp.

smaller than the south island. Buccaneer Bay is popular with sail and power boats, and cottages line its shores, mainly on North Thormanby. L.R. Wright set the murder scene of her novel *Fall from Grace*[12] on the North Thormanby cliffs overlooking Buccaneer Bay.

Paddling back along the Welcome Passage side of South Thormanby can be hairy if wind and tide oppose each other. Sometimes it is preferable to sit in a sheltered cove behind the islands in Buccaneer Bay and wait it out. However, in pouring rain you may prefer to proceed with caution. Incoming tides are constricted at the narrow north end of Welcome Passage, magnifying their speed and creating waves if a northwest wind is blowing. This is what makes it a good area for shakedown trips but disconcerting if you weren't planning one.

35 Half Moon Bay to Pender Harbour

Difficulty Intermediate conditions – moderate risk
Distance 11 nmi from Cooper's Green Park to Madeira Park direct
Duration 4–6 hours
Chart No. 3311 Sunshine Coast No. 3 Howe Sound to Pender Harbour 1:40,000
Tides on Point Atkinson
Currents 3 knots in Welcome Passage

Fortified by an ice cream from the old Half Moon Bay store, paddle back in time past the rum-runners' hiding places of Frenchman's Creek, Smuggler Cove and Secret Cove and on up the rocky coast to the fishing mecca of Pender Harbour.

to Harness Island. On the adjacent mainland, Silver Sands Resort has built a sheltering berm for its sail and powerboat traffic.

A nautical mile beyond Harness Island, Edgecombe Island shelters the

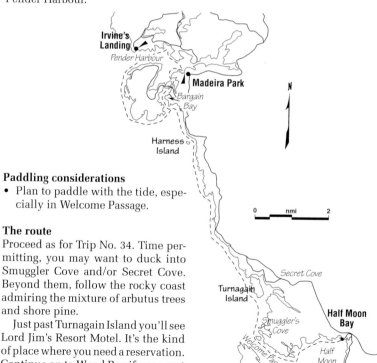

Paddling considerations
• Plan to paddle with the tide, especially in Welcome Passage.

The route
Proceed as for Trip No. 34. Time permitting, you may want to duck into Smuggler Cove and/or Secret Cove. Beyond them, follow the rocky coast admiring the mixture of arbutus trees and shore pine.

Just past Turnagain Island you'll see Lord Jim's Resort Motel. It's the kind of place where you need a reservation. Continue on to Wood Bay if you want to stop. Another 3 nmi brings you

Silver Sands Resort private launch sheltered by Harness Island.

mouth of Bargain Bay. On a high tide, if you choose to paddle to the head of the bay, you pass under a bridge and arrive at Gerrans Bay in the inner part of Pender Harbour. Alternatively, paddle on the outside of the Francis Peninsula. If you land in one of the bays of the Francis Point Provincial Park, watch that low tide doesn't strand you on the wrong side of a mud flat. When approaching the main entrance to Pender Harbour, look out for boat traffic.

On the north shore, in Dingman Bay just past the Skardon Islands, Whittaker's Pinehaven Resort has tenting sites. If you need groceries, liquor or a bank, land at Madeira Park, where there's a shopping centre.

36 Exploring Pender Harbour

Difficulty Novice conditions – minimal risk
Distance 3 nmi length but 82 nmi of shoreline
Duration 1–6 hours, depending on where you go
Chart No. 3311 Sunshine Coast No. 3 Howe Sound to Pender Harbour 1:40,000
Tides on Point Atkinson
Currents Bargain Narrows, also known as Canoe Pass, has a reversing waterfall
and dries at mid to low tide
Gunboat Narrows also has a reversing tidal waterfall.
Whiskey Slough has a reversing waterfall and dries at mid to low tide.
Irvine's Landing has a strong tidal current.

Pender Harbour is a series of inlets and coves lined with marinas and cottages. On windy days, its 82 nmi of sheltered nooks and crannies are a great place to explore, especially at high tide, as Gunboat Bay and Oyster Bay are mud flats at low water.

Paddling considerations
- The open part of Pender Harbour is subject to wind gusts. Watch for this.
- Fast-moving power boats.

The route
Launch at Madeira Park and plan your itinerary based on the state of tide and current. Pender Harbour is lined with marinas and resorts today, but it wasn't always so.

Originally, Garden Bay contained seven huge longhouses where 5,000 Sechelt people wintered. There was also a smaller village on the Madeira Park side. To warn of impending attacks by slave raiders, the people maintained lookout posts at Cape Cockburn and on top of Mount Daniel above Pender Harbour. This is now Garden Bay Marine Provincial Park, where you can still see "moon rings"

of rocks placed there by Sechelt maidens during their puberty ceremonies. All winter, the longhouses rocked with laughter as stories were told and dances performed. In 1862, smallpox killed 90 per cent of the people in a few short months, leaving a vacuum which European settlers eagerly filled.

A decade or two later, loggers, fishers and farmers arrived. Floathouses, net sheds and homesteads replaced the longhouses. When Charlie Irvine sold his land to the Gonzaleses, father and son, they built a steamship dock. With no roads, the large extended families living in pockets around the harbour brought their produce to the dock in small boats propelled by little "kicker" engines. Then the Union steamships—*Comox, Cowichan, Chelohsin* and *Capilano*—brought in supplies and mail and took away local meat and vegetables to market in Vancouver and Victoria.

After the First World War, the sport fishing crowd arrived, intent on pleasure, and marinas sprang up. When the sport fishers retired, they replaced the net sheds with cottages, motels and resorts. The current population is about 2,500.

Pender Harbour from Irvine's Landing.

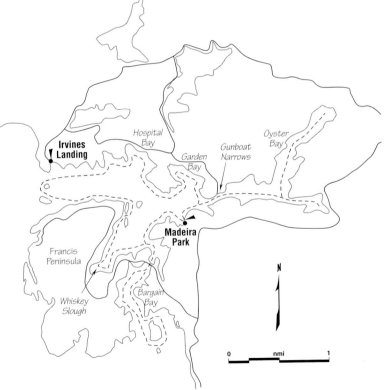

Irvines Landing

Hospital Bay

Garden Bay

Gunboat Narrows

Oyster Bay

Madeira Park

Francis Peninsula

Whiskey Slough

Bargain Bay

N

0   nmi   1

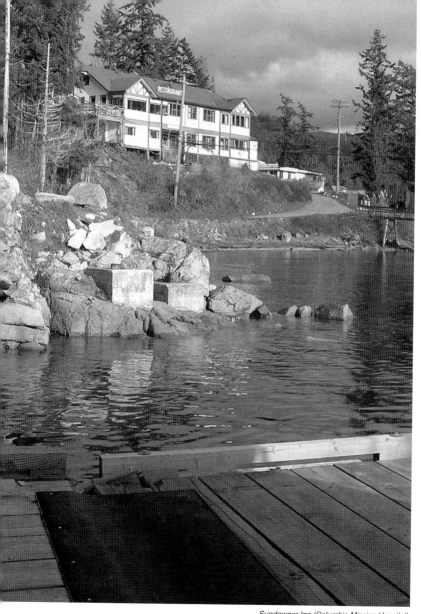

Sundowner Inn (Columbia Mission Hospital).

Personalities of Pender Harbour

– Vancouver's Dr. McKechnie introduced Japanese oysters in 1923, hoping to keep his son, Ian, in gainful employment. Despite Ian's neglect, the oysters flourished and multiplied, much to the chagrin of swimmers who complained about cut feet.

– Sandy McLean, a crusty sealer who may have been the original for Wolf Larsen in Jack London's *Sea Wolf*.

– Bert Sinclair, a writer of westerns who found fishing more lucrative.

– Stewart Edward White, the author of the novel *Skookum Chuck*, which was set in various places along the Coast.

– Allen Farrell, an old-time boat builder of Chinese junks, some of which he sailed to the South Pacific.

– John Antle of the Columbia Coast Anglican mission, who built St. Mary's Hospital in Garden Bay. When the hospital moved to Sechelt, the building became the Sundowner Inn.

– Elizabeth Smart, a society girl from back east, who arrived in 1941 pregnant and in disgrace. Befriended by an elegant Austrian countess who was living in penury, Smart gave birth to a daughter in St. Mary's hospital and finished her novel *By Grand Central Station, I Sat Down and Wept*.

– *New Yorker* magazine writer Edith Iglauer went out on John Daly's fishboat, married him, and wrote the best selling book *Fishing with John*.

– Howard White, author of *Writing in the Rain* and owner of Harbour Publishing. His backhoe operation has dug up many of the smallpox victims.

Madeira Park launch.

37 Pender Harbour to Egmont

Difficulty Intermediate conditions – moderate risk
Distance 12 nmi each way
Duration 4–5 hours
Chart No. 3311 Sunshine Coast No. 4 Pender Harbour to Grief Point 1:40,000
Tides on Point Atkinson
Currents 1–2 knots at the entrance to Agamemnon Channel

At the beginning the trip has a tempting diversion into Sakinaw Lake. As the Nelson Island side has more that's of interest than the mainland, you'll want to cross over to it unless the outflow winds from Jervis Inlet are strong.

Paddling considerations
• Forecast winds in the Strait of Georgia complicated by inflow/outflow winds in Agamemnon Channel from Jervis Inlet.

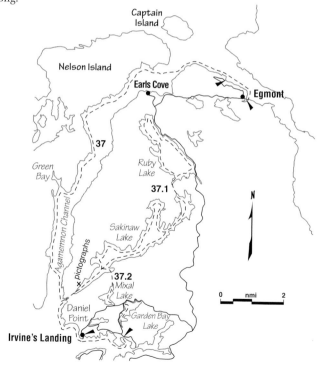

Ruby Lake.

The route

Launch at Irvine's Landing and turn north on exiting Pender Harbour. Follow the shore around into Agamemnon Channel. The island on the left is Nelson Island (see Trip No. 25).

Shortly after Daniel Point there's a small beach within a square on the chart marking an Indian Reserve. The creek running into this empties out from Sakinaw Lake (see Trips 37.1, 37.2).

Continue up Agamemnon Channel. The east side of the channel is somewhat monotonous, with few landings. If the wind is light, cross the channel to take in Green Bay on Nelson Island.

On June 19, 1792, Midshipman Thomas Manby wrote: "My Boats Crew suffered every hardship fatigue and hunger could inflict, in a small cove I passed a Night that abounded with Muscles. A fire soon cooked us enough to make a voracious Meal of. In the course of an hour, the whole of us were taken violently ill, and experienced every agony a poisoned set of beings could feel. I gorged them all with hot water, which had the desired effect, by clearing the Stomach from this dangerous food, it threw one Man into a fever. The rest fortunately recovered." A year later, in the same month, *Discovery* seaman John Carter died of the same malady, the first European to succumb to paralytic shellfish poisoning.[13] See also page 22.

Green Bay, halfway up the western shore of Agamemnon Channel, is where author and publisher Howard White lived as a child. He wrote about it in *Writing in the Rain*. Originally there was a cannery in the bay but this shut down after the 1914–18 War and was replaced by a shingle mill. That didn't last either.

Continue on this side till you're safely past the Egmont ferry terminal and the barge operation before returning to the west side. Ahead, Jervis Inlet begins to open up. There may be strong inflow/outflow winds here. Some of the cottages in Agamemnon Bay have rocky beaches which they prefer you don't land on. The shore curves around into the Skookumchuk Narrows. The famous rapids are about 1.5 nmi beyond your take-out at the Egmont government dock.

The settlement of Egmont lies on both sides of the narrows, and as there is no road access on the far side, people commute by boat. On the south side, a short distance beyond the Back Eddy Pub, there is a government wharf with a general store above it.

One of the early settlers of Egmont was Joseph Silvey (1879–1940), second son of "Portuguese Joe" Silvey (1828–1902) of the Azores who preempted 160 acres on Reid Island in the Gulf Islands in 1881. Young Joe and his wife, Maria King, purchased 40 acres of Egmont waterfront in 1904. Like his father, Joe had his own boat, which he used to earn his living as a fisherman. In 1919, his wife died leaving him to raise seven small children. Two of these died of tuberculosis and a third drowned while on a gillnetter.

37.1 Ruby Lake – Sakinaw Lake Triangle resurrected

9 nmi round trip

One of two interesting side trips involving the short portage from Agamemnon Channel into Sakinaw Lake. It is an all-day affair in the midst of prime cottage country, which can be quite amusing at the height of the season, as most people have a full complement of grandchildren in residence, along with large, colourful beach toys. In days of yore, before someone planted a barge operation beside the Earl's Cove ferry terminal, there used to be a very popular canoe route involving Sakinaw Lake, Ruby Lake and Agamemnon Channel. You can still portage into Ruby Lake but you can't launch at the ferry terminal. Putting in at the north end of Sakinaw Lake is an option but parking is very limited indeed. Try putting in at the restaurant on Ruby Lake, shuttle a vehicle to Egmont and portage from Ruby to Sakinaw Lake and then into Agamemnon Channel, taking out at Egmont.

Landing on the islands at the south end of Sakinaw Lake can be tricky. Once, the Dogwood Canoe Club women decided to camp here. After a sumptuous dinner complete with wine, one of them went to brush her teeth in the lake. She made a wrong step and landed up to her neck in water. The others never let her forget it.

On the western shore of the lake, just south of the islands, look for the dark red stains of petroglyphs on the cliffs. These are said to depict a turtle and a crawfish.

Barge terminal at Egmont in Agamemnon Channel.

Irvine's Landing launch.

37.2 Pender Harbour and Three Lakes Circle

Launch anywhere in Pender Harbour and paddle out and up Agamemnon Channel. Take the portage into Sakinaw Lake and, after viewing the crawfish and turtle petroglyphs on the western shore and the islands, cross to the eastern shore and go into the bay just before the first major point on that side, about 2 nmi. Take out on the small sandy beach next to a private boathouse and several cottages. Carry or wheel the boats 800 m and about 15 m in elevation up Mixal Road to the lake of the same name. Paddle past the island and angle into a bay in the southeast corner, where there is a portage sign. Take out and turn left. Carry or wheel along the road for 460 m to where the Garden Bay and Irvine's Landing roads cross. You are now on the shore of Garden Bay Lake. Put in and paddle along the western shore to the end of the lake. Take out and portage along the road for 600 m. At the junction of Lyons Road, turn left for 150 m to the Garden Bay Hotel and Pub. Perhaps after suitable replenishments, launch back into Pender Harbour at the pub float.

38 Skookumchuk Rapids

Difficulty Advanced conditions – considerable risk
Distance 2 nmi each way
Duration 30 minutes from Egmont to reach the beginning of the rapids, but you may want to stay a couple of hours.
Charts No. 3312 Desolation Sound and Jervis Inlet, page 4
1:40,000 includes a Sechelt Rapids inset 1:20,000
No. 3512 Strait of Georgia, Central Portion 1:80,000
Tides on Point Atkinson
Currents See Tide Tables vol. 5: Sechelt Rapids[14]

These tidal rapids are one of several on the coast that are a prime play place for those with advanced whitewater skills and lots of nerve. If you lack the skills, hike the trail and watch from shore.

Paddling considerations
- Even those who know the rapids are not entirely safe.
- Study the current tables carefully before launching.

The route
For maximum time at the rapids, launch at Egmont. Whitewater paddlers will want to play the rapids. Others may just want to shoot them.

When the Dogwood Canoe Club of Burnaby took a trip here, they arrived at slack tide and camped a night on the island in the middle. They said the whole thing shook at mid tide and was most spectacular. In the morning, they packed up, waited for slack and paddled out again. Before they went, they had the canoe instructors and sailors among them study the current tables to plan optimum times for arrival and departure. As they approached, they watched carefully to confirm that their estimates had been correct.

Coastwise guide John Dafoe says: "Even those who know the rapids are not entirely safe. I have capsized there after years of traversing in all tides. Those who do not know the rapids or are unaccustomed to tidal rapids should use great caution. After studying the current charts, it is also a good idea to stop and study the rapids from one of the islands for a while. Unlike a river rapid, the tidal rapid changes with the height of the tide and of course the change of direction. This makes the tidal rapid seasonally variable and variable within an hour's time and therefore much more complex than river rapids generally. There is of course much more to the rapids than mentioned here." Be warned! People have died here.

Experienced whitewater kayakers thrive on the standing wave at Roland Point. This can be viewed from the 4-km hiking trail which starts at Egmont. It's a good idea to hike in and watch the rapids from shore before trying to run or play in them.

If you want to explore the Sechelt Inlets without going through the Skookumchuk Rapids, launch at the Sechelt end.

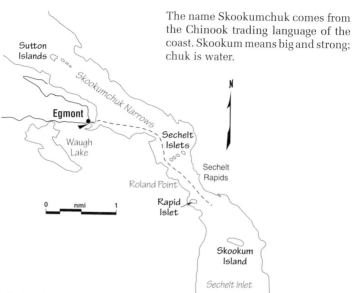

The name Skookumchuk comes from the Chinook trading language of the coast. Skookum means big and strong; chuk is water.

Entrance to Skookumchuck Narrows.

39 The Sechelt Inlets

Difficulty Intermediate conditions – moderate risk
Distance 72 nmi to explore all three inlets in one round trip
              Sechelt to Skookumchuk Rapids 15 nmi each way
              Salmon Inlet 12 nmi each way
              Narrows Inlet 9 nmi each way
Duration 8–10 days
              Sechelt to Halfway Beach (1 day)
              Halfway Beach to the head of Salmon Inlet (2–3 days)
              Halfway Beach to Tzoonie Narrows (2–3 days)
              Halfway Beach to Skookumchuk (1 day)
Charts No. 3312 Desolation Sound and Jervis Inlet pages 4–5 1:40,000
              No. 3512 Strait of Georgia, Central Portion 1:80,000
Tides on Point Atkinson (Secondary ports Storm Bay and Porpoise Bay.
              Add 2.40 and 2.50 at high high water and 2.03 and 2.00 at low low water)
Currents Skookumchuk (Sechelt) Rapids (see current tables)
              Tzoonie Narrows rapids run at 4 knots

The waters of the three Sechelt Inlets are generally calmer than the Strait of Georgia and not particularly crowded. The seven marine park wilderness campsites are both attractive and relaxing. Because the entrance to the inlet system is constricted, there is a difference in the tides of two hours and more.

Paddling considerations
- Inflow/outflow winds are particularly strong in the two side inlets and even stronger in Salmon Inlet, which runs in the same direction as Princess Royal Reach of Jervis Inlet and is subject to the same winds.
- Winds at the mouth of Salmon Inlet and Narrows Inlet can confuse the wind pattern on Sechelt Inlet.
- Afternoon winds are strong. Paddle in the morning or evening.
- The western side of Sechelt Inlet is more sheltered than the eastern.

- Note the weather information emanating automatically from the unstaffed Merry Island light station.

Sechelt Inlet Launches
Sechelt – On entering Sechelt, turn right at the second set of lights (just past a McDonald's) and follow Wharf Road to the Lighthouse Pub beside the government dock. If leaving vehicles on the wharf for more than three days, advise the wharfinger. After launching, watch for seaplanes and other boat traffic.

Porpoise Bay Provincial Park – After turning right onto Wharf Road, drive three blocks and turn right again onto Porpoise Bay Road, which becomes Sechelt Inlet Road. Follow the signs to the park.

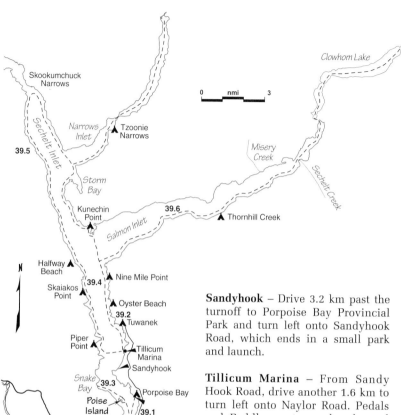

Sandyhook – Drive 3.2 km past the turnoff to Porpoise Bay Provincial Park and turn left onto Sandyhook Road, which ends in a small park and launch.

Tillicum Marina – From Sandy Hook Road, drive another 1.6 km to turn left onto Naylor Road. Pedals and Paddles rents sea kayaks and provides its clients with maps and a wealth of information.

Tuwanek – Continue another kilometre. Bear left after the log sort and follow the road to the water. Parking is very limited and usually occupied by divers. If necessary, be prepared to turn back to one of the other launches.

Campsites

These are administered either by Sechelt Inlets Marine Provincial Park or Mount Richardson Provincial Park. Bring water or boil any water replenished locally. Use the fire rings provided, if at all.

Tuwanek – A day-use site with limited camping above a gravel beach. It is only 1 nmi from Tillicum Marina.

Oyster Beach – Two to three gravel sites. No water. Although the fish farming activities of the previous occupant have been cleaned up, some residue still surfaces on the beach, making this site less attractive than either Tuwanek or Nine Mile Point.

Nine Mile Point – Gravel beach with a creek running through it separating the tent sites into two areas. The trees form a cathedral-like vault over the tents. This is the third and largest of the three Mount Richardson campsites.

Kunechin Point – Heavily used by scuba divers visiting the Chaudière Artificial Reef. No water. No fires. Two tent pads and little space for other tents.

Kunechin Bay – Two sites for four tents. No water. Bears frequent this area, so keep food hung. (No camping on the islets.)

Camping on the north side of the creek at Nine Mile Point. Photo: www.pedalspaddles.com.

Stopping for a picnic on Tuwanek Beach. Photo: www.pedalspaddles.com.

Thornhill Creek – Up Salmon Inlet. Two campsites above a beach of cobblestone and large rocks.

Tzoonie Narrows – Camp on either side of the inlet before the tidal narrows. Bring your own water. Can accommodate up to 10 tents and has a rope bear cache.

Halfway Beach – On the west side of Sechelt Inlet. It has early morning sun, a glacier view up Salmon Inlet and a good swimming beach. 10–15 tent sites. The water supply is apt to dry up in summer and should be boiled before use.

Skaiakos Point – An unorganized campsite a little farther south of Halfway Beach.

Piper Point – An unorganized campsite opposite Tillicum Marina. Gravel beach and space for two to three tents.

Jellyfish

The intertidal world is full of strange creatures that change their sex, eat and excrete in unexpected ways, and grow from one form into another, sometimes in the course of a single season. While the casual observer of jellyfish in the Strait of Georgia may think they see only moon jellies, lion's mane and perhaps water jellies, there are hundreds of different jellyfish (medusae) in B.C. waters belonging to several different groups. Sorting them out requires the use of Latin names.

In phylum Cnidaria there are two main classes: Hydrozoa and Scyphozoa. Both classes have medusae as part of their life cycle and both have a polyp stage. Medusae are free-floating, bell-shaped organisms that are often transparent. Polyps are like small sea anemones attached to a stationary object.

In the Hydrozoa, the polyp is the dominant form and the medusa is small and usually short-lived. Most medusae in this class are less than 10 cm in diameter and are free-floating in the water only for a few weeks in the early spring before becoming a polyp. Aequorea, commonly known as water jellies, are one of the largest and longest-lived of the hydrozoan jellyfishes.

In class Scyphozoa, the medusae is the dominant form and the polyp is only an over-wintering stage. Aurelia (moon jellies), Cyanea (lion's mane) and Phacellophora (egg yolk jellyfish) are the most common of the large scyphozoan medusae that we see all spring, summer and fall in B.C. waters. Cyanea and Phacellophora are often mistaken for each other because they are the same size, but they are quite different if you know what to look for. Cyanea is dark red with eight lappets (indentations in the bell), while Phacellophora looks like a fried egg with a yellow centre and white rim. Phacellophora has about 32 small lappets. Both Cyanea and Phacellophora are about 50 cm in diameter and have very strong stinging cells that will burn the skin.

Cup corals and sea anemones are also members of phylum Cnidaria.

The routes

Local paddlers tend to do short day trips at the south end of Sechelt Inlet.

Trip 39.1

From Sechelt, check out the anemones growing on the marina pilings before paddling over to the Porpoise Bay campsite. In summer, the Department of Fisheries sometimes runs a net through the eel grass and shows visitors the tiny creatures caught in it. These often include long, green pipe fish, which are relatives of the sea horse, several kinds of gunnies, emerald Sitka shrimp and many others. It's quite a sight. To find out when it is occurring, drive out to the park and check the notice board.

Trip 39.2

From Tillicum Marina, enjoy a short trip to explore the tiny, privately owned Lamb Islets, which are also a popular dive site. Land at Tuwanek Beach or Oyster Bay for a picnic. These sites, along with Nine Mile Point, are in Mount Richardson Provincial Park. The area was never logged but fire destroyed some sections 75–80 years ago. Watch for black-tailed deer, turkey buzzards with their tilting V-shaped flight, osprey, eagles, pileated woodpecker and black bear.

Trip 39.3

From Sechelt or Porpoise Bay paddle around privately owned Poise Island and out to land on the good swimming beaches in Snake Bay. The water at this end of the inlet is calm enough to encourage large blooms of jellyfish

Paddling through channel between unnamed island and Tuwenek point. Photo: www.pedalspaddles.com.

Looking up Salmon Inlet. Photo: www.pedalspaddles.com.

equalled only by those in Okeover Arm much farther north. Divers find that these are often a metre or more in thickness.

Trip 39.4

Out of town paddlers tend to want to do more extended paddles, especially as no one likes turning back just as they've reached a prime destination. The most popular route is to launch at Sechelt, Porpoise Bay or Tillicum Marina, check out the Lamb Islets and paddle north watching for the telltale red ochre stain of a pictograph in the form of a face just before Nine Mile Point. If the wind is not howling out of Salmon Inlet, stop and camp above the pretty beach. If the water is calm,

Western Front

The Western Front began as an urban art cooperative in Vancouver in the early 1970s. They came together to purchase and share video equipment for their performance art. To get away from the city, they established land co-ops on the Sunshine Coast at Roberts Creek and Storm Bay. The Roberts Creek co-op was called Babyland and had to be approached on foot. Some residents found it too close to the city and retreated to Storm Bay on Sechelt Inlet. This community is still in operation but has no road access. They like to maintain their privacy, so don't go ashore there.

cross the 1.32 nmi to Kunechin Islets while you can. As you cross enjoy the view of the glaciers at the end of Salmon Inlet. The Kunechin Islets are a bird sanctuary. Keep your distance and use binoculars to avoid disturbing the breeding birds and seals. Behind the islets, Kunechin Point is a popular campsite, but hang food out of reach of the bears.

Another 3 nmi brings you to Storm Bay. Although some people have camped here, the cottagers prefer that you don't. Instead, continue on up Narrows Inlet to just before Tzoonie Narrows and camp there. Both sides of the inlet are possibilities. There is also a private campground with a hot tub if you want luxury. A cabin near the narrows belongs to a commune whose members still use it occasionally.

The tide rushes through the Narrows at up to 4 knots, so time your explorations of the upper end of the inlet accordingly. Look for a hidden waterfall in a grotto of big trees. At high tide you can paddle up the river a short distance. In the fall grizzly bears come down to feed on the homecoming chum salmon.

Returning to Sechelt Inlet, a favourite place to overnight is behind Halfway Islet on the western shore. As the fishing is good, there are lots of seals. This has plenty of camping space and a good swimming beach. Alternatively, continue 0.5 nmi to Skaiakos Point, where, despite the

sandy beach, the remains of old logging equipment make it a less popular camp spot. Another 3 nmi brings you to Piper Point and a third camp spot, directly opposite Tillicum Marina. This one is very small and you look out onto the houses of Sandy Hook.

Trip 39.5

When you come out of Narrows Inlet—and if you possess advanced whitewater experience—instead of returning south, paddle north to Skookumchuk Rapids. Assess the state of the tide before going past Skookum Island, however, and keep to the right of it as well as the other islands. See Trip No. 38.

Trip 39.6

Salmon Inlet is less popular because it is a clear-cut wind tunnel with hydro lines everywhere. Once camped at Thornhill Creek, it is only 1 nmi across the inlet to where Misery Creek thunders down a rock face into the inlet. Beyond it, sheltered Misery Bay is a popular yacht anchorage for those who make it that far. Opposite on the south side, a white sandy beach uncovers in the estuary of Sechelt Creek. At the head of the inlet (3.6 nmi from Thornhill Creek), there's an old logging camp and a road to portage 0.2 nmi into Clowhom Lake which has more sandy beaches and goes for another 6 nmi. It is an area to which troublesome grizzly bears are sometimes relocated.

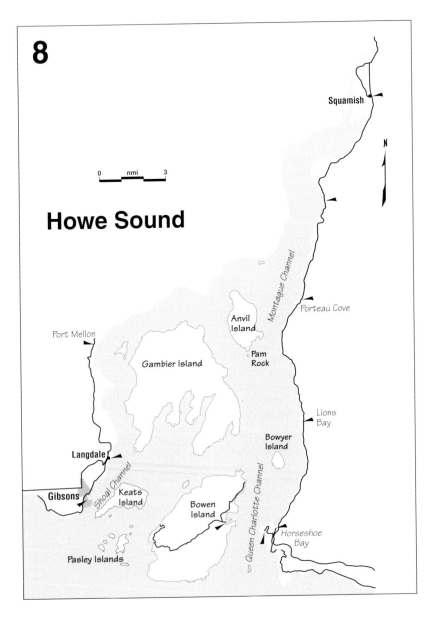

8

Howe Sound

0 nmi 3

Squamish

N

Montague Channel

Porteau Cove

Port Mellon

Anvil Island

Pam Rock

Gambier Island

Lions Bay

Bowyer Island

Langdale

Shoal Channel

Gibsons

Keats Island

Bowen Island

Queen Charlotte Channel

Horseshoe Bay

Pasley Islands

Although Howe Sound is very close to Vancouver, many city dwellers have only seen it from the ferry between Horseshoe Bay and Langdale on the Sunshine Coast. It is a deep, steep-sided inlet surrounded by the sometimes snow-covered peaks of the coastal mountains. Tourists often compare its spectacular scenery to the fjords of Norway or New Zealand. The northern part is wilder than the more populated southern part.

The squalls from its fierce outflow winds, named for the small town of Squamish at the head of the inlet, are legendary. Raging whitecaps come up in minutes, making crossings to the islands hazardous. Some paddlers have been drowned.

In the early 20th century Howe Sound was a favourite vacation place for Vancouverites who built cottages, stayed in hotels or camped. There is a profusion of summer camps for all ages operated by a variety of religious organizations. Due to the problems of keeping children safe in today's environment, unscreened visitors may not be welcome.

A couple of yacht clubs have outstations in Centre Bay on Gambier Island. Others tie up to the log booms and row in by dinghy for beach roasts.

Islands like Bowen and Gambier in particular have seen a change from summer cottages to year-round homes with residents commuting to work daily. Camping is no longer allowed on Bowen. The busy road to the ski resort of Whistler and a railway line run along the east side of Howe Sound. Twenty-five years ago the bridge over M Creek washed

Log Booms

Logs on self-dumping barges as well as floating log booms from all over the coast are towed to Howe Sound and the Fraser River. Before being offered for sale, they may be sorted, usually on dry land but sometimes in the water (to the east of Woolridge Island). Sidewinders—small boom boats with very powerful engines—push the bundles around, sorting them into booms for different purposes such as the manufacture of shingles, plywood, lumber or pulp. Once the bundles of logs are sorted, buyers fly in to inspect them before negotiating a price. Kayakers should observe from a distance without getting in the way of the self-dumping barges, the sidewinders or the float planes.

out on a dark night and an unknown number of cars drove off the end to be lost in the inlet. The creeks have been concreted and contained to reduce the risk of their unleashed fury. However, logging continues on the mountains above.

Landings and launches are scarce. Some of the small communities along the eastern shore have beaches but reserve them for their own residents. Lions Bay is one of these.

Bates exiled marker. See page 219 for story. Photo: Peter Waddington.

Howe Sound Names

In 1792, Captain George Vancouver named Howe Sound in honour of Admiral the Right Honourable Richard Scrope, Earl Howe, who was First Lord of the Admiralty 1783–88. During the Nootka Sound Controversy of 1790, when the Spanish were impounding English ships off the west coast of Vancouver Island, relations between England and Spain became strained to the point of war. Black Dick, as Howe was nicknamed because of his swarthy complexion, commanded the English Channel fleet protecting England from Spain's armada. On June 1, 1794, he won his most distinguished victory over the French. Off Ushant, he sank one French warship and captured six more.

When Captain G.H. Richards surveyed Howe Sound in HMS *Plumper* in 1859–60, he commemorated this "Glorious First of June" battle by naming many islands and points after the participants. *Barfleur, Brunswick, Defence, Latona, Montague, Queen Charlotte* and *Ramillies* were ships. Bowen, Bowyer, Collingwood, Domett, Ekins, Gambier, Gardener, Halkett, Harvey, Hood, Pasley, Graves, Curtis and Thornbrough were admirals or vice-admirals, and Harvey and Hutt were captains who died June 30, 1794, from wounds sustained during the battle.

Launches

On the eastern shore
Whyte Cliff Park

In Horseshoe Bay, find Marine Avenue. The end of it is in Whyte Cliff Park (beside White Cliff Point).

Horseshoe Bay

Access the boat launch ramp from Bay Street, which runs parallel to the shore. Parking is very difficult, which is why most paddlers prefer to use Whyte Cliff Park.

Sunset Beach

From Highway 99, follow the Sunset Marina signs down the hill.

Newman Creek

Although this is marked as a launch on the chart, a gate discourages visitors.

Lions Bay

Local residents like to keep this launch for themselves but others do use it occasionally.

Porteau Cove

38 km north of Vancouver on the road to Squamish and Whistler, has a double, paved boat launch ramp much patronized by power boaters.

Britannia Beach

45 km north of Vancouver on Highway 99, has road and railway running very close to the shore. Across them, the Britannia Beach Boat Club has a launch ramp.

Squamish

Drive the length of Cleveland Road, turn left and the municipal ramp is at the end, beside the Squamish Yacht Club. There is lots of parking.

On the western shore
Gibsons Harbour

From the Langdale ferry terminal, follow the signs for Gibsons, pass Molly's Reach and continue on the road by the water past the marina till you come to a T-junction. Turn left onto Headlands Road. You can drive down onto the beach to launch, but park your car back on the road.

Hopkins Landing

From the Langdale ferry terminal, turn toward Gibsons for 0.3 km. Pass the Salvation Army camp on the left and soon after you'll see the twin entrances to Hopkins Road. At the foot of it there's a small sandy beach beside an old pier. There's not much parking.

Port Mellon

Turn right off the Langdale ferry and drive 11.1 km. Immediately past a three-storey apartment block, turn right on Dunham Road. This tiny community is locally known as Dogpatch. The pavement ends at the end of the block but a rough road continues to the beach, which is a mixture of cobble and rock.

Hopkins Wharf.

Dunham Road launch at Port Mellon looking up Thornbrough Channel.

(If tempted to try Witherby Beach Road, don't bother. After a rough descent, it ends high above the water with a chain and a No Admittance sign.)

The Seaside launch beyond the mill marked on some charts no longer exists and has been supplanted by part of the Howe Sound Pulp & Paper Mill.

Campsites

Porteau Cove Provincial Park, 38 km north of Vancouver on Highway 99, has a campsite that is popular with the RV crowd. Reservations are available for the seven vehicle sites. In addition there are 16 walk-in campsites and a 300-metre trail to a lookout over Howe Sound.

On Gambier Island
Brigade Bay an unorganized campsite.

Douglas Bay an unorganized campsite.

Halkett Bay Provincial Park on Gambier Island.

On Keats Island
Plumper Cove Marine Provincial Park on Keats Island has 20 gravel sites and a 3-km trail to Keats Landing, which has ferry service to Gibsons. Check with the Brackendale branch of B.C. Parks to see if you need reservations.

40 Whyte Cliff Park to Bowen Island via Passage Island

Difficulty Intermediate conditions – moderate risk
Distance 9.2 nmi
Whyte Cliff Park to Passage Island 2.8 nmi
Passage Island to Seymour Landing 1.9 nmi
Seymour Landing to Snug Cove 3.0 nmi
Snug Cove to Whyte Cliff Park 1.5 nmi
Duration 3–4 hours
Charts No. 3526 Howe Sound 1:40,000
No. 3311 Sunshine Coast Sheet 1 Port Moody to Howe Sound 1:40,000
Tides on Point Atkinson
Currents 0.5 knot in each direction in Queen Charlotte Channel. By the time the outflow from the Squamish River reaches here it is almost negligible.

This trip satisfies the urge to cross to Bowen Island without using the ferry. En route, visit little-known Passage Island and test your knowledge of marine traffic.

Paddling considerations
- Strong outflow winds in the afternoon can be a problem at any season.
- Squamish winds of up to 40 knots increase toward the mouth of the inlet and out into the Strait of Georgia. Listen for reports from the Pam Rock buoy.
- Any area in Howe Sound with a long fetch, like Queen Charlotte Channel, can build waves of 1.5–2.5 m, especially when winds and tide oppose tide or river flow.
- B.C. Ferries have the right of way over other craft and, like all ships of that size, can't turn quickly. Take schedules for the Bowen Island and Horseshoe Bay/Nanaimo ferries with you.
- Other fast-moving power boats and sailboat races.

- Two-thirds of this trip crosses major boat traffic routes.
- At least one person on the trip should know marine traffic rules and the others should defer to this knowledge.
- Groups of paddlers should stay together on the crossings so that other boats easily see them.

The route
If winds are low, head directly across from the beach at Whyte Cliff Park to Passage Island (1.8 nmi). If the winds are uncertain, stick to the shore. Poke into the West Vancouver Yacht Club's marina behind Eagle Island, whose residents use a strange, self-operated ferry platform to get home. Enjoy the weird and wonderful West Vancouver architecture. See if you can spy an all-glass home built into the cliff. On the south side of Eagle Harbour, a replica of a certain famous ancient Greek temple stands at the end of Parthenon Place.

Black oystercatchers and pigeon guillemots frequent the Grebe Islets. From there, head across 1.1 nmi to

Passage Island. Passage Island also has interesting architectural structures to observe as well as bird life and a few warm, quiet nooks sheltered from the wind. There is nowhere to land, however. Stop alongside the cliffs to enjoy a snack in your boat. Be careful of cormorants roosting above you. Before you leave, do a last-minute review of the marine traffic rules and the ferry schedules before attempting the busy crossing to Bowen.

Cross 1.8 nmi to Seymour Landing, which is 4WD accessible. After a lunch stop, paddle north along the steep rugged shoreline past Apodaca Provincial Park, which Major J.S. Matthews, Vancouver's city archivist, donated to the province in 1954 in memory of his son who died at the age of 22. It exemplifies the rugged terrain of the island the Spaniards christened Apodaca.

Crippen Park in Snug Cove has a sandy beach where you can land and hike the 4-km trail to Dorman Point. In bad weather, take-out at the boat launch beside the park and walk the boats onto the ferry. If paddling back to Whyte Cliff Park, watch for the Bowen Island ferry coming in or out.

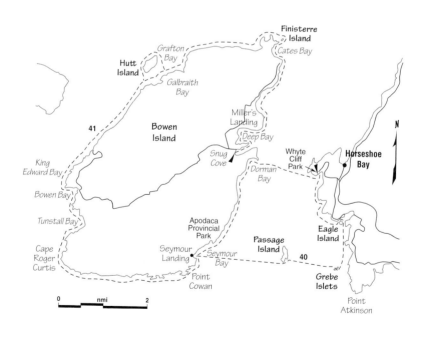

41 Bowen Island – circumnavigation

Difficulty Intermediate conditions – moderate risk
Distance 17 nmi
Duration 6–8 hours
Charts No. 3526 Howe Sound 1:40,000
Tides on Point Atkinson
Currents none

Bowen Island has been a popular getaway for Vancouverites for over a century and still charms those out for a day paddle and a swim. See sketch-map on page 209.

Paddling considerations

- Strong outflow winds in the afternoon can be a problem at any season.
- Squamish winds of up to 40 knots increase toward the mouth of the inlet and out into the Strait of Georgia. Listen for reports from the Pam Rock buoy.
- Any area in Howe Sound with a long fetch, like Queen Charlotte Channel or Collingwood Channel, can build waves of 1.5–2.5 m, especially when winds and tide oppose tide or river flow.

The route

To shorten the trip and avoid the heavy marine traffic of Queen Charlotte Channel, take the ferry over to Snug Cove and launch from there. (Otherwise, see Trip No. 40. Or drive across the island to launch at Tunstall Bay, though parking may be easier at Snug Cove.)

You can also rent kayaks from Bowen Island Kayaking at Snug Cove (see Useful Contacts on page 239). The same company offers short and longer guided paddles around Bowen or to other islands in Howe Sound. For the last five years a "Round Bowen Race" has been held on the first Saturday in June. This attracts outrigger canoes as well as kayaks and finishes with a salmon BBQ.

Deep Bay (also called Mannion Bay), immediately north of Snug

George H. Cowan

Cowan Point was named after Vancouver lawyer George H. Cowan (1858–1935), who built cottages on his property to lease to his friends, many of whom came from the Prairies. He would have their cottages cleaned and groceries laid in prior to their arrival. The families cleared trails, caught salmon, swam in the moonlight and watched the rum-runners and the Japanese fishing fleet. On Sundays they attended church in a big circus tent. Many families returned every summer. Some, like the Russell family, did so for 58 years.

George Cowan hired a farmer for his 12-acre Seymour Bay Farm and rode around the island on horseback comparing notes on livestock with other homesteaders. His neighbours, the Malkin family, to whom Ethel Wilson was related, provided the inspiration for Wilson's novel *The Innocent Traveller*.

Hutt Island and Collingwood Channel.

Cove, was the place where, during the first two decades of the 20th century, Captain John A. Cates (1866–1942) used to bring weary city dwellers on hot summer days. One of five master mariner brothers from Nova Scotia, Cates operated his own steamship line, bringing people here to enjoy picnics and camping "in the ample shade of the deep woods," where he had planted 300 fruit trees and built a store. Cates was also a great teller of tall tales who captivated his audiences with stories of the whale that "sometimes scratched its back on that barnacled rock over there," and others of that ilk. In later years the Union Steamship line took over Cates's hotel, renaming it the Bowen Inn and offering swimming, tennis and a large dance floor for 800.

It was the dance floor that was the focus of the Saturday night booze cruises from Horseshoe Bay which had parents from as far away as the Kootenays warning their teenagers to avoid. No surprise they didn't. During the several decades when these cruises ran, Bowen acquired a somewhat colourful reputation. It's quite different from today's more respectable population of about 3,000 whose municipal government is mandated to keep the island rural and avoid big housing developments. The hotel was demolished in the 1960s to be replaced by private residences.

Leaving Deep Bay, paddle north to the protuberance of Miller's Landing. In 1905, Isaac Miller, who owned a dairy in Vancouver, built a summer cottage called "Moonwinks" with a gazebo on a nearby rock. He liked to watch the cormorants spread their

Exploring the coast of Bowen Island.

George Tunstall

Tunstall Bay is named for George C. Tunstall (1866–1950), sales manager for Western Explosives Ltd., which manufactured dynamite on Bowen Island from 1908 to 1913. He was "a rollicking pianist" who loved to drink and party. But in 1913, when Canadian Explosives bought the plant and moved it to James Island, Tunstall moved to Kamloops never to return. Once the factory was removed, tourists discovered the bay. The Chalmers United Church had a camp there and so did the *Vancouver Sun* for its paper carriers. Bowen Bay Holdings bought 100 acres and shared out the waterfront among its permanent residents.

wings to dry on another rock in the bay. With his children grown up, Miller gave plots of land to various relatives. His eldest son, George Clark Miller (1882–1968), became mayor of Vancouver. Mayor Miller's family spent enjoyable summers at the farm while he was amalgamating Vancouver with Point Grey, dealing with a post office sit-down strike, and opposing fluoridation of Vancouver's water supply. Some of the family used to blast the neighbourhood with Bach and Beethoven, which could be heard as far away as Deep Bay.

Just south of Cates Bay, the Albion Gold Mining Company flourished from 1896–1909 but never produced much bullion, though they dumped untidy heaps of tailings on the beach.

After Captain Cates sold his pleasure cruise company to Union Steamships, he went prospecting in the Okanagan, where he built a large log home. However, he continued to hanker for Bowen, so he had his house dismantled and rebuilt on land on the bay south of Hood Point which bears his name. In 1927 a consortium of Vancouver business-men bought Lot 823 from Cates. They and their successors have operated this land, which com-prises Cates Bay, Finisterre Island, Hood Point and Smuggler Cove, as a private utopia with its own rules of behaviour and architecture over-seen by a resident caretaker.

Between Smuggler Cove and Graf-ton Bay, the coast is pretty rugged with

A.G.R. Seymour

Seymour Bay was named after A.G.R. Seymour, the original home-steader there. He was said to be the disgraced tutor of a noble English family with whose daughter he had fallen in love. As they couldn't marry, he sailed around the Horn to Bowen Island. There he built a log cabin where he lived as a hermit with only his dog for company. Once a year he rowed to Vancouver to buy books, and once a year—tall, barefoot and unkempt—he took tea with the politely correct Cowans, who pronounced him well educated and able to "swear perfectly." In 1906, he sold his property to them and moved off the island.

Arriving at Bowen Island. Photo: Peter Waddington.

few places to get ashore. Little Rock, just north of Galbraith Bay, is where author Ethel Wilson slept on the veranda of her refurbished old house. In her book *The Innocent Traveller,* Topaz sleeps out on the deck but flies back inside when she hears near her head the unaccustomed sounds of deer munching and, in the distance, a log boom squeaking.

Craggy Hutt Island off Galbraith Bay is privately owned. It has only one landing, from which a rough road goes straight up to the dwellings above. Between Galbraith Bay and tiny King Edward Bay, there's a long stretch of rocky coast with views over to Keats and the Pasley Islands (see Trip Nos. 42, 43). Fred Malkin named the bay King Edward because he bought it in 1910, the year His Majesty died. Strewing foxglove seeds, Malkin used to hike over to Cowan Point to visit the rest of his family. His grandchildren still vacation there.

Bowen Bay is where painter Claude Breeze has a house whose veranda is washed by the tide.

A nautical mile south of Tunstall Bay, Cape Roger Curtis was named by Captain G.H. Richards after one of the captains who served with Admiral Howe in his 1794 victory over the French. Hidden among the large rocks just before the lighthouse there's a tiny sheltered beach with a flat spot behind it. Kayakers have camped there in the past but now it's off limits and there is nowhere else to camp on the island.

There are few landing places for the next couple of nautical miles till you reach Fairweather Bay. Between it and Cowan Point are a number of small bays which were all named by the Cowan family one day in 1907 when they rowed along them. Some of the names have changed since then. They called Fairweather Bay Winnipeg Bay, as their nieces came from that city. Echo Cove was so named because an Alpine Club member who was with them yodeled and received an echo. Arbutus Bay was previously called Wilson Bay. Konishi Bay was named after a favourite Japanese caretaker; Alder Cove, because of its trees; Union Cove, for the boundary between the Cowan and Malkin properties; and Trinity Bay, for the school Ethel Bryant Wilson attended in England.

Beyond Seymour Bay, Apodaca Provincial Park was donated to the province in 1954 by Vancouver city archivist Major J.S. Matthews in memory of his son who was killed in an accident at the age of 22. Apodaca was the name the Spaniards gave to Bowen Island.

Just before Snug Cove, Dorman Bay was the scene of a near accident before the days of radar. In dense fog, young Ernie Dorman heard a steamer approach too close. Thinking of the *Titanic,* he ran down to the beach and played "Nearer my God to Thee" on his trumpet. The ship retreated.

Crippen Park in Snug Cove has a sandy beach and a trail to a lookout.

42 Pasley Islands

Difficulty Intermediate conditions – moderate risk
Distance 7–8 nmi
Duration 3–4 hours
Charts No. 3526 Howe Sound 1:40,000
Tides on Point Atkinson
Currents none

These delightful little islands, whose name is pronounced Paisley, are out of sight of Vancouver and have very familiar views to anyone who has watched the *Beachcombers* TV series.

Paddling considerations

- Strong outflow winds in the afternoon can be a problem at any season.
- Squamish winds of up to 40 knots increase toward the mouth of the inlet and out into the Strait of Georgia. Listen for reports from the Pam Rock buoy.
- Any area in Howe Sound with a long fetch, like Collingwood Channel, can build waves of 1.5–2.5 m, especially when winds and tide oppose tide or river flow.
- Crossing of Collingwood Channel to Worlcombe Island 1.4 nmi

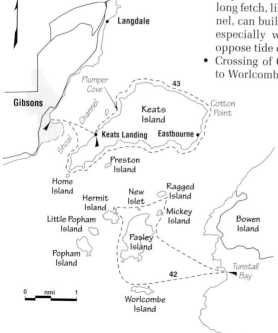

"The New Beachcombers" film used this boat as the "Persephone" which Nick Adonidas' heir (and Peter!) found.
Photo: Peter Waddington.

The route

Launch at Tunstall Bay and cross Collingwood Channel. Sometimes yachts have races through here and are more preoccupied with getting every bit of speed out of their boats than looking out for kayakers. Cross in a tight group without causing the sailors to have to change course or you'll be highly unpopular. If it's too rough to cross, paddle north along the shore of Bowen to visit Hutt Island or, if conditions have improved, cross to Mickey Island and explore the Pasley Islands from there.

The Steller's sea lions that used to inhabit a rock off the west side of Worlcombe Island have disappeared when their population shrank. Roaring, they used to charge kayakers who approached too close so we stayed back as they were bigger than we were. Now, the rock is inhabited by seals.

Marine biology watchdog

The white building on Popham Island is a research centre operated by the Vancouver Aquarium. In addition to studying the marine natural history of Howe Sound, they also monitor the biological effects of local industries like the Howe Sound Pulp Mill. Other studies include glass sponges, prawn nurseries, and bull kelp.

Popham Island has a seal population who like their privacy. No wonder as they are under acute observation from the Vancouver Aquarium's research station on the island. Landing on Worlcombe is difficult and not encouraged due to the fire hazard.

Ragged Island. Photo: Peter Waddington.

In addition to seals, expect to see mergansers with large broods of chicks, kingfishers chittering as they flit from branch to branch above the water and shy Harlequin ducks.

Almost all the islands have one or more cottages on them so stay below the high tide line if you land. Some cottages are being used by the third or fourth generation of owners. The small island at the north end of Hermit has a sign welcoming picnickers to its tiny arbutus forest and sandy beaches. Other islands discourage drop-in visitors.

~

When the Bell-Irving family invited the Vancouver Ocean Touring Kayak Association (VOTKA), the predecessor of the Sea Kayak Association (SKABC), for an overnight trip, our hostess, who was just starting a catering business, instructed everyone to bring different ingredients for an evening feast. Soon we had an incredible buffet of honey garlic chicken pieces garnished with salal leaves. Twenty years later, a guest from Nova Scotia who came on the trip still talks about his wonderful experience. He forgot to bring his asthma puffer but never needed it even when briefly chased by the Steller's sea lions.

~

Mickey Island, northeast of Pasley Island, was named after Malcom Mc-Bean (Mickey) Bell-Irving who died in the 1914-18 War. He and his sister used to vacation on Pasley and named Hermit Island after a tall Norwegian recluse who lived on fish and dressed in seal skins. A tiny driftwood cabin, surrounded by seal skulls, provided his only shelter.

Elevenses at Ragged Island. Photo: Peter Waddington.

Off Worlcombe Island, Pasley Group. Photo: Peter Waddington.

The cove on the northeast side of Pasley Island was a whaling station at the end of the nineteenth century. Visit the Gibsons' Museum to see a few artefacts pertaining to it. "Portuguese Joe" Silvey and three partners: Harry Trim, Peter Smith and Abel Douglas operated it. They built little houses in the bay and a wharf for Douglas' schooner. Douglas' wife was Hawaiian and those of the other three were Indian. Silvey's wife, Khaltinaht, was Chief Kiapilano's granddaughter. Her second daughter, Josephine, was born on Pasley Island in 1872.

Much of the Beachcombers TV series and subsequent movie were shot among the islands so you'll recognize places and even boats. Once we found Relic's boat Persephone, having been a prop in the new Beachcombers' film, ashore on Ragged Island. This island has an intriguing cross cemented onto a rock. The inscription on it reads "Bates exiled 1968-1983." Martin Clarke, owner of Bowen Island Sea Kayaking, thinks "he may have been Richard Bates, a Welsh remittance man who died on Bowen Island 3-4 years ago. He ran a water taxi from Bowen Bay to the Pasleys, built docks for people and resided on Preston Island near Keats for some time." Clarke notes that Ragged Island has been used for other film productions. Once it sported a plywood lighthouse which confused navigators. He's seen a hanged man, lawnmowers on rocks, etc. and he remembers potato guns being fired at kayakers.

Log salvaging is still a viable business for a lucky few. About 100 people in the Vancouver Log Salvage District between Port Hardy and Victoria make their living at it. A more scattered number live outside this area.

Former Vancouver Archivist Major J.S. Matthews thought Popham and Home Islands were named after Rear Admiral Sir Home Riggs Popham, author of Coast Signals (1803). It seems a reasonable supposition.

If you want a longer day, add on a circumnavigation of nearby Keats Island. See Trip No. 43 but check wind conditions in Barfleur Passage as they are part of the Howe Sound inflow-outflow system.

43 Keats Island

Difficulty Intermediate conditions – moderate risk
Distance 9 nmi
Duration 4–5 hours
Charts No. 3526 Howe Sound 1:40,000
Tides on Point Atkinson
Currents none

Once across Shoal Channel this is an easy day paddle from Gibsons or a longer one from Tunstall Bay on Bowen Island. See sketchmap on page 215.

Paddling considerations

- Strong outflow winds in the afternoon can be a problem at any season.
- Any area in Howe Sound with a long fetch, like Collingwood Channel, can build waves of 1.5–2.5 m, especially when winds and tide oppose tide or river flow.
- Shallow Shoal Passage is often choppy, especially when winds oppose tide. Crossing from Steep Bluff to Keats is 0.5 nmi.
- Chop around Home Island; westerlies are bad in Barfleur Passage in summer.

The route

Launch at Gibsons Harbour and cross Shoal Channel. Being less than 2 m deep, Shoal Channel can be very choppy. If so, consider going either farther out into the Strait of Georgia where the water is deeper or up Shoal Channel. After the crossing, paddle north past the dock at Keats Landing where the Gibsons water taxi deposits its passengers and the Baptist Church has a camp.

Charlie Bentall, the developer who built the Bentall Centre in Vancouver, had a farm here. Whenever he would go into the city to chair board meetings, he would wear bib overalls, claiming that business suits were only for men who had not yet made their fortunes. In winter, he would keep his Dominion Construction workers busy building cabins for the Salvation Army camp and doing other good works on the island.

Beyond the tiny Shelter Islets lies the popular yacht anchorage at Plumper Cove. Ashore, the green sward above the shingle beach is apt to be doggy heaven, but on the left there are 20 gravel campsites and a short trail to Observatory Point with views over Howe Sound.

Round the top of the island you'll be able to look left up Thornbrough Channel. You may get wind from that direction. The next section of coastline is rocky with few landings.

The large green open space on the north, which you see from the ferry, used to be UBC Professor C.H. Corkum's farm which favoured students were invited to visit. At Cotton Point the coast turns south toward the small cottage community of Eastbourne. If you land beside the dock, you may explore on foot. The water taxi also can come in here.

Keats Island from Hopkins Landing.

As you leave Collingwood Channel, Barfleur Passage can still be windy, so stick to the shore, where you will find several pocket beaches. The second last one before Home Island is where the CBC sank five boats in the course of filming *The Beachcombers*.

At low tide a shingle spit connects Home Island to Keats. It is a good place to stop and assess the sea conditions for the return journey. The shallow depth of Shoal Channel can cause a nasty chop.

The Beachcombers

The Beachcombers was a television series about a group of ingenious coastal characters who made a living rescuing stray logs off the beaches and selling them. A few people still earn their living this way but their numbers are much diminished. The series, starring Bruno Gerussi, ran on CBC TV for 387 episodes from 1972–90 and has aired in 35 countries.

In November 2002, the CBC premiered a two-hour film called *The New Beachcombers*, which was an updated story featuring some of the original characters and some new ones.

Waiting at Eastbourne, Keats Island, for the wind to die down in Collingwood Channel. Photo: Peter Waddington.

Bowyer Island.

44 Bowyer Island

Difficulty Intermediate conditions – moderate risk
Distance 4–5.5 nmi depending on the launch
Duration 2–3 hours
Charts No. 3526 Howe Sound 1:40,000
Tides on Point Atkinson
Currents none

This is a short trip to visit the seals on the north side of the island.

Paddling considerations

- Strong outflow winds in the afternoon can be a problem at any season.
- Squamish winds of up to 40 knots increase toward the mouth of the inlet and out into the Strait of Georgia. Listen for reports from the Pam Rock buoy.
- Any area in Howe Sound with a long fetch, like Queen Charlotte Channel or Collingwood Channel, can build waves of 1.5–2.5 m, especially when winds and tide oppose tide or river flow.
- Crossing between the Mainland and Bowyer is 1.1 nmi from Sunset Marina and 1.7 nmi from Lions Bay.

The route

Launch at Lions Bay or Sunset Beach. Paddle along the shore till you're opposite the island and then cross. The south side has some rocky beaches sheltered from the winds out of Squamish and overlooked by cottages. The north side is cliffs at the bottom of which seals bask on the rocks.

This is a short trip, and in calm weather you may want to make another crossing to explore Finisterre Island and Hood Point on the north end of Bowen (3 nmi round trip; see Trip No. 41). If so, watch for the Horseshoe Bay to Langdale ferries.

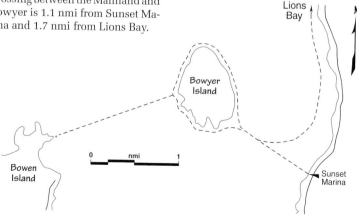

45 Gambier Island

Difficulty Intermediate conditions – moderate risk
Distance 35 nmi to explore all the bays
Duration 1–2 days or longer
Charts No. 3526 Howe Sound 1:40,000
Tides on Point Atkinson
Currents Although the main Squamish River current flows out through Montague Channel, some of it is deflected into Thornbrough Channel.

Larger than Bowen Island and having a smaller population, Gambier is wilder and quieter with four places where camping is allowed. Although the north side is exposed to Squamish squalls, the four inlets on the south side are sheltered.

Paddling considerations
- Strong outflow winds in the afternoon can be a problem at any season.

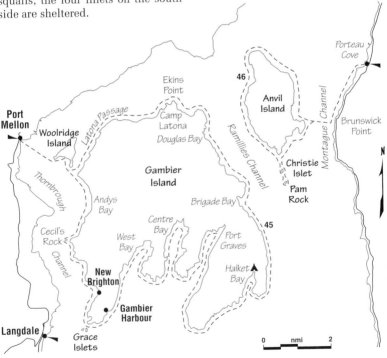

- Squamish winds of up to 40 knots increase toward the mouth of the Sound and out into the Strait of Georgia. Listen for reports from the Pam Rock buoy. Though less of a problem around Gambier than some areas of Howe Sound, Ramillies Channel and the south side of Gambier can be affected by them.
- Any area in Howe Sound with a long fetch can build waves of 1.5–2.5 m, especially when winds and tide oppose tide or river flow.

The route

Launch in Port Mellon at the foot of Dunham Road or at Hopkins Landing. Some people launch at Porteau Cove and come across via Anvil Island (see Trip No. 45), but the Montague Channel winds funneling straight out of the Squamish Valley are fiercer and less predictable than those in Thornbrough Channel. People have drowned making that crossing.

From Port Mellon, paddle across Thornbrough Channel to Woolridge Island. A small beach at the south end of Latona Passage makes a good rest stop. Then head through the in-water log sort in Latona Passage and around the north end of Gambier.

Ekins Point has both a yacht club and a large Christian summer camp which for 40 years was operated as Camp Latona by the Roman Catholic Diocese of Vancouver. In 1996, they sold it to FIRS, a Christian evangelical organization operating out of Washington State which owns several other camps. Behind the camp a logging road provides a great 1½-hour return hike up to Gambier Lake through mature second growth forest. Try yodeling over the lake and listen for the echo. There is a camp spot beside the lake.

Douglas Bay on Ramillies Channel is another popular camp spot, with water available from Gambier Creek, which should be filtered or boiled. You look straight across at the massive cliffs of Anvil Island and the majestic Lions so beloved of Vancouverites. A couple of nautical miles farther on, Brigade Bay has a camp spot but no water. Halkett Bay, a short bay on the south side of the island, is a provincial park and the only official campsite on the island.

If time is short, you may have to miss the three deep bays on the south side of the island, which would be a pity as they are sheltered from Squamish squalls. They also have more cottages. Port Graves, called Long Bay by the locals, contains Camp Artaban, which has been an Anglican church camp since 1923. It has an interesting open-air chapel. Centre Bay has out-stations for the Royal Vancouver and West Vancouver yacht clubs. Several other sailing clubs also use the bay, tying up to the log booms and rowing their dinghies ashore for communal bonfires and feasts. A trail leads up into the interior of the island from the head of it.

West Bay has an unpaved road over to New Brighton on Thornbrough Channel. The estuary of Whispering Creek is muddy quicksand, so land and leave at high tide. At low tide, the sad remnants of boats that got stuck are visible. One of them was a five-masted barque, the *Thomas Lipton*. Gambier Harbour south of the entrance to West Bay is a good

Enumeration by Canoe

In the mid 1980s, long-time Gambier residents Bette Cooper and Carol Constable enumerated 78 people on Gambier by canoe—a Sportspal with a sail and a few leaky rivets.

"It took three days and two nights to do it," said Cooper. "We went into every little nook and cranny. One person met us with a shotgun, so we told him we wouldn't do him and paddled on. Every so often we stopped for Carol to light a cigarette while I bailed the canoe. We spent one night at Ekins Point and the other at Hope Point. In West Bay, the Coast Guard came over and we explained what we were doing, but I didn't tell them we had a leak.

"On election day, everyone came by boat to Gambier Harbour and toiled up "Cardiac Hill" to vote in the community hall at the top. We had hot soup for them and coffee and cocoa. Everyone sat around the warm stove and had a get-together.

"Later on, that hall burned down somehow when we had a party. The new one was built at New Brighton on land donated by Helen Negroponte. We called her the Island Treasure because everyone loved her and she had lived there for 45 years. Gambier is a wonderful community with a fabulous craft fair in August." Cooper lived on the island for 20 years, first in a tent, then in a trailer and then in the house she finally built. Her message to visitors is:

"Take your garbage back with you."

place to stop. You can hike up the hill to where the community hall once stood and over to New Brighton or to Avalon Bay.

The tiny Grace Islands are a joy to explore but the tide drowned the woman they are named after and her body was never found. Little Avalon Bay can provide welcome shelter from the wind and a good view of the Langdale ferry terminal. It is the preserve of the wealthy Killam family after whom one of the peaks on the island is named.

New Brighton is where the ferry comes in. Nearby, the Gambier Island General Store has "everything from anchovies to zucchini" as well as meals.

Cotton Bay, into which Mannion Creek runs, has an interesting old homestead to explore. One of the points beyond has a cave-like overhang in it. In 1979, Cecil's Rock (also called Steamboat Rock) was proclaimed an official Mariner's Retreat where it is legal to scatter the ashes of cremated mariners. It is marked with a cross on top. Out of respect, visitors are requested not to land on it.

Andys Bay has lots of log booms. It is the last one before Woolridge Island and the return journey to Port Mellon.

46 Anvil Island, including Christie Islet and the Pam Rocks

Difficulty Intermediate conditions – moderate risk
Distance 13.8 nmi
   Porteau Cove to Anvil Island 2.8 nmi
   Circumnavigation of Anvil Island 8 nmi
   Irby Point to Christie Islet and Pam Rocks round trip 3 nmi
Duration 5–6 hours
Charts No. 3526 Howe Sound 1:40,000
Tides on Point Atkinson
Currents The main river current flows south from "Stick Point" and into Montague
   Channel though part of it branches off into Thornbrough Channel.

Anvil Island is that big tall hunk of rock in the middle of Howe Sound. Its high point, Leading Peak, reaches 754 m. The cliffs on the west side are fascinating to paddle along and there's the added interest of viewing the bird and seal life on Christie Islet and the Pam Rock. See sketchmap on page 224.

Paddling considerations
- Strong outflow winds in the afternoon can be a problem at any season, especially in Montague Channel.
- Squamish winds of up to 40 knots increase toward the mouth of the inlet and out into the Strait of Georgia. Listen for reports from the Pam Rock buoy just south of Anvil Island.
- Any area in Howe Sound with a long fetch, like Queen Charlotte Channel or Collingwood Channel, can build waves of 1.5–2.5 m, especially when winds and tide oppose tide or river flow.
- Landing places are very limited. Stow your lunch where you can reach it.

The route
Choose a calm day, launch at Porteau and paddle south to Brunswick Point. Enjoy the views up and down Montague Channel as you cross to Anvil. When you arrive, there's a small rocky beach at the south end where landing is possible. The reddish rocks on the beach are the remains of a long-gone brickworks. Behind the beach there used to be a holly farm.

Cormorants nesting, Pam Rock.
Photo: Peter Waddington.

Light beacon and weather station, Pam Rock. Photo: Peter Waddington.

Once on a very hot day when swimming here in the blissful shade of the cliffs, I realized I was not alone. Two tiny birds came within a metre of my head busily nodding their heads like sewing machine needles, and swimming in circles. I was the least of their concerns. Afterwards, I identified them as red-necked phalaropes (Phalaropus lobatus). They were using their spin-and-dab technique to stir up plankton on the water's surface. Although they are supposed to be common, I have rarely seen them since. Look for them offshore where kelp gathers in tidelines.

Paddling around the north end of the island gives views up to Squamish and Woodfibre. Look for sea stars and tunicates on the cliffs and down in the water. On the far side, narrow Ramillies Channel may tempt you to cross over to Gambier Island but I can never bear to leave the Anvil cliffs to do this.

At the southern tip of Anvil, continue south to Christie Islet and Pam Rock. Both are home to numerous harbour seals and gulls.

Returning to Anvil, there is a small bay containing some cottages. When I paddled this area a caretaker lived here. If the wind has come up, you may have to land here and wait till it drops in the evening so that you can cross back to Porteau.

Hopkins Landing.

47 Gibsons to Port Mellon

Difficulty Intermediate conditions – moderate risk
Distance 10 nmi
Duration 3–4 hours
Charts No. 3526 Howe Sound 1:40,000
Tides on Point Atkinson
Currents none

This paddle provides an unusual perspective on the town of Gibsons and the Langdale ferry as well as what used to be a number of separate communities at Grantham's, Hopkins and Williamson's Landings. Once the cottages run out, the coastline becomes very rocky with coves full of log booms.

Paddling considerations

- The tide runs strongly through Shoal Channel, so it's best to start out at slack or on an incoming tide.
- Strong outflow winds can be a problem at any season. They are less strong in Thornbrough Channel, but don't underestimate them here either.
- Squamish winds of up to 40 knots increase toward the mouth of the inlet and out into the Strait of Georgia. Listen for reports from the Pam Rock buoy just south of Anvil Island. They should be less in this area.
- Any area in Howe Sound with a long fetch, like Thornbrough Channel or Collingwood Channel, can build waves of 1.5–2.5 m, especially when winds and tide oppose tide or river flow.

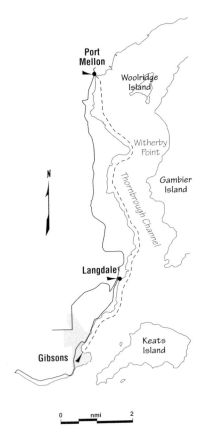

The route

Launch at Gibsons Harbour and after sneaking in and out of the marina floats to inspect the sail and power boats, paddle north past Molly's Reach, home base of the TV series *The Beachcombers*.

At Grantham's Landing in 1909, Frederick Charles Grantham, a Vancouver processor of lime juice, built a summer cottage, subdivided his land and built roads, a pier and a water system.

A nautical mile past Soames Point, Hopkins Landing is named after George H. Hopkins, a retired engineer who built a cottage here and ran a tow boating business with his sons. The red-and-black-funneled ships of the Union Steamship Company called here on a regular schedule. Just beyond is the Salvation Army's Camp Sunrise, which "provides spiritual and physical refreshment" for ages 7–99.

As you approach the Langdale ferry terminal watch for large ferries and small water taxis travelling at high speed. Give way to both. Cormorants often sit on the pilings by the ferry drying their wings and socializing. Just north of the ferry dock a sandy beach provides an easy landing, but pull your boat up beyond the reach of the ferry wash. Then stop to watch a ferry load or unload. The Langdale family homesteaded on this site in the 1890s. It is now Smith Cove Municipal Park.

Boom boat in dry dock showing the cage which protects its powerful propeller.

Sorting logs south of Witherby Point.

Another mile of rocky cliffs and there's the YMCA's Camp Elphinstone. Since 1907 this establishment, with its 1 km of oceanfront, has been "guiding young people through experiences and creating memories that last a lifetime." It is followed by Williamson's Landing. Williamson was another settler like Grantham, Hopkins and Langdale.

Between here and the steep cliffs of Witherby Point and beyond to the Dunham Road launch there are lots of log booms. Expect to hear the constant growl and groan of boom boats as they perform their ballet pushing and pulling the logs into position. You may be lucky enough to see a self-dumping log barge in action. The barge dumps its load by pumping water into the tanks under one side of its deck. This takes about 30 minutes. When the deck is at a sufficiently steep angle, the logs suddenly slide off into the ocean. Don't be too close when this happens.

At the end of the booming area, look for some pilings, a small clutch of dinghies turned upside down above the beach and a rough road down to the water. This is the launch at the end of Dunham Road.

Beyond it, you'll see the Port Mellon pulp and paper mill, opened in 1907–09 and named after Captain Henry Augustus Mellon, R.N., who was the company's first vice-president. The mill was not accessible by road until 1953. The nearby Seaside Hotel preceded the mill and was serviced by the same Captain Cates who ran trips to Bowen Island. In 1958 it ceased to be a hotel and became a pub till the mid 1960s. Now the site is under part of the mill, which has been renamed the Howe Sound Pulp & Paper Mill.

48 Port Mellon to Squamish

Difficulty Intermediate conditions – moderate risk
Distance 19.3 nmi
Port Mellon to McNab Creek 4.3 nmi
McNabb Creek to the Defence Islands 5 nmi
Defence Islands to Woodfibre 5.5 nmi
Woodfibre to Squamish 4.5 nmi
Duration 8–10 hours
Charts No. 3526 Howe Sound 1:40,000
Tides on Point Atkinson
Currents The closer you get to Squamish the more the river current affects you, especially during the summer runoff period. The main river current, often looking white and silty, emerges along the dyke heading out into the Sound till it hits the shore just north of Watts Point. A large clockwise back eddy affects the shore between Woodfibre and the river mouth. From Watts Point, the main current is deflected across to Woodfibre and runs down the coast to "Stick Point" (a local name for the unmarked point on the western shore due west of Minaty Bay and Daisy Creek on the eastern shore), where it leaves the shore and flows down the centre of the Sound. Along the opposite shore, there's a weak return current as a back eddy flows northward to Watts Point.

This rocky shoreline has few places to get ashore except McNabb Creek and there is no road access till you reach Squamish.

Paddling considerations

- Strong outflow winds in the afternoon can be a problem at any season. Between Watts Point and Squamish they blow about 25 knots and produce a short chop.
- The river estuary, which you have to cross, is one of the top ten windsurfing destinations in the world. Windsurfers travel even faster than ferries and are not always looking out for kayaks, so give them a wide berth.
- Squamish winds increase toward the mouth of the Sound, where they may blow up to 40 knots continuing out into the Strait of Georgia. Listen for reports from the Pam Rock buoy just south of Anvil Island.
- Any area in Howe Sound with a long fetch, like Thornbrough Channel or Collingwood Channel, can build waves of 1.5–2.5 m, especially when winds and tide oppose tide or river flow.

The route

Launch at Port Mellon. If a support vehicle is doing a shuttle to Squamish, it may take almost as long for it to reach its destination as for you to do the paddle.

Before paddling northward, take a moment to look across at Mount Liddell (903 m) and Mount Killam (844 m) on Gambier Island as well as the peaks above the City of Vancouver.

Within a mile of Port Mellon there is a nick in the coastline which forms a tiny private cove that is interesting to explore. When I visited it some time ago, a barge rotting and overgrown with salal and moss plugged the rocky beach at the head of it, so it may not be possible to go ashore.

The shoreline between here and McNabb Creek is extremely rocky. Watch for river otters and seals as you pass. McNabb Creek flows out of a wide valley onto a shingle beach 0.8 nmi long. At the west end of the beach, a logging road runs back into the valley for about 15 km but does not connect with the main highway system. Somewhere around the boat basin that has been excavated on the east side of the creek, there is a hard-to-find pictograph. At the turn of the century Asian labourers worked in the logging camp. Occasionally artefacts from that era are to be found. It's a good excuse for a stop.

Potlatch Creek has a beach where landing is possible. On 133 acres here, the Vancouver Boys and Girls Clubs have operated Camp Potlatch from June–August every year since 1944. In 1999, they had their first 1,000-camper year. The camp caters to ages 7–17, including physically and mentally challenged campers.

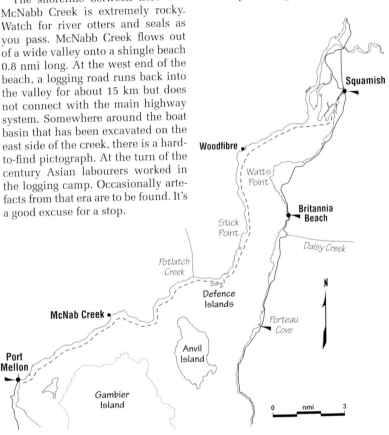

Howe Sound mill at Port Mellon.

If winds are calm, detour out to the Defence Islands and enjoy the view down to Anvil Island and the mouth of the Sound. In the distance, tiny B.C. ferries zip in and out of Horseshoe Bay. Watch for strong easterly currents in the Defence Islands that are not connected to the tides.

About 2 nmi farther on, a tiny isthmus with beaches on either side makes a good stop.

At the next point, not named on the chart but known locally as "Stick Point," and opposite Britannia Bay, expect a head current[15] between here and Woodfibre. This is caused by the outflow from the Squamish River and when combined with an ebb tide could make paddling tough. In this case, cross the Sound to Britannia Beach, where an anticlockwise back eddy will take you up to Watts Point. There you meet the river current again, which, if you let it, will carry you back across to Woodfibre.

At Woodfibre, watch for the ferry coming across the inlet. The workers at the pulp mill live in Squamish and Vancouver, not near the mill. In case of emergency, ask them to take you across to the east shore, where you could thumb a ride into Squamish.

From Woodfibre to the Squamish River estuary another anticlockwise back eddy will assist your progress.

Before crossing the estuary of the Squamish River, estimate the strength of the wind. If the afternoon outflow wind has begun you may need to wait till evening. Use this time to explore the swampy area on the west side. It has lots of interesting channels. When making the crossing you may have to ferry glide across the current.

The Squamish boat launch where you take out is up the Mamquam Channel. This becomes calmer as you proceed up it.

49 Whyte Cliff Park to Porteau Cove

Difficulty Intermediate conditions – moderate risk
Distance 12.4 nmi

        Whyte Cliff Park to Sunset Beach 3.1 nmi
        Sunset Beach to Lions Bay 3 nmi
        Lions Bay to Brunswick Point 4.5 nmi
        Brunswick Point to Porteau Cove 1.8 nmi

Duration 4–6 hours
Charts No. 3526 Howe Sound 1:40,000
Tides on Point Atkinson
Currents none

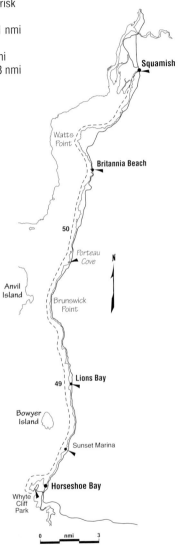

A trip along a rocky shoreline with wonderful views of the islands in Howe Sound and an opportunity to see all the private beaches you can't reach by road.

Paddling considerations

- Strong outflow winds in the afternoon can be a problem at any season.
- Squamish winds of up to 40 knots increase toward the mouth of the Sound and out into the Strait of Georgia. Listen for reports from the Pam Rock buoy just south of Anvil Island.
- Any area in Howe Sound with a long fetch, like Queen Charlotte Channel, can build waves of 1.5–2.5m, especially when winds and tide oppose tide or river flow.
- Landing places are very limited. Keep your lunch where you can reach it.

The route

Launch at Whyte Cliff Park and paddle north. As you come into Horseshoe Bay watch out for the ferries. Stay back from these vessels, as their powerful bow and stern thrusting engines can inadvertently crush an unsuspecting kayak against pilings or other boats.

Leaving Horseshoe Bay.

From the ferry dock onward, the railway and the road run close to the shore. The railway was built in 1956, the road two years later.

Sunset Marina is 1.5 nmi north of Horseshoe Bay. Paddle in to see another potential launch, which will be useful if Bowyer Island is your destination (see Trip No. 44). You'll get good views of it as you paddle along the coast on this trip and you may want to detour out to investigate it. There's also a potential launch marked on the chart at Newman Creek but it is private.

This is a fairly wild bit of coastline so watch for river otters, harlequin ducks, black oystercatchers, bald eagles and seals.

Lions Bay is 2.5 nmi farther on. It has a marina and a small park where residents launch and keep their boats locked to a rack. Once, the creek flowing through Lions Bay burst its banks and drowned a couple of teenagers. A lot of construction has been done to en-sure that this never happens again, but after a heavy rain, don't get too close to where the creek meets the ocean.

After Lions Bay the distant Pam Rock and Christie Islet south of Anvil Island look closer than they are. Save them for another day. Alberta Bay can give welcome shelter if there's a headwind. Continue on to Brunswick Point. In the early 20th century, Brunswick Beach was an exclusive camping community, but it is now part of Lions Bay municipality. The landing is good but there are a lot of cottages. Both wind and water are squeezed through narrow Montague Channel, which at times will mean increased speeds for both. Porteau Cove and the take-out is 1.8 nmi farther on. Somewhere along here you'll pass a camp which groups can book. Sometimes paddlers with disabilities enjoy it for a weekend. As you approach, if you see bubbles coming to the surface, there's likely a scuba diver beneath you.

50 Porteau Cove to Squamish

Difficulty Intermediate conditions – moderate risk
Distance 10.5 nmi
            Porteau Cove to Britannia Beach 4.5 nmi
            Britannia Beach to Squamish 6 nmi
Duration 3–4 hours
Charts No. 3526 Howe Sound 1:40,000
Tides on Point Atkinson
Currents See trip 48 for currents close to Squamish

If you've done Trip No. 49, you may want to continue with this one so that you can see the whole of Howe Sound.

Paddling considerations

- Strong outflow winds in the afternoon can be a problem at any season.
- Squamish winds of up to 40 knots increase toward the mouth of the Sound and out into the Strait of Georgia. Listen for reports from the Pam Rock buoy just south of Anvil Island.
- Any area in Howe Sound with a long fetch, like Queen Charlotte Channel, can build waves of 1.5–2.5m, especially when winds and tide oppose tide or river flow.
- Landing places are very limited. Stow your lunch within reach.

The route

Launch at Porteau Cove. Between Porteau and Watts Point, there's a big back eddy from the Squamish River current, which will give you an extra boost. At Furry Creek there are pictographs up on the rocks behind the old dock. There are gravel pits at Furry Creek and Minaty Bay. Beyond these, Britannia Mines dominates the landscape.

From the unnamed point to the north of Watts Point to Darrell Bay, the main outflow of the Squamish River runs along the coast.

From Darrell Bay to the mouth of the Mamquam Channel on the east side of Squamish, there is likely to be a weak back eddy. The Mamquam Channel is fed by both the Mamquam and the Stawamish Rivers but it's only about a mile to reach the boat launch on the west bank.

Useful Contacts

Kayak Outfitters

Most of these offer or can arrange rentals, lessons and tours. Ask about their instructors' and guides' qualifications.

Bowen Island Kayaking
Tel. 1-800-60-kayak
www.bowenislandkayaking.com

Misty Isles Adventures (Cortes)
Tel. 250-935-6756
www.island.net/~mistyis/

Pedals and Paddles (Sechelt Inlet)
Tel. 604-885-6440
www.pedalspaddles.com

Mitchell's Canoe, Kayak and Snowshoe Sales & Rentals
8654 101 Hwy S.
Powell River, B.C. V8A 5C1
Tel. 1-866-90-CANOE
www.canoeingbc.com

Powell River Sea Kayaks
(Okeover and Lund)
Tel. 1-866-617-4444
www.bcseakayak.com

Sunshine Kayaking (Gibsons)
Molly's Lane
Tel. 604-886-9760
www.sunshinekayaking.com

Terracentric Coastal Adventures
(Lund)
Tel. 604-583-7900
www.terracentricadventures.com

Y-Knot Camp and Charter (Okeover)
2960 D'Angio Road
Tel. 604-483-3243

General Tourism Information

Including current lists of campsites and B&Bs.

Big Pacific Tourism Information
5571 Nickerson Road
Sechelt, B.C. V0N 3A0
Tel. 604-885-5913
www.bigpacific.com and
www.thesunshinecoast.com

Cortes Island has no tourist info-centre. Instead, try the following websites:
http://www.cortesisland.com/tide-line/index.html and
http://oberon.ark.com/~johnwil

Gibsons & District Chamber of Commerce
P.O. Box 1190, Sunnycrest Mall Lot
Highway 101
Gibsons, B.C. V0N 1V0
Tel. 604-886-2325
www.gibsonschamber.com

Pender Harbour Information Centre
P.O. Box 265 Madeira Park,
BC V0N 2H0
Tel. 604-873-6337
www.penderharbour.ca

Powell River Visitor Info Centre
4690A Marine Ave
Powell River, B.C. V8A 2L1
Tel. 604-485-4701
info@discoverpowellriver.com
www.discoverpowellriver.com

Sechelt & District Chamber of Commerce
PO Box 360
#102 - 5700 Cowrie Street
Sechelt B.C. V0N 3A0
Tel. 604-885-0662
secheltchamber@dccnet.com
www.secheltchamber.bc.ca

Camping

In the past many people have paddled from Vancouver or Seattle to Alaska. In the area covered by this book, this is becoming increasingly difficult because the conurbation of Vancouver reaches all the way to Lund. Waterfront cottages and houses line the shore all the way. Official campsites are scarce to non-existent. Paddlers embarking on this trip will be forced to guerilla camp in likely uninhabited areas, arriving at dusk, lighting no fires, showing no lights and leaving at dawn. The best places to look for legal campsites are on islands such as Thormanby, Nelson, Texada, Savary, the Copelands and West Redonda. Any place facing the prevailing southeast or northwest winds may be tough to land or leave without braving surf.

Waterfront Campsites and B&Bs from Gibsons to Egmont
As these change from year to year, get the latest list from the Sechelt and Gibsons Visitors Bureaus.

Bonniebrook Lodge B&B
& attached Chez Philippe Restaurant
1532 Oceanbeach Esplanade
Gibsons, B.C. V0N 1V5
Tel. 1-877-290-9916
info@bonniebrook.com
www.bonniebrook.com

Waterfront Campsites and B&Bs from Saltery Bay to Lund
As these change from year to year, get the latest list from the Powell River Visitor Info Centre. Take collapsible wheels with you for those that are a distance from launches. Sometimes B&Bs situated away from the water will pick up kayakers and their boats and deliver them back in the morning. It pays to ask if this service is available.

Saltery Bay Provincial Campground
42 sites, most away from the water.
Tel. 604-487-4305 or 1-800-689-9025
From the Saltery Bay ferry, drive north on Highway 101 for 1 km. It's on the left.

Kent's Beach Cottages/RV Park
20 campsites including four near the water. Some beachfront cabins. Often full in summer.
14171 Hwy 101
Tel. 604-487-9386 Fax: 604-487-9293
host@kentsbeach.com
www.kentsbeach.com

Seabreeze Cottages and Campground
They want you to camp 200 m from the beach.
Tel. 604-487-9531 or 1-888-771-7776
seabreezeresort@shaw.ca
www.seabreezeresortbc.com

Sandy Shores B&B
1131 Palm Beach Road
Powell River, B.C. V8A 5C1
Tel. 604-487-4402
Right on the water at sea level. Some camping possibilities.

Lang Bay Lifestyles Motel Ltd.
On the water but landing is easier in the adjacent cove.
Tel. 604-487-0111
www.langbay.ca

Suncatcher B&B
8853 Stark Rd.
Tel. 604-487-1087
suncatcherBB@shaw.ca

Malaspina House B&B[16]
9187 Hwy 101
Tel. 604-487-0043 Cell 604-483-8006
malaspinahouse@shaw.ca

B&B by the Sea
Right on the water at sea level.
8711 Hwy 101
Tel. 1-877-711-1377 or 604-487-1377
www.armourtech.com/bbbythesea

Garnet Rock Ocean Front Mobile Home Park
They have pleasant, grassy tent sites at the top of steps up from the beach.
8425 Hwy 101, Black Point
Tel. 604-487-9535

Willingdon Beach Municipal Campsite
On the beach.
Tel. 604-485-2242
www.willingdonbeach.ca

Hog's Heaven B&B
At beach level at Klahannie, just past Sliammon village.
6791 Klahannie
Tel. 604-414-0414
randghughes@shaw.ca

Emmonds Beach
Emmonds Road
Tel. 604-483-9791

SunLund-by-the-Sea RV Park & Campground
Up steps from a rocky beach in Lund harbour.
Tel. 604-483-9220
www.sunlund.ca

Copeland Islands Marine Provincial Park
The first island is about half an hour's paddle north of Lund. The islands have "four framed tent pads, two on the northernmost set of islands and two on the southernmost island."

Websites

BC Ferries
www.bcferries.com
Includes schedules and prices.

B.C. Tourist Information
www.britishcolumbia.com
Maps, accommodation, parks, etc.

Canadian Hydrographic Service
www.charts.gc.ca
Includes tide tables as well as charts of all kinds.

Sunshine Coast Trail
www.sunshinecoast-trail.com
Useful side trip information for the paddles in Okeover, Powell Lake, Powell River Canoe Route, etc.

Tides and Currents
http://www.lau.chs-shc.dfo-mpo.gc.ca/english/Canada.shtml
Gives seven days of tidal predictions for dates in the present and future as well as explanations of tidal phenomena.

Weather
http://www.weatheroffice.ec.gc.ca/marine/marine_e.html?c-sog
Includes links to weather maps and satellite imagery.

BC Parks
http://wlapwww.gov.bc.ca/bcparks
The uniform entry for each park includes a lot of extraneous information. However, the maps are useful and it is sometimes worth looking at the management plan, e.g., Okeover and Malaspina, which have consider-ably more detail than the basic park web page.

Coastal Waters Recreation
www.coastalwatersrec.com
An online place to buy these maps, which are not for navigational purposes. In some cases they mark launches and campsites that I have not included, usually because they are quite difficult to access. They have a few errors, and I probably do too. *Caveat emptor.*

Search and Rescue B.C.
www.sarbc.org/andrew1.html
Includes detailed information on hypothermia treatment.

Further Reading

Barman, Jean. *The Remarkable Adventures of "Portuguese Joe" Silvey.* Harbour, 2004. ISBN 1-55017-326-X

Blanchet, M. Wylie. *The Curve of Time.* Morriss, 1968. ISBN 0-88826-071-7

Carson, Bryan and Southern, Karen. *Sunshine and Salt Air: The Sunshine Coast Visitor's Guide.* Harbour, 1997. ISBN 1-55017-143-7

Drope, Dorothy and Drope, Bodhi. *Paddling the Sunshine Coast.* Harbour, 1997. ISBN 55017-164-X

Graham, Donald. *Lights of the Inside Passage: A History of British Columbia's Lighthouses and Their Keepers.* Harbour, 1986. ISBN 0-920080-85-5

Hadley, Michael L. *God's Little Ships: A History of the Columbia Coast Mission.* Harbour, 1995. ISBN 1-55017-133-X

Hill, Beth. *Seven-Knot Summers.* Horsdal & Schubart, 1994. ISBN 0920663-27-3

Hill, Beth. *Upcoast Summers.* Horsdal & Schubart, 1985. ISBN 0920663-01-X

Howard, Irene. *Bowen Island 1872–1972.* Bowen Island Historians, 1973. ISBN 0-9690638

Keller, Betty C. and Leslie, Rosella M. *Bright Seas, Pioneer Spirits: The Sunshine Coast.* Horsdal & Schubart, 1996. ISBN 0-920663-44-3

Kennedy, Dorothy and Bouchard, Ray. *Sliammon Life, Sliammon Lands.* Talonbooks, 1983. ISBN 0-88922-211-8

Kennedy, Ian. *Sunny Sandy Savary: A History of Savary Island 1792–1992.* Kennell Publishing, 1992. ISBN 0-9696291-0-9

Lange, Owen. *The Wind Came All Ways: A Quest to Understand the Winds, Waves and Weather in the Georgia Basin.* Environment Canada, 1998. ISBN 0-660-17517-7

Lange, Owen. *The Veils of Chaos: Living with Weather along the British Columbia Coast.* Environment Canada, 2003. ISBN 0-660-18984-4

Leslie, Rosella. *The Sunshine Coast: A Place to Be.* Heritage, 2001. ISBN 1-894384-19-9

Mobley, Carla. *Mysterious Powell Lake: A Collection of Historical Tales.* Hancock House, 1984. ISBN 0-88839-983-9

Pacific Weather Centre, Meteorological Service of Canada. *Coastal Weather for British Columbia Mariners; The Quest for Understanding Continues.* Environment Canada. 2000. CD-ROMWC-1411

Peterson, Lester. *The Story of the Sechelt Nation.* Sechelt Indian Band, 1990. ISBN 1-55017-017-1

Southern, Karen. *The Nelson Island Story, Including Hardy Island and Other Islands of Jervis Inlet.* Hancock House, 1989. ISBN 0-88839-196-X

Stanley, Golden. *Pitlamping through Conscription 1916–1923: Memoirs of Golden Stanley.* Powell River Heritage Research Association, 1985. Out of print.

Suttles, Wayne. *Coast Salish Essays.* Talonbooks, 1987. ISBN 0-88922-212-6

Thompson, Bill. *Boats, Bucksaws and Blisters, Pioneer Tales of the Powell River Area.* Powell River Heritage Research Association, 1990. ISBN 0-88925-958-5

Thompson, Bill. *Once upon a Stump: Times and Tales of Powell River Pioneers.* Powell River Heritage Research Association, 1993. ISBN 1-55056-266-5

Thompson, Bill. *Texada Island.* Powell River Heritage Research Association, 1997. ISBN 1-55056-550-8

Thomson, Richard E. *Oceanography of the British Columbia Coast.* Fisheries & Oceans Canada, 1981. ISBN 0-660-10978-6

Walbran, Capt. John T. *British Columbia Coast Names 1592–1906: Their Origin and History.* J.J. Douglas, 1971. ISBN 0-88894-001-7

White, Howard and Spilsbury, Jim. *Spilsbury's Coast.* Harbour, 1987. ISBN 1-55017-046-5

White, Howard. *The Sunshine Coast.* Harbour, 1996. ISBN 1-55017-081-3

White, Stewart Edward. *Skookum Chuck.* Doubleday, 1925.

Wilson, Ethel. *The Innocent Traveller.* McClelland & Stewart, 1982. ISBN 0771093160

Wright, L.R. *Fall from Grace.* Seal, 1991. ISBN 0-7704-2506-2

Quick Metric Conversions

Multiply by

Acres to hectares	0.4
Hectares to acres	2.5
Fathoms to metres	1.8
Metres to fathoms	0.6
Feet to metres	0.3
Metres to feet	3.3
Gallons to litres	4.6
Litres to gallons	0.2
Inches to centimetres	2.5
Centimetres to inches	0.4
Miles to kilometres	1.6
Kilometres to miles	0.6
Nautical miles to kilometres	1.9
Kilometres to nautical miles	0.5
Pounds to kilograms	0.5
Kilograms to pounds	2.2

Fahrenheit to Celsius
subtract 32, multiply by 5/9

Celsius to Fahrenheit
multiply by 9/5, add 32

Treatment of Hypothermia

Cold water kills. Hypothermia sets in when the body's core temperature drops from the normal 37 °C down to 32 °C, resulting in shock followed by cardiac arrest and death at 30 °C.

There have been a few changes to the management of hypothermia in recent years. Consider taking a course in wilderness first aid to be more prepared for what you might encounter in remote areas. The Search and Rescue of B.C. web site, though quite technical, is a good source of up-to-date information. It is www.sarbc.org/andrew1.html. The section on mild hypothermia 34-35 °C is particularly relevant.

Be Prepared

- Always keep your tarp instantly accessible for when you hit shore.

- Always coil tarp guy lines carefully when taking your tarp down—you can't afford the time it takes to untangle them.

- Carry a Thermos of hot drink.

- Carry a stove, even on a day trip.

- Carry a sleeping bag or fleece blanket, even on a day trip.

- Get out of the attitude that help is back in town. Set up your trip so that help is right there. Very few situations need evacuation, and you can do more damage in a frantic rush to get out.

- An ounce of prevention is worth a ton of cure. Ultimately seamanship and good judgment will prevent nearly all incidents. Regard being called "chicken" as a compliment.

- Be aware of the three stages of hypothermia as the treatment is very different in each.

- Wear your PFD at all times.

Symptoms and Treatment

Mild Symptoms

Pulse is normal, breathing normal. Appearance: shivering, slurred speech. Mental state: conscious.

Treatment

In the water

- Get as much of the body surface out of the water as possible and that means getting up and over your upturned kayak or up onto flotsam at once, while you are able to, because you will quickly lose the ability to help yourself (a person loses heat 25 to 30 times faster in water than in air). Find a hat and put it on (we lose a lot of body heat through the head).

- If someone is rescued and back in the boat, get them working as hard as you can, pumping water out of their boat and then paddling, unless hypothermia is advanced. Steady their boat while they reorganize themselves and stay close beside them until you are absolutely sure they are no longer hypothermic. Be prepared to tow and have a support kayak on each side of them in case they become more severely hypothermic before they can get to shore.

- If you can't get out of the water, use the Heat Escape Lessening Position (HELP). Cross your arms tightly across your chest. Draw your knees up close to it. Remain calm and still. Don't swim.

- If others are in the water with you, get into the HUDDLE position: the sides of everyone's chest are close, with arms around mid to lower back and legs intertwined. Put children and elderly people in the centre as they lose heat quicker than others.

- The HELP and HUDDLE positions can lengthen survival time in 10 °C water from 2 hours to 4 hours.

Ashore
- Use a tarp to get the victim out of the cold, wind and rain.

- If one person is hypothermic, look out for others whose body temperature may be going down too. Believe the symptoms, not the victim. They'll often tell you they feel fine. This confusion is one of the symptoms.

Moderate Symptoms
Pulse slow and weak, breathing slow and shallow. Appearance: shivering is violent to stopped, clumsy and stumbles. Mental state: confused, sleepy, irrational.

Treatment
- Remove wet clothing and get the person into warm, dry clothing, including a warm hat.

- Wrap them in a space blanket.

- Alternatively, put them in a sleeping bag, prewarmed if cold (a warm rescuer can get in and prewarm it). Meanwhile, get well-wrapped warm rocks ready for additional warmth if needed. The old idea of body to body contact is out because the second person could go into hypothermia trying to warm the first.

- Give warm, sweet, non-alcoholic drinks. Never give alcohol. It worsens the situation.

- Protect from the wind and insulate from the ground.

- Don't rub the skin. Rubbing extremities brings the warmer core blood to the surface and takes the cold extremity blood back to the core thus intensifying the hypothermia, so rubbing is a no-no.

- Caution the patient not to exercise to rewarm, since exercise or activity (other than in the very early stages) also moves cold blood to the core; but worse than that the heart becomes very sensitive as hypothermia progresses. Rough handling or exercise can trigger a cardiac arrest.

- For the same reason, handle the person very gently as if they were an egg. This is particularly important when moving or removing wet clothing. Just strip off the outer clothes.

Severe Symptoms
Pulse weak, irregular or absent. Appearance: shivering has stopped. Mental state: unconscious.

Treatment
- If semiconscious or worse, try to keep the person awake with warm drinks.

- Any rewarming must be as close to the core as possible; give warm, sweet non-alcohol and non-caffeine drinks if conscious. Use heating pads (or fill nalgene water bottles with hot water and wrap in a T-shirt) and put them close to the major arteries to get the core temp up (between the inner thighs, under the armpits, over the abdomen).

- Monitor breathing and pulse and be prepared to assist either or both if they need it.

- If they lose consciousness, obtain medical help immediately. Check regularly for heart rate and breathing. **Do not** attempt active rewarming unless medical help is delayed; rather, maintain body temperature with insulation (a sleeping bag) and handle them very carefully as the slightest rough handling may cause the heart to stop.

- If signs of circulation are not present give CPR (cardio pulmonary resuscitation) only if it can be maintained without interruption until medical help takes over.

- If no medical help is available, continue to ventilate (rescue breathing, but without the compressions) until the casualty is rewarmed. Never assume that a casualty is dead until their body is warm again and there are still no signs of life. Rescue breathing may bring someone back to life who otherwise would surely have died. If it doesn't work, there's nothing else you could have done.

Equipment List   *Day trips ★*

Kayak Equipment
Kayak★
Paddle★
Spare paddle★
Sponge★
Pump★
Flares (less than 4 years old)★
Paddle float★
Re-entry strap★
Heaving line★
Fine line for moorage★ (100 m)
PFD★
Compass★
Whistle★
Pogies★
Spray skirt★
Cockpit cover
Wetsuit or drysuit★
Thongs
Swellies
Water shoes★
Chart case★
Charts & tide tables★
Carrying straps
Rudder repair kit★
Deck water★
Deck knife★

Cockpit Bag
Binoculars★
Pencil & paper
Sunscreen★
Sun glasses★
Kleenex★
Trail food★
Weather radio & spare batteries★
VHF & charger★
Camera & film★
Space blanket★
Insect repellent★
Current book

Wildlife identification books
Star chart
Small waterproof flashlight★

Camping Equipment
Tarps (2)
Tent
Thermorest
Underfoam
Sleeping bag
Overbag
Pillow
Small flashlights
Big flashlight
Spare batteries & bulbs
Rope & bear hoist
Crazy Creek chair
2 large net bags with zips, to reduce trips up and down the beach with small items.

Clothing etc. in waterproof bags
Fleece shirt
Lifa underwear (2 sets)
Underwear
Heavy wool socks
Lighter socks
Windproof pants/shorts
Sweat suit
Camp jacket
Toque
Swimsuit
Towel
T-shirts
Fleece hat
Hair brush
Alarm clock
Camp shoes
Fleece jacket
Long-sleeved cotton shirt

Washing gear
Shampoo
First aid kit (including sunscreen)
Hydrogen peroxide
Kleenex
Laundry bag
Spare dark glasses
Toilet paper
Trowel
Books
Playing cards

Clothing – worn or loose
Rain gear*
Tilley hat*
Paddling jacket*
Change of clothes in a waterproof bag*

Kitchen Equipment
(1) Kitchen bag
Stove
Fuel
Matches
Large pot
Cutlery
Can opener
Spatula
Metal whisk
Spices
Tea
Coffee
Hot chocolate
Medication
Mug
Plastic mixing containers
Lemon juice
Biodegradable salt water soap
J cloth & scrubber
Dishcloth
Fuel filter funnel
Stove windscreen

First aid kit
Toothbrush & toothpaste
Dental floss
Flashlight
Water purifier
Moist wipes
Pepper & salt
Toilet paper
Cooking oil
Aluminum foil
Pruner
Purelle hand disinfectant

(2) Heavy cotton bag
Pots & pans
Dishes

(3) Lunch kit*
Spare cutlery*
Spare can opener*
First day's lunch*

(4) Water
Pop bottles on strings (2)
Collapsible water carrier (1)

(5) Fuel
Primus (225 g cans) (3)

Food
Breakfasts & lunches in 1 bag
Dinners in 1 bag

x breakfasts
y lunches
z suppers
fish fixings
bread makings

Endnotes

[1] Marshall, Stewart and Scott, Andrew. Painter, Paddler: The Art and Adventures of Stewart Marshall. TouchWood Editions, 2003. ISBN 1-894898-07-9. pp.125–6

[2] Meyer, Kathleen. How to Shit in the Woods. Ten Speed Press, 1989. ISBN 0-89815-319-0

[3] British Columbia Ministry of Sustainable Resource Management, Coast and Marine Planning Branch. Malaspina Okeover Coastal Plan. February 2004. ISBN 0-7726-4911-1 To access this on-line, go to BC Parks website, click on Malaspina and then on Management Plan.

[4] http://www.lwbc.ca/02land/tenuring/commercialrecreation/index.html

[5] Conversation with Dr. Elizabeth Krebs, November 8, 2003

[6] White, Stewart Edward. *Skookum Chuck*, Doubleday, 1925 pp. 177–212

[7] Kennedy, Ian. *Sunny Sandy Savary: A History of Savary Island 1792–1992.* Kennell, 1992. ISBN 0–9696291–0–9. P.35–36

[8] Hancock House, 1984, ISBN 0-88839-9

[9] While Van Anda is spelled as one word Vananda on the nautical charts, the official spelling adopted by B.C. Place Names is Van Anda. Both variations are in common use.

[10] Not the same as the better known Davie Bay, which is farther south.

[11] Harbour Publishing, 1998. ISBN 1-55017-184-4

[12] Wright, L.R. Fall from Grace. Seal, 1991. ISBN 0-7704-2506-2

[13] Vancouver, George. A Voyage of Discovery to the North Pacific Ocean and Round the World 1791–1795. W. Kaye Lamb, ed. London, Hakluyt Society, 1984, 4 vols. ISBN 0-904180-190. Vol II, p. 594 and Vol. III, p. 944

[14] Fisheries & Oceans Canada, Canadian Hydrographic Service. Canadian Tide and Current Tables/Tables des marées et courants du Canada. 2005–, vol. 5, Juan de Fuca Strait and Strait of Georgia. ISBN 0-660-62462-1

[15] Thomson, Richard E. Oceanography of the British Columbia Coast. Fisheries and Oceans Canada, 1981. ISBN 0–660–10978–6. P.182, fig. 10.39

[16] These B&Bs are all perched on a cliff between Albion (Black) Point and Myrtle Point. They have private steps down to the water, where there is space to leave kayaks overnight.

Index of Place Names

In Case of Emergency

In case of an accident, put up one flare and call the Coast Guard on channel 16. Usually they answer right away. If not, call "any boat close to ...(wherever you are)." Don't let off any further flares until you see a rescue boat looking for you. Although Coast Guard stations are located in a number of places in the Strait of Georgia, it can be several hours before help appears. Land and make the best of it. Don't expect to be airlifted to a large hospital. Although it's not impossible, you're more likely to be taken to a small centre and then transferred by road.

Search and rescue costs money. Taxpayers' dollars often do not cover the costs of all the expensive equipment required. Volunteers may have given up a day's pay or more to find you. Although not compulsory, it would be much appreciated if victims and their families contributed to the cause—in thousands.

Search and rescue 1-800-567-5111
Cellular Phone *16
Marine VHF Radio Channel 16